THE ENGLISH LAWYER.

DESCRIBING

A Method for the managing of the Lawwes of this Land.

And expressing the best qualities requisite in the

Student	
Practizer	of the same.
Judges and *Fathers*	

Written by the Reverend and Learned Sir IOHN DODERIDGE Knight, one of the Iustices of the Kings Bench, lately deceased.

THE LAWBOOK EXCHANGE, LTD.
Clark, New Jersey

ISBN 9781584775362

Lawbook Exchange edition 2005, 2011

The quality of this reprint is equivalent to the quality of the original work.

THE LAWBOOK EXCHANGE, LTD.
33 Terminal Avenue
Clark, New Jersey 07066-1321

Please see our website for a selection of our other publications and fine facsimile reprints of classic works of legal history:
www.lawbookexchange.com

Library of Congress Cataloging-in-Publication Data

Doderidge, John, Sir, 1555-1628.
The English lawyer : describing a method for the managing of the lawes of this land, and expressing the best qualities requisite in the student, practizer, judges and fathers of the same / written by Sir John Doderidge.
p. cm.
Originally published: London : printed by the assignes of I. More, 1631.
ISBN 1-58477-536-X (cloth : alk. paper)
1. Lawyers--England. 2. Practice of law--England. I. Title.
KD460.D63 2005
340'.023'41--dc22 2004042386

Printed in the United States of America on acid-free paper

THE ENGLISH LAWYER.

DESCRIBING

A Method for the managing of the Lawes of this Land.

And expressing the best qualities requisite in the

Student
Practizer of the same.
Judges and *Fathers*

Written by the Reverend and Learned Sir IOHN DODERIDGE Knight, one of the Iustices of the Kings Bench, lately deceased.

LONDON,
Printed by the Assignes of I. MORE Esq.
M DC XXXI.

The Printers to the READER.

THE later part of this Volume was heretofore obſcurely printed by an imperfect Copie from a then unknowne Authour, under the Title of *The Lawyers light*: We now reimprint it in faire light, by the Authors owne Copie, written (for the moſt part) with his owne hand; wee vouch his name and intitle it, as hee himſelfe did, *The Engliſh Lawyer*: The other part hereof, which was not formerly printed, wee now alſo put forth according to the Authors owne Copie, and place it, as hee did, in the formoſt rancke; There are other parts alſo (which are expreſſed on the next leafe) requiſite to the making up of the whole intended worke; but becauſe they are not made, or not found as yet, they can bee but deſired untill ſome happie hand ſhall either ſinde or finiſh the reſt of this good worke, whoſe worth wil recommend it ſelfe upon the reading.

This

This Whole Treatise is divided into three Parts.

The first concerning the Student: And that also divided into three distinct Sections.

THE first Section containeth a disquisition with what Naturall gifts and faculties the Student of the Law ought to be furnished withall.

The second Section containeth what acquired Qualities are required in the Student as well touching the Vertues intellectuall, and the liberall Sciences, wherein the Student should be informed, and other Knowledges necessary for the rectifying of his understanding, as also touching the Morall vertues for direction of his Conversation.

The third Section containeth the best manner and Methode that may be used for the most delightfull and most usefull study of Law, and whereby most profit may be gotten in profoundnesse of Iudgement in the knowledge of our English Lawes.

The

The second Treatise touching the Counseller or Practizer of the Lawes, is also subdivided into three principall Parts or Sections.

THe First concerneth his Private Counsell given at home in his Chamber to his Client, which is one part of his duty Consulendo, *by way of Counsell.*

The Second Part or Section concerneth the drawing of Assurances and Conveiances, which are of sundry sorts; which is his dutie Cavendo, *by way of Caution.*

The Third Part or Section concerneth his Pleadings for his Client; And that is threefold: In point of Law: In Argument of Demurrers: In matter of fact, as in giving or delivering of Evidence. And the Patronage of Causes in Courts of equitie: all which are his duties Agendo, *by way of publike Action.*

In

In the Third Treatise concerning a *Iudge*, are contained these particulars, in two generall parts divided: first, his Preparation in his person, Secondly, his Practice.

IN *his Preparation, or consideration of his Person, the qualities required in an upright Iudge are these: first, that hee bee Religious, according to the Counsell of* Iethro *unto* Moses, *Provide men fearing God.* 2 Chron. 19.7. Exodus 18.21.22.23.

Secondly, They ought to bee men of Courage. Provide thee among all the People men of Courage. Deut. 1. 17.

Thirdly, They ought to be men of Integrity, Iust men, dealing truly: They shall be iust, if first they hate Covetousnesse, so will they not be corrupted, For rewards and gifts doe blinde the eyes of the wise; Exod. 23.8. Deut. 16. 19. Ecclus. 20. 28. 2 Chron. 19.7. *Secondly, if they have no respect of persons.* Lev. 19.15. Deut. 1.17. 2 Chron. 19.7. *Thirdly, if they be free from passions and perturbations of the minde, as anger, favour, desire of revenge, &c.*

Fourthly, Iudges ought to be wise, men able to discerne circumstances, and to foreknow the mischiefes and inconveniences that may ensue of inconsiderate Iudgements. Deut. 1.13.

Fiftly, Iudges ought to be learned, especially in the Lawes, Be ye learned that judge the earth.

The Second Part, which is the Practice of the Iudge, generally considered is twofold, first either Sedentary, in the Court wherein he sitteth: or Itinerate, in the Circuite wherein he rideth.

The

THE CONTENTS.

THE

THE ENGLISH LAWYER.

Cap. I.

FOrasmuch as the Exercise of all such as enterprise the Profession, and doe intermeddle with the Knowledge of the Lawes of this Realme, consisteth, 1, either in the obtaining, study, or speculation thereof. 2, Or in the practice, prosecution, or direction. 3, Or in the full and finall decision and determination of causes therein called into question: behoovefull it were (as mee seemeth) for such as have already entertained a love to that faculty, and covet to contemplate with their inward eye the *expresse and perfect Image of an English Lawyer*, to view each of these in their particular charge and duty, and therewithall to consider what things were requisite, and what course were most convenient to be holden for the better and more full accomplishment of that which is, and must be expected. And as the persons whom our speech concerneth, and whose charge we have here briefely touched, are three in number, *The Student, the Practizer, and the Judge:* (For as touching the Pronothory or Clark, and the Attorney, they are rather Ministers to follow others, then Managers to direct:) So will the matters incident to every of their duties yeeld us a threefold Treatise, and give us large scope of Discourse in the prosecuting of such things as are requisite and incident unto the same.

And first as touching the *Student*, & his speculative search of our English Laws (wch is his indeavour and study) as it is in *order formost*, and by Nature the ground of the proceedings of both the other, being that indeed without the which the rest cannot subsist. *Reason* in this point requireth, that due consideration, and carefull forethought should be had for the obtaining and triall of those things which are esteemed as *Viatica necessaria*, needfull implements behoovefull in the person of him that shall undertake to deale therewith. *Authors* which have written Institutions for the better information and direction of the learner, have required at the hands of such their Auditors and followers as were to be instructed; these three things, *Nature*, *Arte*, and *Exercise* or *Use*, each of wch they would so have, & indeed so ought to be linked to other, that seldome hath bin found perfection in any one person in whom all these three have

have not bin conjoyn'd: For *Nature*(though of her ſelfe excellent) yet without *Art* or *Exerciſe* is as the Gold in the droſſe, or as the precious ſtone taken out of the bowels of the earth, rude, and unpoliſhed: *Art* without *Nature*, bare, barren, and defective (as being indeed nothing elſe but an obſervation of *Nature*) And both without *Exerciſe*, voide of fruit: *Nature* reſembleth the ſoile; *Arte* or *Method* whereby wee are directed, the Huſbandman; *Precepts* or *Inſtitutions* in the Science which we meane to profeſſe, are as the ſeeds, which induſtry and exerciſe doe bring unto growth, ripenes & perfection: ſo that *Sane Beatus, dijsq; acceptus eſt, cui Deus iſta omnia tribuit*. But ſithence that diviſion wch conſiſteth of two parts is holden moſt Artficiall, all theſe three (as me ſeemeth) may aptly be drawne and reduced into two originall Branches. The one concerning the *Qualities*
lities wherewith it is convenient our Student ſhould be adorned before his intended enterpriſe attempted, and with the which he might be ready furniſhed to ſet upon the ſame. The other diſco- 2
vering the manner, method, and direction of the courſe of our ſtudy once entred, the meanes of furtherance thereof, and how, and in what manner to hold on therein without intermiſſion untill the wiſhed fruit, and expected end ſhall bee obtained.

In the former we ſhall include *Nature* and ſuch 1
other habiliments as ſhall bee required for the full furniſhing and adorning thereof.

In the latter, *Arte, Exerciſe*, and other inci- 2

dents and adherents unto the ſame.

Concerning therefore the conſideration of
thoſe former qualities that are to be before had,
and obtained, *Philoſophers* led by the rule of rea-
ſon have diſtinguiſhed the tranſitory gifts that
God hath beſtowed on us in this life, to be either
Bona animi, bona corporis, or *bona fortuna*. *Qualities*
either reſident in us, or externall benefits beſtow-
1 ed upon us. Thoſe which are *inherent in us*, con-
cerne either our mindes or our bodies, which
good gifts of our mindes are either *Naturall* given
by God unto us, without our labour bred toge-
ther with us, and within us from our Cradles,
growing and increaſing with our age, as firſt *ſharp-
neſſe, pregnancy*, and *dexterity of wit*: Secondly,
Sound and *exquiſite memory*: Thirdly, *ready, copi-
2 ous*, and ſweet *deliverie of our words*. Or *gotten and
gained by long induſtry* and travell, grown to a perfit
habit, either firſt illuminating our knowledges,
as the *Sciences Liberall*, and other the ſpeculative
vertues of the minde: Or elſe ſecondly directing
our lives and converſations as *the vertues Morall re-
poſed in our wills*.

CAP. II.

TO diſcourſe therefore of theſe particulars (I mean principally the gifts of the minde) in ſuch order as is before ſpecified. The firſt and chiefeſt *Naturall gift* is *sharpnesse*, and *dexterity of wit*, the excellency whereof surpassing all praise, needeth no commendation, being the thing indeed without which nothing can be throughly sifted as it should bee, or sufficiently set forth as it ought: but to speake more particularly thereof, and for the purpose in hand, none can well denie that doe consider the depth of knowledge reposed in the Lawes of this Realme: none I say can deny, which doe consider how many cases of much conformity, and resemblance doe daily happen, wherein neverthelesse dexterity of wit upon some circumstance of matter, espieth a difference: None can deny, which doe consider that many in the Patronage and defence of causes, are oftentimes pressed upon the sudden, presently to reply to the adversaries unexpected objections, (which effect *Promptnesse* and *readinesse of wit* onely worketh :) but that the excellency and dexterity thereof were almost alone sufficient to make a ready and prest Lawyer; for it behooveth the Lawyer with a quicke conceit to comprehend the cause of his Client once opened, throughly to understand the drifts of his Adversaries reasons at the first urged, readily both to invent, and fitly to apply his provided proofes and arguments to the point in question: all which are the effects of an excellent wit, and with the which we doe so much desire *our learned Lawyer* should be adorned.

The consideration therefore of wit, or of the light of humane understanding which Almighty God hath given unto man, whereby hee excelleth

all other living creatures, may bee conſidered of
us by the view of two ſeverall faculties, or ſundry
1 operations of our minde; the one for diſtinction
2 ſake may bee called *Apprehenſion*, and the other
Iudgement (not that the minde is diverſe, or mani-
fold, but that theſe are the divers affections, and
proper paſſions of one and the ſelfe ſame cauſe.)
1 The firſt is the quick, ſpeedy, and lively vigour,
the ready ability of our underſtanding, and as it
were the hand by which our minde taketh hold of
the knowledge of things propoſed, being indeed
the very ſame the Latines call *Ingenij acumen.*
2 The other (before called *Iudgement*) is the faculty
whereby we doe as it were give ſentence of the
thing conceived, and cenſure our owne underſtan-
ding concerning the ſame. And as unto the firſt
may be attributed (as the true enſigne and peculi-
ar qualitie thereof) *Sharpneſſe*; So from the other,
which is *Iudgement*, in like manner followeth (the
proper qualitie wherewith it is inveſted) *Sound-
neſſe*; of which it is evident (to ſpeake briefly) that
the one is the ſharpnes of conceit, the other is the
ſoundneſſe of conceit; reſembling and alluding to
that *Philoſophicall* diſtinction, *Intellectus agens*, and
intellectus paſsibilis, ſeu poſsibilis. And as theſe ope-
rations of the minde are in duty ſeverall; ſo are
they for the moſt part ſunderly and ſeverally di-
ſtributed by God unto men; not that the one can
be wholly, and alone without the other, but that
the excellency of the one is ſeldome ſetled, and
contained in one perſon with the excellency of
the other, whereof daily obſervation may yeeld
abundant examples.

The Iudgement of *Plato* touching his two Disciples, *Aristotle* and *Theophrastus*, was grounded upon the diversitie of their naturall gifts, in this respect the one surmounted in sharpnesse of understanding, namely *Aristotle*; The other (though that way inferiour) yet every way comparable in sharpnesse of *Iudgement*.

There lived at one time in the Common weale of *Athens* two notable Orators, *Demosthenes* and *Demades*: the one through his care, premeditation, and soundnesse of *Iudgement*, by speech to please the humour of the people, was a man renowned. The other, namely *Demades* for his quicknesse of wit, and ready utterance upon the sudden, most excellent.

There were likewise wont to come into the Counsell Chamber of the said City, at one the selfe-same season, two famous Counsellors, *Aristides* for his sound counsell greatly esteemed, and *Themistocles* for his sharpe and witty policies highly regarded. At one time there were in the field two famous Captaines, each against other in a quarrell, which concerned either the flourishing, or the downfall of both their States and Common-weales, *Hannibal* the *Carthaginian*, and *Quintus Fabius Maximus* the *Roman*, in which their conflicts the *Carthaginian* was not more commended for inventing a Stratagem, wherein he excelled, then was the *Roman* reverenced for staid and advised *Iudgement* in preventing the same, wherein he surpassed: The one of them was not more wilely, then the other wary ry; But thus much of the Heathen. In the Church of God, and as concerning the writings of ancient Latine *Doctors*, there is found in the stile of *Augustine* an excellent and peculiar sharpnesse: In the books of *Ambrose* & *Ierome* a plain, full, and familiar soundnesse, and *Bernard* addeth to both a delectable sweetnesse. Among the Schoolemen, who racked reason as farre as it would reach, one man in one age for his sharpnesse of wit was called *Subtilis Doctor*; and another neere the same time for his soundnesse of *Judgement*, *Doctor Angelicus*. But to come to the Lawes of the Land, and to exemplifie our discourse in our owne faculty (purposely refraining to speake or publish the excellent gifts of many famous men now living in this profession) let us call to our considerations two notable Ornaments of one Bench or Court, of one time, of reverend remembrance, and now both deceased, Sr *Anthony Browne*, and Sr *Iames Dyer* Knights: both having beene Chiefe in their places of *Iustice*. In the one did shine an incomparable sharpnesse of wit, and in the other was found in a manner an irrefragable soundnesse of *Iudgement*. But to leave examples, and to descend to a subdivision, we are to note, that sharpnesse of wit is againe observed by two properties, that is to say, *Quicknesse of capacity*, and *readinesse of discourse*, for *Ingenij acumen non solùm concipit, sed discutit*. And yet these qualities are likewise by God oftentimes sunderly disposed; for some men there are which can of themselves soone conceive any difficulty by others proposed in speech or writing,

ting; but they are not alſo indowed with the naturall gift of promptneſſe of diſcourſe and argument; And, ſome others on the contrary are excellently gifted for Oratory or diſcuſſion, but defective, and come farre ſhort of others in the former property, I meane, in mentall conception.

And yet though a Student of the Law bee by nature unfurniſhed with theſe gifts of the minde aforeſaid, he muſt not be diſheartened, but rather incouraged; which incouragement may take good ground;

Firſt, upon conſideration with himſelfe, that ſeldome is ſeene ſuch excellency of quick capacity in any one perſon unmated with the blemiſh of ranging lightneſſe and inſtabilitie: That the more fertile the ſoyle is, the more prone it is to beare and bring forth (without painefull manurance) unprofitable, and ſometime moſt noyſome weeds; that as waxe is apt to receive whatſoever impreſſion, ſo is it apt eaſily againe to looſe it, and to be new framed into whatſoever faſhion; where on the contrary part the form which is engraven in Marble is as hardly worne out as it was with much labour imprinted: for quicke wits (ſaith one) are apt to take, unapt to keepe, ſoone hot, ſoone cold, more apt to enter ſpeedily, then able to pierce farre, like edges of ſharpe tooles, ſoone turned; For we may finde true by experience, that among a number of quicke wits in youth, few be found in the end either very fortunate for themſelves, or very profitable to ſerve the Common-wealth; such was *Hermogenes* the *Rhetoritian*, who (as it is written) being in manner a Child but eighteene yeares old, compiled an excellent Treatise of *Rhetorique* savouring more of *Iudgement* then is commonly found in that age; but afterward attaining to the yeares of 28. hee became madd and utterly forgot all things.

Secondly, the mindes of Students are incouraged, and their wits consequently increased, as well by due commendation given them for their good endeavours, as also by commemoration of the utility, profit, and excellency of the things they covet to obtaine. Touching the first of these well saith *Aristotle*, *Adolescentiam gloria studio duci*. Wherefore to be short, and to speake of this in a word, what a spurre Praise is to pricke forth the minde in every good attempt, is seene and perceived even in bruit beasts. The Hound hunteth best when he is incouraged with the cry of the Huntsman, that Hauke is made more eager to pursue her prey, to whom the Faulkner hath used to impart some part of the prey taken: But what course or tenor ought to bee holden herein, *Plutarch* giveth good instruction: *Cum exultant animi, reprehensionibus ad pudorem redigantur; cum dejecti sunt, rursus laudibus erigantur.*

Touching the second, which is the commemoration of the thing coveted; true it is, that the consideration of the excellency thereof is a most wonderfull provocation to set forwards the due meanes with all industry which serve for the obtaining

taining of the ſame, which for as much as in the tract we have in hand, is the exact knowledge of the Law, a briefe narration of the neceſſity and utility thereof is able ſufficiently to vanquiſh all tediouſneſſe of ſtudy, and all irkſomeneſſe to be endured and borne in the obtaining thereof: So that although (by the way, and nothing out of the way) apt occaſion be here offered to ſpeake in the commendation of the Law, ſurpaſſing all praiſe that my poore ability can beſtow upon it, yet let it ſuffice ſomewhat to have ſaid herein, and nevertheleſſe no more than another hath ſpoken in the like kinde many hundred yeares agoe; *Iuris-prudentia ſine controverſia, & magna eſt, & latè patet, & ad multos pertinet, & ſummo in honore ſemper fuit, & clariſſimi Cives ei ſtudio, & ſemper præfuerunt, & etiam hodiè præſunt.*

Cap. III.

THe next naturall gift to be considered of, is *Soundnesse of Memory*, which is the receptacle wherin is reposed and laid up whatsoever thing the Vnderstanding hath apprehended and judged worthy of receipt or entertainment: for what doth it profit with great labour, dexterity, and industry to get together, when the thing gotten is not carefully kept and preserved, but loosely let goe, or negligently lost? What booteth it to reade much, which is wearinesse to the flesh; to meditate often, which is a burthen to the minde; to learne daily with encrease of knowledge, when as the matter learned is to seeke, at that time especially when we have most need of the use therof? *Memory* therefore is the Chest of an inestimable treasure, given from God for the preservation of all kinde of knowledge: it is as *Plutarch* saith, the store house of all our understanding; and as *Plato* saith, *Mater Musarum*, the Mother of the

the Muses: as *Aristotle* saith, it is the guide of our experience, and the ground-worke of all our wisedome, for that fore-passed experiences called to remembrance doe ingender advised circumspection, and are able to direct all our future atchievements through the consideration of fore-passed events. *Tully* saith it is *Signatarum rerum in mente vestigium*, the character of things imprinted in our minde. S. *Augustine* (as it seemeth) ravished with the contemplation of this wonderfull facultie, useth these words thereof, *Omnia recipit recolenda cum opus est, & retractanda grandis memoriæ recessus, ac nescio quid secreti, atque ineffabilis sinus ejus, cum omnia suis quæque foribus intrant ad eam, & in eam reponuntur:* Memory is a store-house infinitely capable, and can never be overfilled, wherein by the most cunning Work-master of Nature are hoorded up all kindes of acts and accidents that either the outward senses have perceived, or the inward understanding conceived; wherein things of like kinde and quality, as in a large treasury, are orderly composed and laid up together by themselves in certaine, sure, and seposed cells, from thence to be drawne and deduced wheresoever fit and apt occasion is offered; which Art of Memory doth manifest by this or the like instances ensuing: for when wee doe call to minde any one particular, the same so remembred doth for the most part bring to light his like, so that wee doe remember the one by the commemoration oftentimes of the other: of the which one hath written

written very well in this manner; *In memoria omnia ita collocata & ordinata sunt, ut unumquodque separatim, & cuncta confertim, & singula ordinatim exposcere & digerere valeamus.* The truth is, that some things there are which we can remember easily and with great facility, some other things with more difficulty, as hoorded up in the bottome of that Chest, and doe require more search (as the rumaging of wares in the bulke of a ship) to be unladen and brought to light; some things doe offer themselves, and some other things after long seeking are hardly found: And thus much may here suffice to have been written concerning the effects of humane Memory.

But for the better and deeper discovery of the nature thereof, (for then we shall the better addresse our selves to the use of Memory, when we doe truly comprehend the kindes, causes, and nature of the same) we are to conceive that the learned who have written hereof have observed a double faculty of Memory; the one concerning things comprehended by the outward senses, and therefore called by them Memory Sensative: The other concerning things conceived by the Vnderstanding and Power of wit, and therefore called Intellective Memory. The first, namely Sensative Memory is common to Man and many other living Creatures, resulting from the sense: Hence it is that the Horse knoweth and remembreth the way wherein hee hath beene often travailed,

vailed, many times better then his Rider; The Dog after many yeares absence can call to memory his Master, and by fawning upon him renue his old acquaintance: The fowles of the ayre, how farre so ever they flie can readily returne to their Nests, by Memory of the place where their young are reposed: The Bee can resort to his owne Hive, and in the Hive to his proper hole; and the little Ant retire to her Denne whence she first issued, neither forgoing nor forgetting it at her returne, with innumerable occurrences of like nature, all which are effected by the Art and operation of Memory Sensative.

Memory Intellective followeth the use of reasō and therefore is found in no other Creature then Man, which is indued with the faculty of reason. And whether, and in what manner this kinde of Memory doth differ from the Vnderstanding it selfe, I doe remit to the Philosophers, to the contemplation of whose learned discourses I doe commit the curious desire of the Reader that seeketh farther satisfaction herein.

But to proceed: as there is a twofold Memory, Sensative and Intellective, as hath beene said, so is there also a double operation of the Memory Intellective: The one is called *Actus memorandi*, the other *Actus reminiscendi*. The first of these is the representation of things past, as if they were still present, representing the Image of things forepassed in the same manner as if they were now

now actually & really present. *Actus reminiscendi* is as it were a kinde of discourse of Memory; for as before was said of understanding, that there is one operation to conceive and comprehend, and another operation to inferre, collect and discourse thereupon, and to draw conclusions from a thing conceived to another thing concealed, and to extract out of things knowne the knowledge of things unknowne; so is it likewise in these operations of Memory, the one doth remember the other, *viz. Actus reminiscendi*, out of one thing remembred discovereth another thing in manner lost and forgotten: so that the one draweth the other as the severall linkes of a Chaine draw and depend one upon another: Examples will make it manifest. If a man doe relate unto me a matter done in time forepassed in his and my presence, and with our privities, if I doe remember the same, and thereby doe acknowledge the thing to be true, for that the same is now represented unto me by the Act of Memory, as if it were really present, this is called *Actus memorandi:* But if I have forgotten it, and he bring me in minde of it by quickning and reviving my Memory by the circumstances of time, place, company, or such like other occurrences, and by that meanes at length I come to repaire that decay of Memory, this is called *Actus reminiscendi*; so that the last mentioned operation may aptly bee called the Discourse of Memory.

The

The objects of *Memory* are things passed, as *Aristotle* recounteth, *Memoria est rerum præteritarum.* And as hope is of things to come, sense and understanding of things that are present; so *Memorie* is employed and worketh upon things past: And thus much shortly by the way of a *Philosophicall* discourse (*rudi Minerva*) touching *Memorie*. *Objects of Memory.*

Now that out of these things thus knowne we may make some use for the better establishing and encrease of the students Memory, and to teach as it were a true Art Memorative, not out of forraigne precepts, or by the helpe of Imaginary places, but out of the nature of Memory it selfe, which may be *tanquam vivida præcepta*; I shall exhibite to your consideration some few remarkeable circumstances, and so much the rather, by how much the more this facultie (although excellent in it selfe) yet is the sooner lost, and with the losse thereof, it maketh all our studies but lost labours. For true it it is, and too true which *Seneca* affirmeth, speaking of Memory, *Res est ex omnibus partibus animi maxime delicata, & fragilis, in quam primum senectus incurrit*: The most delicate and fraile part of our Minde, the which old Age doth first assault. And as *Pliny* saith, *Nec quicquam æque fragile in hominum vita, morborum & casus injurias, atq; etiam metus sentiens*; Nothing so fading in all Mans life, subject to decay by the injuries of sicknesse, chances and feares: therefore for the better accomplishment of our intended purposes; let us first consider the instrument or organ, which the qualities or faculties of the mind or ſoule do worke withall in this life, which is the body; for the body is *vehiculum animæ*, the chariot, wagon, or ſhip of the ſoule, if not the ſepulchre thereof, as *Plato* affirmed, σῶμα ὅτι τῆς ψυχῆς σῆμα, and the aptneſſe of the inſtrument is a great furtherance to the facility of the workmanſhip, and to the beauty of the worke. Mans body being compoſed of elementall qualities requireth in the perfection thereof a temperature of humors, which alſo conſiſteth in the temperate diſpoſition of heate and moiſture, for that *in humido, & calido conſiſtit vita*, and hereby it is made a more apt inſtrument and organ for the operation of the powers of the ſoule, and ſo conſequently of Memorie, naturall moiſture muſt not abound as in children, whoſe memory is therefore in tender yeeres moſt commonly not of the beſt. And againe, naturall moiſture muſt not on the other ſide be almoſt in a manner exhauſted, as in old men, whoſe Memorie is therefore worne, but it muſt hold the golden meane, for fluide things are apt to receive but cannot long retaine any impreſſion, by reaſon of overmuch moiſture, which makes the impreſſion looſe, and at length utterly loſt; And aride and dry things can receive no impreſſion for want of moiſture, the one receiveth but retaineth not, the other receiveth not at all; wherefore as this golden meane muſt be preſerved in the temperature of moiſture, ſo muſt it bee held indifferent betweene cold and heat, nothing ſo hurtfull to *Memory* as overmuch cold, nothing more harmful

to

to *Memory* then overmuch heate, the which how to mitigate in the diſpoſition of the body I leave to Phyſitians by medicine and diet; and therefore I reſort to precepts agreeable and correſpondent to the nature of Memory without medicine.

Firſt therefore, whoſoever deſireth to remember that ſcience, facultie or propoſition which he learneth or readeth, let him bee well aſſured that he firſt throughly underſtand and apprehend the ſame with ſome kinde of delight, for no man did ever remember that perfectly, which hee underſtood not throughly; in as much as the well underſtanding is the Character, and ſeale of the thing underſtood, which the Memory receiveth imprinted in her. Things are then ſaid to bee throughly underſtood, when the effects are known by their cauſe, *tùm enim ſcimus, cùm per cauſas cognoſcimus*, as ſaith *Ariſtotle*; or when the cauſe is known by the effects, when the reaſons thereof are throughly apprehended, and the conſequents truly diſcerned, namely, when the judiciall part of our underſtanding reſteth ſatisfied, and giveth a ſentence within our ſelfe, that it doth fully comprehend. This perfect underſtanding muſt bee joyned (as I ſaid) with delight, which dilateth the vitall ſpirits, and quickneth Memory; whereas things conceived in contrary paſſions can hardly be retained long through the perturbations occaſioned therby.

Vnderſtanding with delight is drawne from the excellency of the knowledge apprehended, from the rareneſſe, ſtrangeneſſe, or elſe of the good conformitie and coherence thereof, with other things, or out of a naturall inclination wee have thereunto; For it is true, *Quæ magna æstimamus magis memoriæ insigimus*, therefore first covet to understand well and with delight, and you shall remember the better.

2 The next precept is, often to meditate upon the thing so understood with a diligent disquisition and search through all the parts thereof, for whatsoever is by perfect understāding imprinted in the Memory, the same is more deeply ingraven by meditation therein; and as spice swallowed doth neither give taste to the tongue, nor heat to the stomacke, but when it is first broken and chewed in the mouth; so, much reading doth not increase learning except it be whetted and sharpned with meditation, which is the chewing of the cud after the mindes repast. And hereof it is that *Aristotle* affirmeth that *Meditatio confirmat memoriam*, and hence springeth the Proverbe, that it hath beene seldome seene that ever an old man forgot that place where hee had hidden his gold, for where our treasure is, there is our heart and meditation also.

3 The third consideration is to use and keepe a method, and to analyze the matter with all his parts and incidents which wee doe desire to remember, a course which notably establisheth, confirmeth, and strengthneth Memory. For in as much as Method consisteth much of division, that saying is very true which the glosse hath observed, and *Bracton* out of the same transumed,

Divisio

Divisio sive partitio triplicem operatur effectum; primo enim animum legentis incitat, secundò mentem intelligentiæ præparat, & tertiò memoriam artificiosè reformat.

The fourth consideration or precept is, to eschew and avoyd the troubling and incumbring the Minde at one time with sundry different and uncohærent matters, except it be done with much moderation, and at set times and houres, for recreation onely, and for the reviving of our understanding with variety, when it beginneth otherwise to be weakned, dulled or cloyed: so shall our Memory not bee pestered with manifold impressions; for when it seeketh to apprehend the one, it often and most commonly doth lose the other, according to the usuall and true saying, 4

Plurimis intentus minus est ad singula sensus.

The fift precept is daily to exercise Memory, that is, daily to commit things to the faithfull custody of our Memory, and after a time passed, most curiously and carefully to recall the same to an account thereof, and to render backe againe the things so received. And this kind of exercise maketh Memory very ready, and doth much increase the same; For *Quintilian* hath very well noted of Memory, that *Nihil æquè augetur cura, vel negligentia intercidit*; Nothing is so much encreased by diligence and care had thereof as Memory, and then the same nothing sooner lost by negligence thereof. As touching a true use hereof, we are to consider a distinction of things to bee remembred; for either we doe desire to remem- 5 ber the matter or ſubſtance onely which in all kinde of learning is to be obſerved, or elſe we alſo deſire to commit to Memory the frame and compact of the words alſo, as when we doe covet a penned Oration, ſet Sermon or Speech.

As touching the firſt, as the morning is a fit time to ſtudy, ſo is it alſo to commit matters of ſubſtance to Memory; for as the Memory is ſaid to be *Muſarum Mater*, ſo is *Aurora Muſarum amica*, for then are our bodies diſcharged of all ſuperfluous burthens that may hinder our ſtudies and meditations, and our ſpirits are more quicke after their received reſt.

As concerning the ſecond, many doe not unfruitfully commit their penned orations, ſet ſpeeches, laboured Sermons, and ſuch like which they covet verbally to pronounce, to Memory in the evening, being ſilent and quiet, and to give it harbour and lodging with them overnight, that they may more readily recount the ſame in the morning. And thus much touching theſe few, ſhort, eaſie and familiar precepts and obſervations touching that operation which we have called *Actus Memorandi*.

Now as touching the other called *Actus reminiſcendi*, the ſame is incited by divers circumſtances, as of the place, whereof *Ariſtotle* ſaith, *à locis videntur reminiſci aliquando*; So likewiſe of the perſons, times, the manner of doing, or as ſome other memorable accidents ſubject to the ſenſe, not ordinary or accuſtomed, doe occaſion: for things ſtrange and unfrequented are beſt held in

Memory

Memory, because they were first received of the Memory with admiration, as a new welcome guest into an Inne or lodging, about the entertainment and good usage of whom there is ordinarily most care and industry bestowed and conferred; And therefore no doubt, and upon this reason, those things which children doe first apprehend with an admiration and delight, they do retaine best and hold when they come to age. To these considerations there are those which do adde the precepts of Art Memorative, so often treated of by such as have written of Oratory, by appointing certaine places, conceived and imagined unto themselves, which being carefully disposed in convenient order, they doe fixe thereupon those things which they would remember in apprehension, and by consideration thereof do call to minde such forepassed matters in due and direct order, and so with much facility doe and can recount the same, upon which places so in their imagination fixed and apt for the matter in hand, it behooveth that they cast their carefull consideration and frequent meditation.

CAP. IIII.

THe third gift given from God by the courſe of nature unto Mankinde, wherewith the Student of the Lawes ought to be adorned, is a prompt and ready delivery by way of ſpeech, of thoſe things which are conceived in the minde, which is as it were the hand that doth communicate the former gifts ſpoken of, and participate unto others; and is that which the excellent Romane Oratour affirmeth to bee *bene conſtitutæ Civitatis quaſi Alumna quædam,* I meane not an elaborate curioſity of words, or an affectation of phraſe, which is practiſed by none, and wherewith none are mooved, but ſuch as are of vulgar judgement. But that I meane which the ſame Author commendeth, *Ea dicendi facultas quæ eſt plena dignitatis, grandis verbis, ſapiens ſententijs, accommodata cauſæ, genere toto gravis:* for of him that is adorned therewith ſaith he, *hujus enim eſt in dando conſilio de maximis rebus cum dignitate explicata ſententia, ejuſdem etiam languentis populi incitatio & effrenati moderatio:* That kinde of eloquence which is full of dignity, ever worth hearing, in ſpeech pure without affectation, ſententious and diſcreet, apt, anſwerable and agreeable to the matter in hand, and throughout beautified with

with gravity: Of this required quality let us also consider some advertisements (as we have done of the former).

Eloquution doth consist of three things, first, of the voyce as the instrument, 2, the words that are the subject; 3, the manner of doing, which is the forme of delivery. In the voyce are required two principall qualities, soundnesse and sweetness: this thing the same Oratour expresseth thus, *Cum orationis judicem vocem habeamus, in voce autem duo sequamur, ut clara sit, ut suavis sit, utrumq; omnino à natura petendum est, verum alterum exercitatio augebit, alterum imitatio praesse loquentium & leviter: litterae neq; oppressa sint ne aut obscurum, neque nimium expressa ut putidum:* In the words two things are required, purity and propertie; *Eloquution.*

First purity, that is, that neither the words bee old or outworne, neither newfangled or affected, in the which *non solum rusticam asperitatem, sed etiam peregrinam insolentiam fugere discamus*, that we may learne to eschew not onely forlorne rusticity, but all new affected outlandish vanity. 1

Secondly, property, that is, they are to bee made apt for the matter in hand, having few translations, Metaphors or borrowed speeches, but where they are needfull and doe illustrate. 2

In the third, the manner of composition of the speech and delivery, there are also two things considerable; first, perpetuity, secondly, exornation. 3

Our speech is made perspicuous if our words and sentences be not doubtfull in the compositiō,

E if

if they be free from Amphibology and ambiguous reference, if they be cleere of idle Taurology and vaine repetition, if our periods and clauses be not over long, nor interlaced with too many Parentheses; Lastly, if the copiousnesse and superabundance of words unnecessary hinder not the apprehension of the hearer, a fault whereinto many fall, that neverthelesse doe thinke they doe exceeding well.

Secondly, exornation is to bee performed by amplifications, extenuations, and such other Rhetoricall precepts as that Art teacheth, unto the which for this point I doe referre you; onely here giving you this caution, that the exornation exceed not the quality of the cause, *ne materiam superet opus*, for as it is vaine to overguilde excellent Marble with gold, so gold beseemeth not everie materiall; And many things shall and must passe the Lawyers pen and speech, which are *facundia minimè capacia cum sint tantum contenta doceri.* And having thus much said of these three gifts which proceed from God by the gift of nature, I will conclude with that saying of *Tully* which doth comprehend all three, *Animi & ingenij celeres quidem motus esse debent, qui ad excogitandum acuti, ad explicandum ornandumq; sint uberes, & ad memoriam firmi & diuturni.*

CAP. V.

THus with as convenient brevitie and perspicuity as I could have I declared those natural abilities that I wish him that shall undertake the study of the Law to bee furnished withall. There doth now farther remaine a consideration of those qualities that are acquired by industry, and not ingrafted by nature, wherewith it will (doublesse) be behoovfull also, that our student should be adorned; Those acquired qualities whereof I speake, are of two sorts, some of them perfecting our understanding, and inriching our knowledge, and others rectifying our wills, and directing our behaviours and manners. Of the first kinde are the *Vertues Intellectuall*. Of the second sort are the *Vertues Morall*.

First of all therefore let us speake in order of those *Intellectuall Vertues*; And let us a little fall into dispute, whether any other knowledge bee needfull for a Lawyer, save onely that of his selfe profession, I meane the knowledge of the Law; And if there be any of those *intellectuall* endowments necessary, Then, which and how many of them are needfull, and in what sense, measure and under-

understanding they bee conceived and adjudged so to be behoovefull.

Ob. prima. Some men there are which thinke that a Lawyer should not need much to bee troubled with any other learning then that which is their owne, whose reasons and motives thereunto, let us propose and thorowly weigh and examine the same, so that as well such as are of the one part, as of the contrary, may be thereby the better called into consideration.

Ra. prima ab experientia. Their first reason is drawne from experience; for it hath often hapned and appeared in every age (say they) that there have beene many excellent Lawyers within this land, of deepe judgement, great understanding, profound knowledge in their profession, of ready and apt eloquution, and yet no schollers at all; utterly ignorant of any other additionall erudition, then their homebred naturall gifts. These men have beene famous in their times, have undergone great affaires, as well in the Courts of our Soveraignes, as in the Tribunalls, wherein they have been worthily placed, and also generally in the greatest businesse of the Kingdome and Common wealth; so that the number of these men from time to time have not beene few. Therefore if the knowledge of the Law may be gotten without other learning, what need then to bestow time in the obtaining of those Arts, when as the Grammer Schoole yeeldeth as apt Plants for this profession, as the University.

Ra. secunda à subjecto juris. Secondly, they say that the knowledge of the Law

Law is affirmed to be *Rerum divinarum humanarumque Scientia,* it doth containe the knowledge of all divine & humane things; & therfore he that hath obtained that knowledge, hath therein comprised, included, and contained all other knowledges, and need not to busie himselfe farther with the search of any other, as having obtained the knowledge of the Law, which is truly stiled The Science of Sciences; for the knowledge of the Law is as large, and as ample as the materiall subject, and the matters and causes whereof it treateth, whereof contention or strife may grow, or upon which they may bee grounded: for the end and finall scope of the Law is, *ut sopiantur jurgia*; so ample is this subject, as all those things whereof men may have property or possession, or whereupon or concerning which injuries and wrongs may be offered or inferred.

Thirdly, they say that we should consider, that *Ars est longa, vita brevis,* the study of the Law is, *multorum annorum opus,* it is the worke of many yeares, the attaining whereof will waste the greatest part of the verdour and vigour of our youth, and therefore the sooner we doe apply our selves unto the study of the Law, it will be the better for our ease; for in a long journey, hee that hath found out the shortest way, with much ease and in lesse time commeth to his journeyes end. And to conclude with the Orators words; *Is autem concludatur in ijs quæ sunt in usu Civitatum vulgari ac forensi, remotisque cæteris studijs quamvis ea sint ampla atque præclara. In hoc uno opere (ut ita dicam)* *Ra. tertia dicitur à diuturnitate juris.*

 noctes

noctes atque dies urgeatur, (What hee saith of his Oratour, these men apply to the student of our Law) Let therefore our student of the Law be concluded and compassed within the bounds of his owne profession, and exercised in things of vulgar and ordinary use in civill causes, and all other forraigne studies being relinquished, let him bee night and day employed in this sole worke. These and the like are the allegations and arguments of those men that remove the knowledge of all forraigne Arts and Sciences liberall from the student of the Law.

But, what of the other part may be said, what reason may be produced and verified, and how these objections may be answered, let us observe; leaving all other particular enforcement to their proper and peculiar places.

Resp. ad primam object. First therefore, that is very true which hath beene affirmed, Many excellent men there have beene, that by their gifts alone which nature hath bestowed upon them without other addition of Art or learning, have attained to a profound and deepe knowledge of the Lawes of this land. But to conclude thereof, that all other men may bee so exquisite by their example without farther helpe and furniture then their owne, were much like to him that would affirme, because some men by their strength have travailed a long journey on foot, therefore no other man for that purpose should need the helpe of an horse; But if those men of such naturall vigour in their foot-journey had led (as the Proverbiall speech is) their horse in in their hand, that is, had beene assisted with the helps of other learning, they had beene much more excellent, and attained that knowledge with more facility and certainty, for their gold oare comming out of their naturall Mine, and of their home-brood, was not sufficiently cleered of his drosse; Their speeches have wanted perspicuity and brevity, their arguments although deeply learned and full of excellent matter, yet have oftentimes beene tedious, confused and perplexed, and their opinions wavering and unsetled, and could not neatly, and expeditely deliver themselves; because some men are by nature skilfull Painters, Carvers, or excellent in any manuall occupation (as some there are) therefore none should be bound Apprentices to those trades were a wonderfull absurd allegation: Men are musicall by nature, many have good voyces which Art cannot yeeld, therefore artificall Musicke (which is the perfection of the naturall) should be banished, were a strange illatiō? Although a man may goe alone, yet he were unwise to refuse the helpe of a staffe where occasion required the use, and opportunity offered it selfe. It hath beene said by us in the former part where occasion was offered, that Art truly used is the perfection of nature; Art hath also naturall grounds, and was invented for Natures furtherance; For mans wisedome devised meanes out of frequent use and long experience, to ripen natures operations, by precepts; and precepts layd together have ingendered Arts. Men naturally

rally can number, yet they have deviſed many wayes, by cypher, by Counters, and by other formes to aſſiſt nature, and to deale with ſundry formes by the exerciſe of Arithmeticke, the Art of numbring, and to bring to paſſe ſtrange effects far beyond the ability, nay to the marvell and aſtoniſhment of men onely holpen by the power of nature. Surely ſometimes ſuch circumſtances have happened (if not often) to thoſe men of ſuch excellent gifts naturall without other learning, wherein they have for want of good literature ſo much beene miſ-led, that they have at unawares bewrayed themſelves, ignorant even in triviall things, and expoſed themſelves to no ſmall ſcorne and obloquy.

This hath beene anciently obſerved, and is obvious every day; but becauſe I will lance no new ſore, I will ſet downe what the Roman Oratour obſerved, ſpeaking of ſuch naturall excellent men of his time, let mee therefore uſe his words; *Quid ergo hoc fieri turpius aut dici poteſt, quam qui hanc perſonam ſuſceperit ut amicorum controverſias cauſaſque tueatur, laborantibus ſuccurrat, agris mediatur, afflictos excitet, ita labi, ut alijs miſerandus, alijs irridendus eſſe videatur*. What can bee more unſeemly either to be done, or to be ſpoken, thē that he which ſuſtaineth & hath taken upon him that perſon, as to defend the cauſes and controverſies of his friends, to ſuccour the oppreſſed, to relieve the grieved, to raiſe the afflicted (which are the properties as well belonging to the Lawyer, as to the Oratour) ſo much in ſmall and triviall things

to

to erre and be deceived, that some should hold him worthy to bee pittied, and others make him the subject of dirision; And hence is it that in our owne times so farre this matter hath beene urged, that in scorne some have called the crew of unlearned Lawyers, *Doctum quoddam genus indoctorum hominum:* But to returne that reproach from whence it sprang, to the honour of the study of our Lawes be it spoken, that the Profession of our Lawes hath now, and formerly hath had great numbers of students that have had as long, and as ample institution in those sciences called liberall, as any of thẽ. And if I might remember old Originalls from the time of the *Norman Conquest*, untill the latter dayes of King *Henry* the third, as well the Iudges itinerate through the Counties, as those that were sedentarie in the Kings high Courts of Iustice (which then for the most part followed his person) were men excellently skilled in all generall good learning, as doe witnesse the works of that worthy Iudge *Henry de Bracton*, and *Iohn Britton* sometimes a learned Bishop of *Hereford*, skilfull in the Lawes of this Realme, who writ a treatise by commandement, and writ of King *Edward* the first, as an Institution to the study of the lawes of this Realme, serving that time. So also was *Martyn de Patchull* sometimes Deane of *Pauls* in *London*, of whom the said *Bracton* maketh honourable mention, together with divers other noted men of rare learning, not onely in the Lawes of this Realme, but in all forraine knowledge fit for their places. And these men exercised

Henry de Bracton, Io: Britton Bish. of Hereford, Martin de Patchull Deane of Pauls.

sed judiciall functions in the Temporall Courts of this Realme, whereof our records being *& vetustatis & veritatis vestigia*, the lively representations of time and truth, and reputed the Treasures of the Kingdome, doe yeeld plentifull testimony. What should I farther commemorate the names, and revive the memories of our worthy Ancestors, *Herle, Bereford, Thorpe, Finden, Belknap*, flourishing in the victorious times of King *Edward* the third? Whose deepe, short, subtile, pithy and learned Law-arguments; argue moreover thus much, that they were sufficiently furnished in that Schoole-learning, which in those times was in most esteeme. Let me not here forget or passe-over in silence those excellent Iudges in the raigne of King *Henry* the sixt, *Newton, Prisott, Fortescue*, which man last named, was first Chauncellor to the Prince, and after chiefe Iustice of the Kings Bench, and was excellently learned in Divinity, Philosophy, Law both Ecclesiasticall, and the Lawes of this Realme, as the little Treatise written by him in the praise of our Lawes, in the Latine tongue, and some other Manuscripts I have seene of his worke of a higher subject, doe evidently declare. But I will represse my selfe, resting in this place upon that which now is already spoken, leaving other particularities untill we come to determine of other peculiar Sciences.

Herle, Bereford, Thorpe, Finden, Belknapp tempore R. Ed. 3.

Newton, Prisot, Fortescue, tempore H. 6.

Resp. ad sec. ob.

To the second objection it may well bee affirmed, that the knowledge of the Law is truly stiled, *Rerum divinarum humanarumque Scientia*; and wor-

worthily imputed to be the Science of Sciences; and that therein lies hid the knowledge almost of every other learned science: But yet I pray consider, that those forraine knowledges, are not inherent or inbred in the Lawes, but rather as a borrowed light not found there, but brought thither, and learned elsewhere by them that have adorned and polished the studies of the Lawes. For since the materiall subject of the Law is so ample (as indeed it is) containing all things that may be controverted. The study of the Lawes then must of necessity stretch out her hand, and crave to be holpen and assisted almost of all other Sciences; Therefore this objection may well bee inverted against them that doe urge the same, and proveth rather that the Professor of the Lawes should be furnished with the knowledge of all good literature of most of the Sciences liberall; for if a man may observe the use of those sciences to lie hidden in the Law, who then may better use them or observe them, then he which is already furnished with them. And if the knowledge of the Law, doe receive ornament by those eruditions (as I think no man can denie) it shall be very expedient and well befitting the student of the Lawes, to have first familiarity and acquaintance with them, and to bee instructed in the same.

But it may bee objected, that the Lawyer shall not need the knowledge of those Arts himselfe, but when opportunity shall be offered, and when question shall arise, wherein the Lawyer shall ſtand in need of reſolution of any of thoſe Sciences, he may conferre, and bee informed by the Profeſſors of the ſame, to his good ſatisfaction, although himſelfe be not expert therein. Many times there have beene (and may bee hereafter) Appeales of Mayme brought by ſuch parties as in private fight and otherwiſe by violence have received maime, that is, mutilation and loſſe of a member of his body ſerviceable for offence or defence againſt thoſe parties that ſo have hurt them, and many times queſtion & debate ariſeth, whether the hurt ſo received, be to bee adjudged a Maime, yea or no? So that the Iudges are oftentimes enforced to conferre with Chyrurgians for their ſuffrage and reſolution; will you therefore require your Iudges, Profeſſors and ſtudents of the Law to be alſo Surgeons, or skilfull in the Art of Chyrurgery? that were altogether uncomely.

Reſp. This objection is eaſily anſwered and avoyded, for firſt there is a great difference in this reſpect betweene manuall Arts and occupations wrought by the dexterity of the hand, and thoſe that are ſciences and vertues intellectuall adorning the Minde, as are the Liberall.

Mayme. The Lawes of this Realme doe appoint no other trial of a Maime, then the view of the Iudge, for a Mayme is ſuch as for the moſt part is viſible and ſubject unto ſenſe; And therefore if upon ſome doubt or occaſion conceived, by reaſon of the view, the Iudges doe deſire the conference of expert Chyrurgians for the better ſatisfaction

of

of their conſcience. This is no matter of neceſſity to import the Iudges, but matter of diſcretion onely, in not being too precipitate, but rather mature in their judgement, as they ought; and to ſhew themſelves rather willing to goe onward with others, then to run alone of themſelves. And herein the Iudges are not tyed to the opinion of the Chyrurgian, otherwiſe then hee findeth the ſame to be conformable and grounded upon ſuch good and apparent reaſon as may yeeld full ſatiſfaction and contentment: But when the queſtion ſhal be moved wch ſhal require informatiō of any learned ſcience which is gotten by diſcourſe of reaſon; Although in thoſe caſes the laudable courſes have ever beene in our Courts of Iuſtice, to heare the Profeſſors of thoſe ſciences to diſpute and debate the matter controverted before our Tribunall and judgement ſeats, yet no man can deny, but it is better to draw one draught out of the pure fountaine it ſelfe, then to quench our thirſt out of derived ſtreames, for

Dulcius ex ipſo fonte bibuntur aquæ.

For in every Science which doth depend upon diſcourſe of reaſon, there are many fundamentall Maximes and Principalls not to bee changed in any future reſolution, but rather to be received as guides to direct, which at the firſt will ſeeme harſh to ſuch as have not beene inured unto them, and therefore it were perillous to the Iudge and Profeſſor of the Lawes, and he ſhall not bee able either to receive to himſelfe, or to give to others ſatisfaction, except hee can by his proper knowledge discerne of the controversie. For we surely know *Non ex relatis aliorum, sed cum per causas cognoscimus*, and if wee have knowledge in those sciences our selves, we shall the better apprehend and understand the reasons of those matters so disclosed by debate: And thus I leave the second objection.

Resp ad tertiam Object. To the third, last, and maine objection, this may be produced for an answer, that though true it bee *Vita brevis est, ars longa*, our life is short and full of calamities, and learning is a long time in getting, yet may wee not in respect of short life shut up all our endeavours for feare of an end; for therefore the Period of our life is sealed up from mans knowledge, first for that wee should bee alwayes ready when we are called hence; Secondly, for that the feare of a knowne death should not daunt or interrupt our endeavours; Likewise the verdure of our yonger yeares is best imploied and spent in obtaining of those sciences, for then are we most apt thereunto. And as the study and practice of Morall Philosophy (as Art doth witnesse) is not fittest for men over yong; so likewise the study of the Law which hath his foundatiō in Morall Philosophy (both having one end generall, namely, the rectifying of our manners) doth require some maturity of yeeres, and not to bee set upon by infants in yeeres, judgement, and cariage. And so likewise shall wee finde in a long journey, that the fairest way is better although somewhat farther about, then a shorter rough way, hard to finde and difficult to keepe; and in the

the end also to answer that close or upshot drawn from *Tullies Orator*; I would you should likewise remember for conclusion of this question that which he affirmeth, *Non enim Causidicum nescio quem, nec proclamatorem aut rabulam hoc sermone nostro conquirimus, sed eum virum qui primùm sit ejus Artis Antistes,&c.* We seeke not hereby to institute I know not what manner of vulgar professor of the Lawes, no common blatterer or temerist, but that man which may prove in the end an excellent and chiefe Pillar, Prop and Ornament of his profession.

CAP. VI.

The necessity of the Latine Tongue in a Student of the Law.

HAving hitherunto proceeded in the generall, it shall bee now requisite to descend to particulars. And first of all to consider, whether the knowledge of the Latine Tongue, and the use of Grammar, tending to the obtaining of the same, be necessary for a Lawyer: not proposing it by way of doubt, question, or difficulty, that it should need any large dispute, but by way of manifestation and disquisitiō onely; for there is no man (as I suppose) that can or will deny, but that the knowledge of the Latine tongue is right necessary for our English Lawyer: which may be made apparent by many evident

evident and eminent arguments and allegations, easily to be produced for that purpose.

Ra. prima. First of all, many of our old Statutes, and ancient positive Lawes were written and formed in the Latine tongue, and so doe still rest and remaine in our Records and Bookes; as that Act called *Magna Charta*, The great Charter of *England*, great indeed, not in respect of moulde, but matter, not great in quantity, but in weight and worth: Containing many the fundamentall points of our Lawes, bought with the blood of our Nobility and English Ancestors, in those troublesome times of King *Iohn*, and *Henry* his sonne. And although many of the Constitutions contained in that Charter, first introduced in part by King *Henry* the first, (then called for his learning *Henry le beu Clarke*,) comming in and putting by his elder brother *Robert* of *Normandy*, and as it were by restitution and renovation of the old Lawes of *Edward* the Confessor King before the Conquest, and in tract of time sought to be enfringed, yet neverthelesse not without trouble it was afterward againe both revived & enlarged, first by another Charter of King *Iohn*, and lastly by King *Henry* the third his sonne in Parliament established, and sundry times afterwards by succeeding Parliaments, also confirmed and commanded to be put in due execution.

Magna Charta.

Hen. 1.

Stat. Marton 20. H. 3. Marlebridge Glouceſter. In like manner these severall Lawes of note, as the Statute made at *Marton Abbey* in *Surrey*: That also made at *Marlebridge*, that likewise at *Glocester*, and sundry others were all originally framed

med in the Latine tongue in the reigne of the ſaid *Henry* the third: Alſo the Acts made in the firſt, certaine in the ſecond, and the Acts made in the third Parliaments all holden at *Weſtminſter* in the raigne of that victorious and renowued Prince King *Edward* after the Conqueſt ſurnamed the firſt, compiled by Parliament for the good government of this Kingdome, were written alſo in the Latine tongue. *Weſtm.* 1. *Weſtm.* 2. *Weſtm.* 3.

Secondly, many learned Writers have compoſed divers excellent Treatiſes of the Lawes of this Realme, in the Latine tongue, as namely, that ancient Treatiſe compoſed by *Ranulphus de Glanvilla*, a learned Iudge of this Land, who is ſaid to have gone in perſon with King *Richard* the firſt into the holy Land, and to have ended his dayes at *Ptolomais* then called *Acon* or *Acres* a Maritine Towne of that Country. Treatiſes of Law in the Latine Tongue. *Ra. Glanvill.* Ended his dayes at *Ptolomais* in the holy Land.

I will here adjoyne the learned Treatiſe (and as the times then ſtood) I might well call and affirme the eloquent Treatiſe of the Common Lawes framed by *Henry de Bracton* a moſt learned Iudge of this Land, living in the latter end of the raigne of King *Henry* the third, and in the entrance of King *Edward* the firſt his regiment: This Treatiſe is repleniſhed with many excellent ſentences, fitly and aptly compoſed in Latine; and by the reading of this worthy worke, the ſtudent ſhall truly underſtand not onely the conformity our Nationall Lawes then had with the Civill, Cannon, or Eccleſiaſticall Lawes, but alſo ſhall well perceive what the Common Law of this our Coun- *Hen. de Bracton.*

trey was before the making of divers Statutes which have altered the same, whereby great light may bee had, and a great helpe obtained for the better understanding and true interpretation of the same.

Likewise, there is a learned Treatise composed by a learned yet unknowne Author whiles he was a Prisoner in the Fleet, and therefore the said *Fleta.* worke or tract is called *Fleta*, in the time as it seemeth of King *Edward* the first, and although there doe now remaine but a few Manuscript copies thereof, as having beene never imprinted yet is it worthy to see the light, and for the furtherance of the student of the Lawes to be divulged, and this also was written in the Latine tongue: I might remember two Treatises, the greater, and the lesser, gathered by *Radulphus de* *Ra. Hinghã.* *Hingham*, sometime Chiefe Iustice of the Common Pleas, whose monument yet remaineth in the Cathedrall Church of Saint *Paul* in *London*, and written in Latine, but in corrupt language as the times then afforded.

But passing over many other in silence, I will conclude with that little Treatise made *de laudibus legum Angliæ*, in praise and commendations of the Lawes of this Land by comparison with the forreigne Lawes of some other Countries devised and written in the Latine tongue by that sincere and most learned Iudge, Sir *Iohn Fortes-* *Io. Fortescue.* *cue* Knight, thereby to incite by many arguments the Prince, sonne and heire to King *Henry* the sixt, to the knowledge of the Lawes of this Country:

it

it ſeemeth by many paſſages of this Treatiſe, that the ſame was contrived in the Kingdome of *France,* during ſuch time as the Queene with her ſaid ſonne the Prince remained there to ſollicite ayde for her husband. This Author at the writing of this Treatiſe was as it ſeemeth Chauncellor to the Prince, and afterward Chiefe Iuſtice of the Kings Bench: This little worke is well worthy the peruſall, plentifully ſhewing the learning of the Author in Divinity, Philoſophy, and other good literature, beſides the knowledge of the Lawes of this Realme, a man I ſay who for the fidelity he bare to his Maſter, taſted of the tempeſt then ſtirred in the end of his time, having had both his riſing and his ruine in that fatall fall of his Lord.

Thirdly, all the formes of writs are and ought to be framed in the Latine tongue, and if they do containe falſe Latine, they are abateable, and to be defeited, and the party plaintife who purſued the ſame, ſhall bee driven to purchaſe a better writ, and to begin a new. For the better underſtanding whereof, let mee obſerve ſomething of the nature of Writs. *Writs ought to be framed in true and congruous Latine.*

A Writ is the commandement of the King, formed in Latine, directed either to ſome Miniſter of his Courts; or ſometime to the partie Defendant, at the purſuite of the Plaintife, for the better adminiſtration of Iuſtice. This Deſcription concerneth all manner of writs, which as touching their forme, are ſhort and briefe; and therfore in Latine are called *Brevia,* in French *Briefes* *Definition of a Writ.*

The Etimologie. for their ſhortneſſe in Engliſh Writs, for that they are Mandates in writing. The latine Etymology of the name, *Bracton* yeeldeth thus: *Brevia dicuntur (per modum Regula juris) quia rem quæ eſt & intentionem Petentis brevitur enarrat:* And yet ought they not through brevity to bee obſcure, but cleare and in a compendious manner to comprehend the matter therein contayned: They ought to be formed in words, proper & perſpicuous, free of ambiguity, no prepoſterous order, no doubtfull reference, no idle repetition, no omiſſion of needfull matter, and ought to bee formed in apt, true, and congruous Latine.

Diviſion. Writs are in ſundry manners divided, (1) ſometime in reſpect of their matter; (2) ſometime in reſpect of their forme; (3) ſometime in repect of the efficient cauſe; (4) and ſometime againe in reſpect of their finall cauſe.

In reſpect of their matter, all Writs are of three kinds, that is, (1) Originall, (2) Meane Proces, (3) Iudiciall.

Defin: An originall Writ, quid? An Originall Writ is the Commandement of the King, formed in Latine, iſſuing out of the Chauncery, ſealed with the great Seale of *England*, contayning the cauſe of ſuite directed to a Miniſter of the Court to compell the defendant to appeare and anſwer at a day prefixed for the returne thereof.

Etimology. The Originall Writ is the foundation of the ſuit, and therefore is called originall, for that it is the firſt writ ſued forth at the beginning of the ſuit, to bring the defendant in Court to anſwer.

In

In respect of their matter, they are divided thus; They are either (1) Reall, (2) Personall, (3) Mixt, or (4) neither, as the Appeale. *Divisio in materiam & formam.*

In respect of their forme, they are either of a setled and composed forme, and therefore called *formata:* or without a setled forme, but doe vary according to the circumstance of the cause, and called by *Bracton, Brevia Magistralia*; the other *Brevia de cursu.*

In respect of their efficient cause all these Originall Writs doe issue, as hath beene said, out of the *Chancery*, which is the shop and forge wherein for the most part they are framed. The Magisteriall Briefes, because they vary with the case, require a Masters hand to compose them in respect of skill. But the other *De cursu, Writs of course*, because they have a setled forme prescribed in an ancient booke therefore called the *Register of Writs*, and vary not but *in mutatis mutandis:* they are written by a society of Clarkes of the Chancery called therefore *Cursitors:* But I purpose not here to make a full and liberall discourse of writs, this alone may suffice in this place, and for the matter in hand. *Causa efficiens.* *Cursitors, unde dicitur.*

Fourthly, it is manifest, that all the returnes of Writs, all manner of proceedings, all Counts or Declarations of the Plaintiffes or Demaundants, all Pleas, defences or exceptions of the Defendants or Tennants, either to the Iurisdiction of the Court, or to abate the writ, or in barre of the Action all replications thereunto by the Plaintife and demandant, all rejoynders or surrejoynders, all issues taken, all verdicts, demurrers, continuances and entries of the judgements of the Court in sundry formes, according to the severall nature of the writs and actions in controversie: Likewise all the proceedings in criminall causes and Pleas of the Crowne which concerne life or member by way of indictment or presentment, the Arraignment, Tryall, and Iudgements thereupon had, are entred, written, and engrossed in the Latine tongue; And therefore without the knowledge of this language, the student of the Lawes, the Practizer, and the Iudge must of necessity walke thorough a vale of darknesse and palpable ignorance in the superlative.

By this which hath beene already affirmed may easily be conceived, that Grammar being the first Liberall Sciences is very behoovfull & needfull for a Lawyer, as by sundry instances may bee made manifest in every part thereof. *Grammar* hath beene divided into these foure parts; *Orthographia, Etymologia, Syntaxis*, and *Prosodia*.

Orthographia. In *Orthographie*, which concernes true writing, we are taught that from the knitting together of Letters are made sillables, of sillables significative words. These words are twofold, Primitive, which were composed at the first to denote and signifie this or that thing, and words derivatives drawne from those Primitives, which in writing ought to containe the radicall letters of those Primitives, that thereby may be discovered and discerned the root and of-spring from whence they were drawne and deduced.

First

First therefore, as touching letters and syllables, sometime a letter is omitted which maketh the word written, no latine at all,

In a *Scire fac*: the writ was abated for want of a letter, for the writ was *ex insinatione*, which is no latine, whereas it should have beene *ex insinuatione*. So in a *precipe quod reddat*, the words were *precipe quod reddat hari*; where it wanted a syllable and should have beene *hæredi*, and this writ was abated. And sometimes for placing one letter for another, as in a writ of waste, the same was *ad destrictionem*, whereas it should have beene *ad destructionem*. So likewise an Inditement of Burglary was avoyded, for that it was *Burgaliter*, whereas it should have beene *burglariter*, although no perfect, yet allowed Lawyers Latine, and an artificiall word, a word of Art.

24. E.3.7.

41. E. 3.21.

Cooke 2 part. lib. 5.

The second was of Grammar called *Etimologia*, hath two parts, for it doth not onely concerne the derivation of words, but also the forming of words in all the principle parts of speech, as of the Nounes, Pronounes, Participles, in number, case, gender, termination, declination, & such like; but also of verbs in declination, moode, tense, nūber, person, and such like, and in these things also the Lawes of this Realme require congruity to bee observed, according to the rules of Grammar. The writ was *hos breve*, where it should have been *hoc breve*, and therefore was abated, and could not be amended; one case for another.

Etimologia.

In a *Precipe quod reddat*, the writ was *quas*, where it should have beene *quod*, one gender for ano-

another, and therefore was abated. In a writ of
12.H. 4. 10. *Iuris vtrum*, the writ was *fit* where it should have
Fitz. n.br. beene *sint*, one number for another, with divers
466. others, such like examples.

Syntaxis. The third part of Grammer is Syntaxis or Composition of speech, and hath these parts (1) the conformity betweene the verbe and the casuall word; (2) betwene the substantive and the adjective; (3) betweene the Antecedent and the Relative which part hath sundry examples in the Law, and would be tedious to remember.

Ob. prima. These things notwithstanding, there doe remaine certaine objections to be cleared; for first it may be objected that in the Courts of Iustice, the Clerks in the entring and enrolling of their Records, forme up their words in a short kind of writing by certaine abreviations, by which are knowne the words intended; And therefore in this course which is most usuall there can be but a slender observation of true Orthography.

Resp. To this I answer, that among all the *Cursitors* and *Prothonotories*, and all other Clerkes in our Courts, there is observed a briefe and short kind of writing for the better dispatch of an infinite masse of businesse in that kinde, and heape of writings which they termly undergoe, yet the same is not voluntary, or at pleasure, or as every man will or shall devise, fashion, or frame unto himselfe, but such onely vulgar, and well known both among themselves, as all other that intermeddle therewith, which tract of time hath made famili-
4.H.6.16. ar from age to age by expert observation. And here

here may I remember that almoſt every of our Courts of Iuſtice hath his ſeverall ſet forme of handwriting, as the Chancery hand, conveyed in a faire forme of letter, little inferior to the print; and the Court hand ſomewhat diſtinguiſhed in forme of letters frō the ordinary ſecretary or ſet hand uſed among the vulgar, which our Auncestors at firſt invented, and ever ſince to great purpoſe have practiſed, thereby giving the greater impreſſion, ſo that it may remaine legible to poſterity many hundred yeeres, as by our ancient Records, and many Monuments of Antiquity yet remaining of ancient occurrences before the *Norman Conqueſt* is evidently declared.

Secondly may be objected, that ſince the time that the Latine tongue was vulgarly uſed among the *Romans*, and other the Nations, that they ſubdued to that Empire (for they much endeavoured the propagation of their language) ſundry new things have beene invented, whereof thoſe ancient people had either no intelligence, or no uſe, and therefore where ſuch things doe occurre, there doe want words proper and peculier in the Latine tongue to denote the ſame, and men muſt of neceſſity bee enforced either to uſe barbarous words farre from the purity of the Latine ſpeech, or to invent new to expreſſe their meaning. *Ob. ſecunda.*

For ſatisfaction and full declaration whereof, we are to conſider that uſually in courſe of Law foure kind of words are caried under the colour of latine in Law proceedings; as firſt, the true native and proper latine word if they bee found for *Reſp.*

the present purpose, whereof our Iudges have e-
Coke lib. 10. fol. 133. ver beene carefull, as by their sundry conferences with Grammarians, and men learned concerning the true and naturall signification of Latine words almost every way extant in our books doe declare.

Secondly, there are words of Art in the lawes, as in other faculties.

And thirdly, certaine other words drawne from the ancient Idiome and language of our predecessors, the former Inhabitants of this Land, vulgarly and sufficiently knowne, which receiving latine formes passe in our Lawes, as *felonia, felonice, Murdrum, Burglaria, Warrantia, Esnitia, pars mulier, pro sobole ex legitima uxore nata,* with many others of like derivation, as *mesuadgium* for an house, *toftum* for a decayed house, *gardinum* for a garden, *bruera* for furse or heath, *maromium* for timber, *bastardus,* for *nothus,* a base borne childe, and the like.

And fourthly, for new invented things not known to the Ancients, new words likewise haue had their originall, as *Bombardum* or *tormentum* for a gunne, *Pulvis tormentarius,* for gunpowder, *Stapedia* for a stirrop, *velvettum* for velvet, and many of such like making, wherunto for better understanding we doe permit the English usuall words to be adjoyned in our latine pleadings.

Ob. tertia. Lastly, there remaineth this scruple, where it hath beene affirmed, that there is much respect had of the true propriety of latine words, it seemeth nothing lesse, for those formes are conceived in in a base stile farre removed from purity of speech so that the professors of Law within this land can challenge no great commendation in this kinde.

To this is answered, that the Lawes of this Land neither doe, nor desire to affect Eloquence in the Latine tongue, for wee have no use of the speech thereof in our arguments, for as much as the Statute made 36. *E*. 3. *cap*. 15. hath ordained that all pleadings, and all arguments and disputations of Law should thenceforth be performed in the English tongue, whereas formerly as it seemeth it was put in ure in the French, remaining untill that time, as a badge of the *Norman Captivity*, whereof there is now no use but in the arraigning of an Assize, and an Appeale, and such French Arguments as are used for exercise in the Houses, and Societies of Court and Chancery. Neverthelesse the former usage hath still remained, that is, that all proceedings Iudicial shold be entred and enrolled in the Latine tongue, so that the Latine serveth to convey to posterity our Memorialls and Records, and not our debate and speech: The Antiquity whereof, whether it first grew in respect of the use thereof, retained among all Nations subject to that Empire upon like occasion even unto this day; or whether for the Majestie of that language wherein all Arts of literature are still promulged, or whether it may be reached unto the *Romane Conquest* of this Land, who long held it under their government, and reduced many parts thereof into Provinces, endeavouring (as their manner was) to propagate

Resp.

36. E. 3. 15.

their language as largely as their Empire; or whether it happened in respect our Anceſtors the *Brittons* with good affection embraced that language, as *Tacitus* reporteth, I doe surceaſe in this place to determine.

But for farther ſatisfaction in this poynt, the Entries and enrollments of our Writs, Pleas, and all other our Law proceedings are neither baſe, abject, or horrid, as hath beene imported; for our Originall Writs of ſet forme are from ancient memory, have ever beene preſerved in the booke called the Regiſter, from the which our Clerkes may not ſwerve, to avoyd the infinite variety of formes which might otherwiſe enſue, and were firſt conceived and deviſed in as proper Latine, as the times wherein they were firſt invented, and the matter it ſelfe was able to beare. And as touching the other mentioned proceedings entered in the Latine tongue, although not eloquent, yet *ſatis laudato forenſi ſtilo,* as in any other Kingdome perſpicuous and ſignificant.

Let not the ſame therefore be a blemiſh to our Lawes, which hath invaded almoſt all other Sciences; for what horrid and incompt words hath Logicke and Philoſophy endured, introduced by their Dunces devices, as *Ens, entitas, quidditas, cauſalitas,* with a multitude of others impertinent to be remembred? with what improper tearmes and barbarous ſpeeches have the Schoolmen daubed Divinity? What hath beene in this kinde brought in upon the pure and cleare fountaines of the Digeſts of the Civill Lawes? which being

being compiled out of ſundry moſt excellent ſentences, drawne out of the workes and paſſages of the ancient *Romane Lawyers*, doe retaine the ſame purity and conformity of a cleane and neat ſtile, as though all had beene penned by one man; and yet are in a manner defiled by the *Feudary Tenurist* writers of the middle age in their *Glosses* and *Commentaries*, as thoſe learned Lawyers of this latter age *Alciatus*, *Budæus*, *Cujacius*, and the reſt have undergone an *Herculean* labour to clenſe the ſame.

But to conclude this matter; the Students of our Lawes, and the profeſſors thereof may well defend themſelves by the teſtimony and authoritie of the beſt Writers in this behalfe: For firſt of all *Ariſtotle* himſelfe giveth warrant, *Quod nova vocabula ſunt facienda cùm ad res explicandas nullæ ſuppetunt voces:* And herein they may bee bold to ſtand to the judgement of *Tully* himſelfe who affirmeth, *Omne quod de re bona dilucide dicitur, mihi præclarè dici videtur: iſtiuſmodi autem res dicere ornatè velle, puerile eſt; planè autem & perſpicuè poſſe docti & intelligentis eſt viri.* And I know no cauſe why wee may not ſay the ſame of our Lawyer which he affirmeth in that Booke of the Philoſopher, *Philoſophum ſi afferat eloquentiam non eſſe aſpernendum, ſi non habeat non eſſe ab eo admodum flagitandum, dum tamen complectatur verbis quod vult, & dicat planè ut intelligatur.* And ſo let me ſay, if our Lawyer or Pronotorie in drawing up his pleadings can uſe a good phraſe and pure Latine, I will

Ariſt. in Catego. Relationis.

never blame him, if not, I will not expect it at his hands, so that that which he hath drawne bee congrue, plaine, familiar, sensible, and easie to be understood.

Thus have wee produced two of the best Authors for our defence, the one for wit and knowledge the worlds wonder; The other for eloquent and excellent speech in his native language the chiefest ornament. It shall suffice to conclude with a sentence of a Christian Father inferiour in humane learning to neither of them, whose speech because it is excellently to the purpose, I cannot let passe; *Bonorum ingeniorum insignis est indoles, in verbis verum amare non verba; Quid enim prodest clavis aurea, si, quod volumus aperire, non potest? aut quid obest lignea, si hoc potest? quando nihil quærimus nisi patere quod clausum est?* It is an excellent Argument of the best wits, not to hunt compt and filed words, but in words to embrace the truth, for what profiteth a Golden key, if it cannot open, and what hurt is it to use a wodden key, if it will open, when there is no other end of both, but to open that which was shut.

CAP.

Cap. VII.

THe next ſucceeding *Science Liberall* is *Logicke*, and therefore order doth require wee ſhould here alſo make inquirie whether the Art of Logicke be neceſſary for the attaining to the knowledge of the Law. The queſtion hath beene diverſly debated by ſundry of *Ariſtotles* Interpreters, and ſuch as have written of that Science both touching the peculiar inſtance or *Hypotheſis*; as alſo more at large in the generall *Theſis*, namely, whether Logicke bee neceſſary for the better obtaining of other learned Sciences. In handling of this debate, we will hold our former propoſed courſe, and firſt of all let us object againſt the neceſſity thereof. *Logicke.*

Experience is a ſure foundation: many excellent Lawyers both in the civill Lawes of the Empire, the Cannon Lawes of the Church, and the Common Lawes of the Land have not beene skilfull in Logicke, and therefore Logicke is not neceſſary for the knowledge of the Lawes. *Ra. prima.*

Law Arguments are deduced more from authority then reaſon, for the Engliſh Lawyer in arguments requireth moſt the ſtrength of Caſes apt to the purpoſe, and Preſidents of former *Ra. ſecunda.*

times,

time, then diſcourſe of reaſon; and therefore Logicke which reſpecteth onely the inference and diſcourſe of reaſon, is not ſo needfull for a Lawyer.

Ra. tertia. The Lawes deale with particular inſtances, and individuall Caſes, where the ſundry circumſtances accompanying the fact, make maniteſt difference, *inter æquum & iniquum; juſtum & injuſtum;* whereas Logicke dealeth not with univerſalities abſtracted from the particulars, and exempt from their circumſtances, and therefore Logicke not neceſſary for a Lawyer.

Ra. quarta. A great part of Logicke doth treat of Propoſitions, and the framing of Syllogiſmes, but the Lawyer doth not argue ſyllogiſtically, and therefore needeth no Logicke.

Ra. quinta. Man is a living creature, by nature reaſonable, and can by the gift of nature alone, apprehend, underſtand, inferre, collect, diſcourſe, reaſon, prove, diſprove, order, and diſpoſe things conceived, and truly judge of them; and therfore where theſe things are by nature, what neceſſity is there to learne them by Art? for *ſicut pupilla ineſt viſus, ita animæ Intellectus; Ariſt. 1. Ethic. cap. 6* And againe the ſame writer, *homines à natura Dialecticos & Rhetoricos eſſe; Ariſtot. 1. Rhet. ad Theodoctum, & 1. Elenchorum.* Every faculty and diſcipline of it ſelfe hath a diſtinct and peculiar manner of proceeding, and therefore a ſpeciall Logicke muſt be framed for the ſtudy of the Law if any bee neceſſary at all, for the generall Logicke will not ſuffice.

The

The full handling of this queſtion will give occaſion of a large diſcourſe, and incite us to ſet out and declare the principall parts of Logicke, and the true uſe thereof in the knowledge of the Lawes; wherefore leſt our ſpeech thorow multiplicity of matter might be confuſe, wee will hold this order:

First, we ſhall endevour to produce the teſtimonies of moſt approved Authors of the part affirmative, wherein they have delivered the neceſſity or profitable uſe of Logicke. 1

Secondly, wee ſhall undertake by reaſons drawne from the moſt parts of Logicke, to prove the neceſſity, at leſt the utility thereof. 2

Thirdly, wee ſhall propound thoſe places out of our owne Bookes of the Common Lawes of this Land, where the uſe of Logicke hath either beene acquired, admitted, or practized. 3.

Then handling that part of Logick which concerneth Method, wee will diſpute whether the knowledge of the Law may bee brought into a Method yea or no? 4

Then wee ſhall conſider the ſtate of this maine queſtion according to the different opinions of ſuch as have written thereof. 5

And laſtly, Anſwer the arguments and objections at the firſt propoſed on the contrarie part. 6

As touching the firſt of theſe; although Logicke was not brought to perfection in *Platoes* time, yet is the ſame greatly commended by him in ſome places of his works, as in *Phadro* & *Parmenide.* *Ra. prima.*

aide. In *Phædro* after some use of Logicall division expressed, *Socrates* falleth into a wonderfull commendation of Logicke. *Iamblicus* in his Epistle to *Sopratus* affirmeth, That *nulla scientia Philosophiæ absque Dialectica ratione comparari potest*.

How necessary the use of Logicke is for the obtaining of other knowledges of other sciences, is made knowne by explicating the parts thereof in divers passages by *Aristotle* himselfe as 1. *Poster. cap*.2. 1. *Topic. cap*. 2. and in *Elenchis sophisticis, cap*. 3. and in sundry other places of his workes, and in 4. *Metaph. textu* 8. he sheweth, that the ancient *Philosophers* fell into many errours through the ignorance of Logicke.

Marcus Tullius Cicero the great *Romane Orator* in many places of his workes extolleth the necessity and use of Logicke. In his *Tusculane Questions* thus, That it is the Art *quæ rem definit, genera dispertit, sequentia adjungit, perfecta concludit, vera & falsa dijudicat, ex qua cùm summa utilitas existit ad res ponderandas, tum maxime ingenua delectatio & digna sapientia:* Logicke is an Art that defineth and setteth forth the nature of things, it divideth the generall into its particular parts, it sheweth the necessary coherence and dependancy of the consequent deduced from the antecedent, it discerneth betweene truth and falshood, out of which ariseth as well an excellent profitable use in the search of things, as also an ingenuous delight a worthy wisedome.

In his Booke *de Finibus*, he calleth Logicke the *Rule of knowledge, Quæ quasi delapsa de cælo sit ad cognitionem*

cognitionem omnium, ad quam omnia judicia rerum dirigantur: qua servata, nunquam ullius oratione victi, sententia desistamus: A rule of knowledge I say sent or slidden downe from heaven for the obtaining of the knowledge of all things, by which all judgements are directed, and which rule being truely observed, we can never by whatsoever powerfull speech of any, be vanquished or diverted from apprehended truth, and a setled judgement. To the like effect he affirmeth by the example of *Servius Sulpitius* a famous *Romane Lawyer* who was *Iuris-consultorum eloquentißimus, & eloquentium Iuris consultißimus*; That Logicke is an Art *Quæ docet rem universam tribuere, in partes, latentem explicare definiendo, obscuram explanare interpretando, ambiguum, primùm videre, deinde distinguere, postremò habere regulam qua vera & falsa dijudicarentur, & quæ (quibus propositis) essent, quæque non essent consequentia.* Hee saith, That this *Sulpitius*; *Ad ea quæ confusè ab aliјs aut responsa aut acta sunt, disertè & respondisse & egisse; quòd is ad juris civilis cognitionem Dialecticam omnium artium maximam quasi lucem attulerat.*

Thus much out of the ancient Heathen; Let us now descend unto the Fathers of the Church: *Origen* in his second *Homily* upon *Exodus* hath these words, *Eruditio ista* (speaking of Logick) *ad omnem pervenit sensum, & per eam quisque meditatus & fotus, ad divinorum intelligentiam paratior venit.*

Clemens Alexandrinus thus, *Dialectica velut manuducit ad veram æternamque scientiam, & ad cognitionem supremæ veritatis.*

Saint *Ierome* thus; *Vere quicquid perversorum dogmatum est, & putatur esse robustum in terrena sapientia, hoc Dialectica arte subvertitur, & instar incendij in cinerem favillasq; dissolvitur.*

Saint *Augustine* is also evident in many places as *li. 2. de ordine. Ad religionis Christianæ cognitionem nemo aspirare debet sine Dialectica.* And againe, *lib. 2. de Doctrina Christiana: Disputationis disciplina, ad omnia genera quæstionum, quæ in literis sanctis sunt penetranda & dissolvenda plurimum valet! tantùm ibi cavendum est, libido rixandi, & puerilis quædam ostentatio decipiendi.* And in sundry other parts of his works, as *lib. 1. contra Crescomum Grammaticum*; and *lib. 3. contra Academ:* And he hath defined Logicke to be *Ars artium, Scientia scientiarum, qua aperta omnes aliæ aperiuntur, & qua clausa, omnes aliæ clauduntur.*

By these Fathers of the Church, it may appeare how needfull they held Logicke to bee for the knowledge of Divinity.

The Interpretors of *Aristotle*, and the Writers of latter time *pleno intonant ore.*

Avicenna in his Treatise of Logicke, *Cap. 2. Natura & prima inchoatio hominis, non fuit sufficiens ad verum cognoscendum, fuit ergo opus aliqua arte, per quam, modum procedendi in cognitione haberemus, ut tali modo perspecto, postea ad rerum speculationem accederemus, hæc autem ars fuit Logica, seu Dialectica, quæ modum universalem tradit, rem quamlibet speculando.*

Aquinas saith it is, *Scientia rationalis, actuum rationis directiva.*

Albertus

Albertus magnus likewise: *Logica est quæ à Phantasiis, quæ videntur & non sunt, liberat; errores damnat, falsitates ostendit, & lumen rectum in omni opere contemplationis præbet.*

I will conclude with that which *Barth. Kickerman:* hath in *Gym. Logico, lib.* 1. Logicke saith he, amongst other things promiseth, *Tria maxima bona, Veritatem, perspicuitatem, & ordinem, quibus nihil est in humanis rebus, aut sublimius, aut pulchrius.*

But it will here be objected, That I have strayed from the question, which is, whether Logicke be necessary for the obtaining of the knowledge of the Law? *Ob.*

To the which I answer; That otherwise those Writers have laboured in vaine, who have published the Art of Logicke adapted for the Civill and Common Lawes, some in part as the *Topicks*, or places of invention legall; as *Tullij Topica ad Trebatium* a Romane Lawyer: *Claudius Cantiuncula, Nicholaus Everarde*, in their bookes intituled *Topica legalia, Hottaman* and others. *Resp.*

And some others the Precepts of the whole Art, as *Christopherus Hegendorphinus, Iohannes Thomas Fregius: Petrus Gambræus*, and others, as *Apellus, Bellonus, Oldendorpius, Nevisanus, Grammara, &c.* And how the same shall be needfull to the Common Law; That which we are further to declare will better manifest.

Concerning the Third proposed matter, These may be the reasons following to prove Logicke

 neceessary

necessary or at least behoovfull to the study of the Law.

Ra. prima. The Art of Logicke is the Art of reasoning, *Ars argumentandi*, as one of the properties thereof, teaching to find out truth by argument and disputation. But the Common Law of this Land (which is often stiled in our Bookes by the name of common reason) is deduced from principles evident and knowne, for the decision of such things as are drawne into doubt, and are unknowne. The precepts thereof are taught by Logicke in the bookes of Demonstration and Topicke parts of the Art of Logicke; and therefore is Logicke necessary for the obtaining of the knowledge of the Law, especially for that all points debated or controverted in our Law, are either matters in fact, and so triable by a Iury : or doubts in law, determinable by disputation and argument.

Ra. secunda. Againe, Logicke teacheth a man to collect the Axiomes, principles, grounds and rules observed in that Art which he studieth, and being so collected aptly to dispose the same, which yeeldeth diversity of matter, and ready furniture for disputation : but those things are very necessary to be observed in the study of the Law, therefore is Logicke a very necessary science for the obtaining thereof in this respect.

Ra. tertia. Our Lawyer in his Law-arguments, the better to demonstrate and strengthen his opinion is driven not onely to define or describe the thing disputed of, but to divide the same into parts, to distinguish

diſtinguiſh the divers ſignifications of the words, but alſo to ſearch and indigate the difference of matters and caſes propoſed: all which the Art of Logicke profeſſeth to teach; and therefore Logicke is neceſſary.

Every man in his Argument ought to covet to bee underſtood of them that heare him; for to what end elſe ſhould he ſpeake. *Ra. quarta.*

But a man is beſt underſtood when in obſcure matter he doth propoſe firſt, the moſt generall propoſitions, of eaſie apprehenſion, and out of them deduce others, and ſo to combine and knit all together, as all the parts in orderly diſpoſition may cohere, of which reſult thoſe three excellent things, *Brevity*, *Perſpicuity*, and *Verity*, all which Logicke promiſeth; and therefore is Logicke neceſſary.

When a doubtfull queſtion is propoſed, the truth is found out by Argument, debate, and diſcourſe of reaſon on both parts, as in all our law-arguments appeareth; and therefore ſuch debate and conflict of reaſon is ſaid to be the flayle whereby the corne is ſevered from the ſtubble, truth is tryed from falſhood (for there can be but one truth;) and therefore when there is diverſity of opinion, the truth can reſt onely but of one part, and the others muſt bee deceived thorow the deceipt of a faulty forme of their manner of reaſoning. *Ra. quinta.*

But *Logicke* teacheth a man to know the falacies of deceiptfull and imperfect Arguments, and to reſolve them into better formes,

or

or to disclose their imperfection; *Ergo*,

Ra. sixta. Every Artificer is made more expedite when he is furnished with apt instruments prepared to his hand, *Sed sciendi instrumenta sunt forma discerendi*. The Instruments of knowledge are the formes of discourse; therefore our understanding which is the Artificer, is made more ready, when it hath right and fit grounds of argument reduced and prepared, which Logicke provideth, *Ergo*;

Ra. septima. To obtaine the knowledge of any Science two things are required, first, the certaine dependency and coherence of the parts of the matter to bee knowne, and secondly, the aptnesse of the instrument whereby we doe apprehend and know the same. The first of these doth result on the necessary consequence, that is, betweene the causes and their effects; the latter dependeth of the knowledge of that discourse of reason and argument which is used in the apprehension of Science, and giveth satisfaction and assurednesse of truth to the learner. And these things doth Logicke minister unto us; *Ergo*.

Ra. octav. It is the saying of *Aristotle*, *Scire arbitramur cum cognoscimus rem ex sua causa, & quod alitèr se habere non potest*. Then wee are assured to know when the effect is known by his true cause, whose consequence cannot faile: but these things wee learne by those Arguments which we call *Demonstrations*, which *Logicke* informeth us in. And therfore *Aristotle* truly observed, 2. *Metaph. cap.* 3. *Est impedimentum ad scientias capessandas non prius tenere modum sciendi*. Where his Commentator

Averois,

Averois, and the most of his Interpreters doe understand *per modum sciendi*, the Art of *Logicke*.

These things considered and laid together, it will not be hard or difficult, to answer the Reasons shortly of the opposite part.

As to the first: *Experience* indeed is a sure foundation, and many excellent *Lawyers* haue beene without *Logicke*: But yet if *Logicke* had beene joyned to their *Law*, they would have beene better strengthned in their knowledge, and more perspicuous in the delivery thereof. *Resp. ad primam object.*

To the second: *Law-arguments* are often drawne out of Authorities: but Authorities prove two manner of wayes; 1, sometime directly, and then is Authoritie called an inartificiall Argument: 2, but most commonly, by inference and consequence, which *Logicke* directeth. *Resp. ad sec. ob.*

To the third: *Lawes* deale with particular Cases, *Logicke* with universall Precepts. But when particular Causes are brought to argument, they are drawne to more generall *Theses* and *Propositions*. *Resp. ad tertiam Object.*

To the fourth: it is true that the *Lawyer* doth not argue syllogistically concise, and yet many times with a Syllogisme at large. *Resp. ad quar Object.*

To the fifth Objection: Reason is naturall, but yet it is polished by Art, and therefore best by the Art of Reason, which is *Logicke*.

It resteth now then, that wee examine *Logicke* by his parts, and try the use, utilitie, or necessitie thereof by examples out of our *Lawes*. *Res. ad quint. object.*

Logica quid? Amongst sundry definitions or descriptions of *Logicke*, this is one vulgarly received, *Dialectica est recte definiendi, dividendi, & argumentandi ars*: An Art teaching the true meanes of right Definition, Division, and Argument. Wee will distinguish therefore these into parts, and speake first and formerly of Definition.

Definitio quid? But before wee define what Definition is, because there is an ambiguitie, and duplicitie of the signification thereof, wee should first distinguish the same. There is therefore *Duplex Definitio*. 1, *Nominis*: 2, *Rei*. *Definitio Nominis est qua vocis significatio explicatur*. The reason is added; *Sunt enim verba notæ aut signa rerum*. And this also is twofold: The first called commonly *Etimologie*, of the Greeke words ἔτυμον & λόγος: whereby is imparted the property, waight, and signification, or Emphasis of the word: and the reasons drawne therefrom are called in our bookes, Arguments, *ex vi verbi*. Thus *Tully* in his *Topickes*, and the *Latines* after him, have called *Notations*, *a notatione*;

Etimologia quid? Or, Etimologie *est cum vox ex sua origine explicatur*.

2 The second kinde is called *Antilexis*; and is *cum vox ignotior vel obscurior voce notiore vel clariore idem significante declaratur*. And of both these we have plentifull examples.

Etimologies of the first kinde, which are most effectuall, are diversly deduced; sometimes from the matter, sometimes from the scope or end, some-

ſometimes from the effect, ſometimes from the properties, ſometimes from the object, & ſometimes from the oppoſite.

From the ſcope or end wee have ſundry examples; as a Colledge is in *Latine* called *Collegium, a cohabitatione, & quia ſimul colliguntur.* 9 & 10. *Eliz.* 267. *b. n. Dyer.*

So likewiſe wee call him an Executor of a laſt Will and Teſtament, of executing and performing the will of the dead; not that hee alwayes doth ſo, but that in reſpect of his power and duty he is bound ſo to doe. *Com. Pl.* 2. 280. *b.*

So a Iudgement or Sentence of a Court is called *Iuditium quaſi Iuris dictum,* The finall ſaying, judgement and doome of the *Law.* For that every Iudgement is taken and received for law, untill it be reverſed for error; for that is the ſcope and end of the *Law.* *Coke lib.* 10. 42. *a.*

Likewiſe a *Preband* is called *Prabenda, a prabendo auxilium & conſilium Epiſcopo:* for to that end were *Prebends* ordained in Cathedrall Churches, that the Prebendaries therof ſhould be Aſſiſtants and of Counſell to the Biſhop in his Epiſcopall function. *Coke lib.* 9. *fo.* 75.

Likewiſe ſaith *Bracton, Rex dicitur a regendo, non a regnando.* *Lib.* 3. *cap.* 9.

And the French word *Verdict* uſed in our *Law* for the reſolution of thoſe that are impanelled to try matters in fact, *eſt quaſi vere dictum,* as the ſaying of truth; and ſo to be received without contradiction untill it be defeated by an attaint. *Lib.* 1. *cap.* 8. *Bracton.*

Sometimes Etimologies are drawne from the effect or operation: whereof *Bracton* ſaith well, *Bract. lib.* 3. *cap.* 1.

 That

That an Action or Suit in law may well be called an Action, *quum agitur de injuria:* for it is a complaint of an injury received.

*Coke li.*10. *ca.*116. 117. So *Damnum*, Damage (ſaith one) is derived *a demendo, cum diminutione res deterior fit.*

Littl.con.caſ. 520. A Confirmation is ſo called, as *Littleton* affirmeth, *& idem eſt quod firmum facere*, of the operation it hath to make ſtable or firme a former Grant.

14. *H.* 7. So is a Surrender, *Quia ſurſum redditio*, and of the two French words *ſuiſe & rendre*, or yeelding up of an eſtate againe to the Leſſor or his aſſignee to the immediate Reverſion from which it was derived.

*Bract.*112. 413. To like purpoſe a Writ is called in Latine *Breve*, and in French a *Briefe*, for the brevitie of it, and for that, (as *Bracton* ſaith) *rem quæ eſt & intentionē petentis breviter enarrat.*

So, a *Fine*, whereby lands or inheritances are conveyed in Courts of Record by concord and agreement of the parties, in reſpect of their operation, ſcope, and ſtrength to make peace, and

Glanvil. ſettle the Inheritance: Of which *Glanvil* the moſt ancient writer now extant of our *Law*, giveth an intimation when hee writeth, *Dicitur talis concordia finalis, quia finem imponit negotio, adeo ut neutra pars litigantium ab eo poterit recedere.* Which is al-

21. *Ed.*1. ſo affirmed by the Statute of 21. *Ed.* 1. *de finibus levandis*, where the words are, *Quia Fines in curia noſtra levati, finem litibus debent imponere: & ideo Fines dicuntur maximè.*

*Coke li.*10. *fo.*26. So wee ſay that the foundation of a Colledge, Hoſpitall,

Hospitall, or such like is called *fundatio, quasi fundi datio, vel fundamenti locatio.*

Likewise a Villeine, a man of servile or base degree is called in our Law in Latine *servus*; for as *Bracton* saith, *dicitur servus à servando, non à serviendo, antiquitùs enim solent Principes captivos vendere, & ideo eos servare & non occidere.* And in English we call him Villeine *à villa*, from a Country Farme, whereunto they were deputed to doe service, as our *Villeines regardant* to *Mannors* were, as old Records and Authors affirme, *gleba ascripttitia*, tyed to the Turfe: Or rather of the word *vilis* of his condition vile and base. And the woman Villeine as *Littleton* saith, is called a *Neefe*, *quasi nativa*: The making free of both which, or their Infranchisment, is called in Latine, *Manumißio, à manu mittere, quod idem est quod vel extra manum aut potestatem ponere vel dimittere*; For *manus* in the Law Metaphorically signifieth either power or possession, alluding to the old Ceremonie used in the infranchisment of Bondmen, whereof *Isiodorus* speaketh, *manumitti servus dicebatur, cum Dominus ejus, aut caput ejusdem servi, aut aliud membrum tenens, dicebat, Hunc hominem liberũ esse volo, & remittebat eum è manu.* The ancient forme and Ceremony thereof among our Ancestors the Saxons was in this manner: *Si quis velit servum suum liberum facere, tradat eum vicecomiti per manum dextram in pleno Comitatu, & quietum illum clamare debet à jugo servitutis suæ per manumißionem, & ostendat ei liberas portas & vias, & tradat ei libera arma, scilicet lanceam & gladium &*

Bracton li. 1. ca. 60. pa. 3.

Lambert. ΑΡΧΑΙΟΝΟΜΙΑ. *fo. 126.*

& deinde liber homo efficitur.

So the word *Remitter*, which is an ancient tearme of the Law as *Littleton* saith of the word (*mitter*, or rather of the French word *remitter* to restore) and importeth a restitution of possession unto a mans ancient right.

Litt.li.3.cap. 12.Remitter. P.Com.139. ca.P.Weston.

Likewise *Mortmaine* which is a gift of Land or other hereditaments to a Corporation, which hath a perpetuall succession, and therefore never like to returne to the Lord by Escheat or Donor by *Reverter*. And therefore as one sayth, it seemeth to be taken into a dead or dying mans hand which holdeth fast whatsoever it claspeth. Or as the *Feudists* affirme; *In mortuam manum vocarunt, quod res sic data tanquam mortua, usui illorum mortalium in perpetuum adempta essent*: or else as another of the contrary: *Quia possessio quasi immortalis est, quia nunquam heredem, vel successorem, vel possessorem habere desinit.*

Pol. Virgil. lib.17.

Hottomanus de verbis Feudalibus.

So we call a *Rent* paid yeerely for Land or other things *Redditus, à reddendo*, because it is yeerly yeelded or restored for the Lands, &c. Or rather as some will *à redeundo*, because it doth returne to the Lessor or Donor for the issues and profits of the Land: And in English it is called a *Rent* of the French word *Rentor* to rate or Assesse at a price.

Coke lib. 10. f. 28. a.

As concerning these *Derivations* or *Etymologies* drawne from the finall cause or effect, I was not minded curiously to distinguish, for that in these things which doe depend of humane Acts, wherein the finall cause and effect is all one; for that the

the operation is attempted and atchieved for the effects sake.

But to proceed; Sometimes also Etymologies are drawne from the forme or manner of doing or working.

So we call a Common, to be a right whereby we take some kinde of profit in the land, or soyle, or inheritance of another, together in Common with the Owner or others, which *Bracton* expresseth by way of Etymology thus: *Comunia ex virtute vocabuli componitur ex una & cum (& subintelligitur alio) Quia comunia est in alieno & una cum alio & non in fundo proprio, quia nemini seruit suus fundus proprius.* *Bract. lib. 4. c. 33. f. 223. 13. H. 8. 16. a.*

Likewise wee call certaine Lands Copyholds of the forme and manner of Tenure, because the Tennants thereof doe hold the same *per copiam rotuli Curiæ Domini*, they have no other evidence or writing of their Tenure; but the Copy of the roll of the Lords Court.

But of these we have said sufficient, let us now speake of the other kind which is called *Antilexis*, when an obscure word is explained by another more familiar or better knowne: This is performed when an English word is expounded by a Latine word, or in any other language from whence the word was first derived.

As administration of goods of an Intestate is said to bee *ordinatio seu dispositio*, 1. *Eliz. Dyer.* 166. b. *Lamberts Iustice li. 1. ca. 17. 22. b.*

An Assault upon a mans person by another, is so called of the Latine word *assultus* and doth import *Ass pla. 6. P. 6.*

port the offer of any hurtfull blow or fearfull ſpeech.

An Arreſt is ſaid to be the reſtraint of a mans liberty by power or colour of a lawfull Warrant, derived as ſome thinke from the French word *ar-*
Lamb.Iuſtic. *reſter* to ſtay, or elſe farre fetched from the Greeke
li.1.cap.16. word ἀρέστον a Decree or ſentence of the Court.

So *nomen à noſcendo, quia notitiam facit*, where-
Bract lib.4. upon ſaith *Bracton*, *Ideò impoſita ſunt nomina ut*
ca.20.f.188. *demonſtrent voluntatem dicentis, & utimur notis in vocis miniſterio*. So that we may eaſily obſerve; That many of theſe of this latter kinde are meere
17.E.4.fo.2. Derivations, as *Contract à contrahendo*, *Deodand, quaſi Deo dandum, id eſt, in eleemoſynas erogandum*; *Divortiū à divertendo*, *Dureß ex duritia*, of ſtraight impriſonment or hard intreaty. *Larceny, id eſt, la-*
Lamb.Iuſt. *trocinium*, *homicidium ab homine & cadio*. *Para-*
Bract.lib.3. *pherna, id eſt, præter dotem*, and ſignifieth *mundum*
120.b. *muliebrem*: Peace *à vocabulo latino Pax*. *Lamb. Iuſtice, lib.1.cap.2.f.67*.

A Court of Pypowder, a Court belonging
12.E.4.9. and incident to Markets and faires, to yeeld Iu-
Lamb. de ſtice to the buyers and ſellers comming thither,
curijs. which becauſe they are moſt frequented in Summer, the word was given of the duſty feet of the commers.

A Preſentment which is preſented by an Inqueſt containing ſome crime or neuſance, wherof they had to enquire, is derived of the French word, *preſenter*.

Lamb.Iuſt. *Records* are ſo ſaid of the verbe *Recorder* to re-
lib.1.ca.13. member, becauſe they are *Remembrances, & vetu-*

ſtatis

statis & veritatis vestigia, the lively representations both of former time and truth : *Reversion* of the word *Reverterr*, or as *terra revertens*. Coke lib. 2. fo. 5.

An estate Tayle, of the French word *tailer*, to docke, or cut, limit or appoint in certainty, and many such like, whereon I need not to insist. Litl.l.2.c.2.

Sometime the Derivation of the word is deduced from some ancient word in old time used although now antiquated and growne out of use, and yet neverthelesse such as giveth light to the present knowledge of the word, as *Constable* an ancient Officer of this Kingdome, derived of two old *Saxon* words, *Kinning* which signifieth King, and *stable*, stability, as the stabilitie of the King and Kingdom; So the word Farme in one signification importeth Lands, or other inheritances, holden for a yeerly rent, *quasi feormian*, which is an old *Saxon* word, signifying to feed, or render victuall; for that in ancient time they rendred victuall for the most part, and not money. Lamb. de Constables. cyng. Feormian. Lambert in Archionomia

So warrantisure, of the old word which signifieth to defend or acquit, for so saith *Bracton*, *Warrantizare nihil aliud est quam defendere, & acquietare tenentem, qui warrentum vocavit in seisina sua.* Bracton li. 5. fo. 380. b. Paragraph. 2.

So *Gavellkinde*, a custome whereby every sonne or heire male inheriteth a portion alike in his Ancestors estate, and is derived of two old *Saxon* words *gife eal cyn*, that is, given to all the kinne; *Quasi omnibus cognatione proximis data hereditas*. gife eal cyn.

So *Gulda Mercatoria*, an ancient word found in old Charters and monuments, and signifies *contuberrimum* : or a Corporation of Merchants. Lam. Arch. Coke li. 10. fo. 30.

L So

So Steward derived of two old words, *Steed* and *Ward*, and is as much to say, as a man appointed in my steed or place.

Coke lib. 9. fo. 45.

So the word *Wythernam*, yet much in use, drawne from two old and outworne *Saxon* words *Wither, alterum*, & *Nam, pignus*; *quasi altera pignoris oblatio*.

pyþeр & Nam. *Lam. Arch.*

Sometimes Derivations are made of some old words, whereof the use from which the Derivation was made, is now utterly changed, as *socagiū, id est, servitium soca, id est, caruca*, for that the word *soca* was used for a plough. But this service was after by generall consent of Lord and Tenant, redeemed by payment of a yeerly rent, and yet the signification remaining still, as Land giuen to plough the Lords Land, although the use of that service be abrogated, except upon Creation of the Tenure, it should bee reserved and so renewed.

So saith one, the houses of the devoted religious were called *Monasteria*, of the solitude or solitary life there led, which in latter dayes was nothing lesse, *Quia pleraq; monasteria nil minus sunt quam solitudines*.

Claudius Cantiun. de la legal.

Sundry other Derivations there are, which are but onely allusions strained and framed by the wit and industry of man, rather then from the native signification of the word, and therefore of lesse regard and moment, as *testamentum, quasi testatio mentis*, first devised by *Servius Sulpitius* the old *Romane Lawyer*, and used in our bookes, although impeached by *Aulus Gellius* in that age, or shortly

Aul. Gellius lib. 6. ca. 12.

ſhortly after as a ſtraine of wit, and not out of any true denomination of the word.

So likewiſe of that ſtraine is *agreamentum*, which one would frame as *aggregatio mentium*. Com. Fogeſſ. 17.

So *æquitas, quaſi æqualitas, quia eſt rerum convenientia, quæ in paribus cauſis paria deſiderat jura & omnia bene coæquiperat*. Bract. lib. 1. ca. 3.

So have they derived felony, *quaſi felleo animo factum*; ſo another deriveth Robbery of the word *robe*. And another *terra, à terendo, quia vomere teritur*, and many ſuch like, with the which I will not meddle. Lambert. Coke l. 4. 124 Lam. Iuſt. l. 1 ca. 20. Coke li. 4. 37.

There reſts a few words of the uſe of theſe Etymologies, Notations, and alluſions, and ſo an end.

Etymologies if they be rightly uſed and drawne from the finall cauſe or from the effect, doe not onely yeeld an Argument of good conſequence, but alſo offer much illuſtration and delight; And therefore it is well obſerved by one, That *Etymologia eſt reſolutio vocis in verum & proprium effectũ, & verbi veritatem notificat, & ob id, eam Cicero veriloquium appellat*: And hence grew among the Græcians that uſuall ſpeech of the which *Iſiodore* ſpeaketh, [illegible] to learn aright it is principally neceſſary to ſearch out the ſignification of the word. Clau. Cantiuncula de loc. legal.

Firſt therefore, we are for the right uſe of them to obſerve; That theſe derivations are not to be obſerved in every word; For there are and muſt be in every language many primitives which have

 their

their native significations according to the impo-sers pleasure for that of the Poet is to purpose;

Multa renascentur, quæ nunc cecidere, cadentque
Quæ nunc sunt in honore vocabula, si volet usus,
Quem penes arbitriũ est, & mos & norma loquendi.

They are Derivative words which out of composition may beare interpretations.

Secondly, Arguments from Etymology are not to be used at all times and upon all occasions, but rarely, and where necessity doth require the same, or delight, or apt consequence doth offer fit occasion; and therefore saith one, *Etymologia usum habet necessarium, quoties interpretatione res de qua quæritur eget.* *Clau. Cant.*

3 Thirdly, that your allusions be such, *non abhorrentes ab ipso vocabulo, sed à sono vocis provenientes:* not harshly or hardly drawne or wrung out, but answerable to the sound of the word, and application to the sense.

It is not my purpose to set forth here when arguments and reasons drawne from Etymologies, doe hold their consequence, and when not, for therein the student of the Law must bee formerly instructed by the Precepts of the Art of Logicke; for this plaee will not permit the same, lest I should treat of Arguments before I come to Argument. But let me not here forget that Etymologies are most used by the Authors of our Lawes in their Treatises and Tracts which are of *Simplicis Thematis.*

Having

Having done with the derivation of words, we come now to the explication of the nature of the thing by definition.

Definition it selfe is thus defined, *Definitio est* *Definitio*
oratio, quæ quid sit, de quo agitur, ostendit brevissime. *quid?*
It is a Proposition which doth expresse the nature of the thing shortly. And therefore *Aristotle* *Aristo. 1.*
saith aptly, ὁρισμὸς ἐστι τῆς οὐσίας γνωρισμός: or as in ano- *Post.*
ther place to the like effect: *Definitio est oratio, quæ* *2. Post. c. 10.*
quid est significans. And therefore it is truely said of another, That *Fons totius explicationis est vera Definitio; nullus enim rem melius noscere videtur,* *Kickerm.*
quam qui quid eam sit aperte possit explicare. A true Definition is the fountaine of explication: for no man knoweth any thing better then he which can aptly and briefly expresse the nature thereof, and what it is.

Of Definitions there be two kindes: the one perfect and absolute; the other lesse perfect. The
perfect Definition is that which doth consist *Ex* 1
proximo genere, & vera differentia; as that whereby they doe define a man to be a living creature mortall endued with reason, the *Genus* whereof is a living creature mortall; which our English tongue cannot well expresse in one word, as it is by the *Latine* word *Animal*. But because this word is generall to many other living creatures besides, endued with sense, therefore that perfect difference, *endued with reason, rationale*, is adjoyned, whereby man is distinguished from all other things. For although Angels be indued with rea-

 son

son, yet are they not *animalia*, and there is nothing which may be called *animal rationale* but man alone. This rule I here remember, *Quod genus & differentia ex Prædicamento sumantur*.

But these things I leave to the *Logicke-schoole*: And for that our dull understanding can hardly discerne the true essentiall difference of things, we are driven, and especially in accidentall matters, to expresse by their properties, parts, causes, or accidents; which a *Logicall* writer hath well conceived in these words, *Cùm certum sit, hominem internas rerum formas perfectè non cognoscere, ideo loco differentiarum seu formarum, propria accidentia tanquam, scilicet, sensibus viciniora in definitione sumimus*. Another in this manner, *Nullius rei majori laboramus inopia quam differentiarum*. And another, *Laboramus plerumque vel maximè omnibus è rebus verarum differentiarum penuria, quaq; hic ut in rebus cæteris pro veris habeamus, quæ proximè veris videntur accedere*. Therefore the imperfect Definition, which is called a description; is thus set forth:

Definitio imperfecta est definiti per terminos minus essentiales explicatio. Of this there are, as some do teach, these kindes; *Causalis, Partialis, & Accidentalis*. Others somewhat more fully thus, *Imperfecta definitio sive descriptio, est principalis vel minus principalis. Principalis, definitum explicat genere & accidentibus, vel causis, vel effectibus proprijs, vel partibus*. And therefore that which is given of them *ex causis*, is called *causans*, and is nothing else but *Oratio rei proprias causas manifestans*: so that

that they doe affirme, That such descriptions are causall, and given *per materiam & formam* to be essentiall.

Descriptio, or *Definitio minus principalis*, which is, *ex accidentibus*, and therefore called *accidentalis, est definiti ex merè contingentibus terminis, vel etiam externis explicatio, sive generis accurata assignatione*. And here I thinke it not amisse to observe some rules for good definition or description. And therefore.

First, every good definition or description ought to containe two principall parts: 1, That which is generall, and therefore called *Genus*, wherein the thing defined hath communitie with other things: And 2, that which may more particularly expresse the nature thereof, to distinguish the thing defined from all other things *loco differentiæ*. And therefore saith *Tully ad Trebatium*, *Sic veteres præcipiunt, cum sumpseris ea quæ sunt rei quam definire velis cum alijs communia, usque eo persequi dum proprium efficiatur, quod nullam in aliam rem transferri potest*. Another setteth the same downe in this manner: *Primò quærendum est Genus, deinde dividendum donec tandem veniatur ad eam orationem quæ cum definito convenit*.

Some men there are, which though they extoll the true definition (where it may be had) before the description, as it deserveth; yet hold they the description more familiar, and apter to teach, then the former, whereof *Lodovicus Vives* writeth thus; The perfect Definition (saith hee) *Verior quidem est, sed tamen obscurior: hinc fit, ut essentiales*

essentiales definitiones parùm doceant mentem hominis non exactè docti, cui quidem longè utilior fuerit descriptio ab externis accidentibus, quæ sensu poßint percipi. And againe, *essentiales, & exactißimæ definitiones parùm nos docent, & idcirco apud authores bonos sunt raræ.* For (saith one) *Definitio essentiam, descriptio intelligentiam rei claudit.*

Authors have given certaine rules also appliable to both these kindes, which I may not let passe: because in this place they stand (as I conceive) to good purpose. Whereof the first is thus: *Removeri debet à definitione omnis ambiguitas, & omnis obscuritas, quæ fit duabus causis: primò, ex translatione Tropi, & Metaphora: secundò, ex insolentia vocis, omnis vox inusitata est obscura.* To this effect hath *Aristotle* these words, *Oportet eum qui definit, maximè omnium clarißima interpretatione uti: siquidem cognoscendi & intelligendi causa traditur.*

Arist. Top. 6. ca. 1. Wherefore the first rule as you see, *ut clarior sit definitio, & debet dari per notiora*: for that *Definitio prolata sensui discentis notior & magis obvia esse debet.*

The second rule is, That every good Definition *debet reciprocari cum definito*, it ought to be reciprocall and convertible with the thing defined or described. For the better understanding whereof, it is to be observed, that every thing needeth not a definition or description: for particular and individuall things subject to sense, need no definition or description: for that *Definitio debet*

9. Metaph. ca. 6. *esse de universalibus.* And hereupon *Aristotle* affirmeth, *Omne quod definitur est species.* And although there

there be five universalities or Prædicables as they tearme them, as *Genus*, *Species*, *Differentia*, *Proprium*, *& Accidens*, yet are there but foure *Prædicata Topica*, for *species* is the thing defined, and wherein, and whereby the rest are verified. And againe, *Definitio est de rebus compositis a natura & finitis*.

The third rule is as a consequent of the former, *Nihil habeat superfluum aut diminutum Definitio*: for if the definition or description be convertible, and reciprocall with the thing defined, or described (as it ought) it cannot have either superfluity or defect; this Precept I thought necessary in this place, because the student might be the better enformed to frame his Definition or description.

Let me here say a word of the efficacy and use of definitions and descriptions; And after shall I endeavour to yeeld some examples out of our Lawes: A Definition is said to be one of the Instruments of knowledge, and that two manner of wayes; *Primo in ordine ad definitum*, whereby the thing defined or described is knowne, not by discourse of reason but in a manner by contemplation intuitive, resembling the Angells knowledge; and therefore it is said well by a Writer, *Definitio est intuitiva cognitio*; And hence it is that *Kickerm.* *Aristotle* so highly in many places of his workes *Arist. 8. Topic. ca. 3.* commendeth the same *Difficilis est omnis disputatio, nisi id de quo ea instituitur rectè ab initio definiatur*. And againe in the same place, *Omnis quæstio de qua disputare difficile est vel definitionem requirit*, *vel distinctionem nomine*. And in the fourth booke of his Physickes, *Text*.31. *Arist*. setteth forth the effect of a Definition, *Quod per eam omnia dubia solvi poßint & debeant*.

Whereupon one writer groweth so confident that he thinketh, that out of a full definition of a Mariage, and of an Oath, all controversies concerning either of them may bee fully decided; these be his words : *Hujus utilitatis duo exempla sunt valdè conspicua, unum in doctrina de conjugio, alterum in disputatione de juramento, omnes quaestiones de his materijs facilius & certius possunt explicari*. And therefore *Tully* in his Offices would have everie orderly treatise *à definitione proficisci*.

Strigellius.

De officijs lib. 1.

Secondly, a Definition is an Instrument of knowledge, *In ordine ad demonstrationem, ad sciendam conclusionem, hoc est, ad proprietatem demonstrandam paßionem de subjecto*. But of this more hereafter, when we shall speake of Arguments necessary, which are called Demonstrations.

Sungletius l. 2. *lo. in proœm.*

Let us now exemplifie what we have said, by instances drawne out of the Common Lawes of this Land.

Feoffment, quid?

If I would define or describe a Feoffment, I must first seeke out a Generall or *Genus*; as thus, A Feoffment is a conveyance, but because there be sundry other conveyances, I must proceed further to distinguish the same from all other conveyances; and therefore I adde and say, A Feoffment is a conveyance which passeth an estate in

Fee-

Fee-simple by Livery of Seisin; And hereby I have distinguished it from all conveyances of record, and conveyances that inure by way of grant; But because likewise Leases for life are likewise passed by Livery of seisin; and likewise a gift in Taile, passeth by Livery and seisin, I have added the last complement and full difference in these words, in fee simple. Wherfore in every feoffment two things are of necessary regard; First, that it is performed by Livery of seisin. And secondly, that it passeth an estate in Fee simple: for Lands given in taile and executed by a Livery, we doe not call a Feoffment, but a gift in Tayle.

If I should define or describe a fine, whereby Lands, and other hereditaments are conveyed, I would thus describe the same. *Fine, quid?*

A fine is a conveyance of Record by Concord betweene the parties upon licence obtained in a suit depending betweene them in the Kings Court of Common Pleas. Where a Conveyance is the Generall or *Genus*, The words (of Record) make a difference from other conveyances passed in the Country in Pais. And because there are also some other Conveyances of Record, there is added further the essentiall difference, which is the forme of a Fine, namely, the concord upon licence obtained; for otherwise such concord cannot be admitted in an action depending between them: for without Action, there can be no Fine, which action or suit, must concerne Lands or Hereditaments, whereof the fine is levied, or upon an action of Covenant to levie such fine; And this suite must be depending: And next of all is added the Kings Court, for such fines as by Custome may be levied in Courts of ancient *Demesne*, or the like if any be, are not true fines, but similitudinary onely.

Lastly is added the Kings Court of Common Pleas, for that in ancient times, before the Court of Common Pleas was erected, fines were levied, (as among the old Records thereof appeareth) in any of the Kings great Courts of Law; But after the erection of the said Court, because fines are levied upon *Original Writs* that are *Common Pleas*, and therefore onely to bee dealt withall in that Court, fines are and ought to bee levied in that Court onely.

I may describe a fine shorter thus out of *Glanvills* words;

Finis est amicabilis compositio & finalis Concordia, ex licentia terminans loquelas motos in Curia : for his very words are these : *Contingit autem aliquando loquelas motas in Curia Domini Regis per amicabilem compositionem & finalem Concordiam terminari, sed ex licentia Regis vel ejus Iusticiariorum.*

These like Concords have beene in use in the Civill Lawes, and are called by them Transactions; whereof they say thus, *Transactiones sunt de eis quæ in controversia sunt, à lite futura aut pendente ad certam compositionem reducuntur, dando aliquid vel accipiendo.*

Or shorter thus; *Transactio est de re dubia & lite ancipite ne dum ad finem ducta, non gratuita pactio.*

Where

Where note that it may well be ſaid *non gratuita Pactio*, becauſe in the end of the concord of the fine, which is the forme thereof, there is contained a certaine ſumme of money under this forme, *Et pro hoc fine habendo, &c. I. S.* the cognizee *dedit* 20. *li. ſterlinguorum*. So likewiſe there is mony paid unto the King, which is called the Kings Silver, *pro licentia concordandi*.

Thus much have I added out of the Civill Law, That the Student might as well in this, as in many other Titles of the Law obſerve the great conformity that is betweene the Common Law of the Land, and the Civill Law of the Empire.

If I ſhould define *Homage*, I may ſay, That *Homage* is a ſervice corporall of moſt reverence done by the Tenant unto his Lord, whereby hee doth acknowledge himſelfe to become his man, and to doe him all earthly honor. *Homagium quid?*

Where *Service* is the *Genus*, or moſt generall word, limited by the word corporall, to diſtinguiſh from other ſervices not corporall, for, that it is to bee done by the Tenant himſelfe in perſon and by none other to the Lord: All thoſe words that follow in the ſaid deſcription are added in ſtead of the difference drawne from the forme and manner of the performance of the ſaid *Service*.

Bracton hath a larger deſcription hereof, taken from the effects proceeding on both ſides, thus; *Homagium eſt Iuris vinculum, quo quis tenetur & aſtringitur ad warrantizandum, defendendum, & acquietandum tenentem ſuum in ſeſina ſua, verſus omnes*

 per

per certum servitium in donatione nominatum & expressum, & etiã vice versa; Quo tenens re obligatur & astringitur ad fidem domino suo servandam, & servitium debitum faciendum. And after setteth downe the forme and manner of doing thereof. The *Feudists* in the Civill Law, doe render it shorter thus; *Homagium seu hominium (hac enim vox communior est) est veneratio (si vim verbi strictè consideramus) cùm se eo nomine hominem, id est, Clientem ipsius fore profitetur.*

Estate in Dower, quid? If likewise I should yeeld a generall descripti-on of an estate in *Dower*, which might agree to all the several kinds of *Dower* by *Littleton*, I would describe it thus:

An estate in *Dower* is an estate of Freehold during the life of a lawfull wife, appointed out of an inheritance whereof she is dowable, which estate beginneth upon and after the death of her husband for her maintenance.

The Generall of this description is an estate of Freehold during the life of a lawfull wife. There is added, appointed, for that an estate in dower
1 is appointed two manner of wayes; First, either by act of Law, as a gift of the Law upon a lawfull mariage, as is the Estate in Dower at Common Law, of the third part to bee assigned by metes, and bounds by the Law, and generall custome of
2 the Realme: Or else of more, as of the moity, &c. according to the custome of the particular place.

It is said moreover, lawfull wife, for except the wife be a lawfull wife, and the mariage a law-

full

full mariage, *Dower* cannot be had, for the estate in *Dower* is in regard of the mariage.

The second way, That Dower is appointed, is by act of the partie, and that is, either at the mariage at the Church doore, when they come to be maried, and therefore called Dower *ad ostium Ecclesiæ*; or by consent of the Father, or other Ancestor of the husband, and therefore commonly called Dower *ex assensu Patris, &c.* But both these Dowers are almost worne out of use. *2. Way.*

These words (after the death of her husband, for her maintenance,) doe containe the finall cause and purpose wherefore it was put in use.

Dower by the course of the Common Law, which is the most usuall kinde of Dower, may in this manner be described.

An estate in Dower by the course of the Common Law, is an estate of Freehold for the life of a lawfull wife, of the third part of all those inheritances dowable, whereof the husband was seised of an estate of inheritance, during the Coverture, given by the Law to be compleat after the death of the husband, for her maintenance.

This description is drawne from all the causes: the *Materiall* cause is set forth unto us by the persons; the husband and wife; the forme is the estate of freehold for the life of the lawfull wife. The efficient causes are, The Act of the Law, and likewise the seisin of the husband during the Coverture, and lastly, to be compleat after the death of her husband; And the finall cause in these words, for her maintenance.

So

So that by lawfull mariage the estate in *Dower* hath commencement; by the seisin of the husband during the Coverture it hath his progression; and by the death of the husband his consummation, and accomplishment, whereof ensue the three

3. *Barres.* maine barres to be pleaded by the Tenant of the land in a writ of dower.

1 The first against the mariage, *ne unques loyalment accouple*, wch plea is triable by the Ordinary.

2 Against the Seisin, *ne unques saise, &c.* tryable by a Iury.

3 And against the consummation, that the husband is yet living, which is triable onely by proofes of witnesses.

Although the Civill Law doe call that Portion which is brought by the wife, or given with the wife in mariage (which we commonly call the mariage portion) *Dos*, her *Dower*: And they call the estate in Dower, *Donatio propter nuptias*, yet have they this agreement or conformity, *quod neuter sine matrimonio esse potest*.

And because wee have had occasion to speake of mariage, let us here define or describe the

Bract. lib. 4. f. 298. b. Lib. 5. f. 420. same, *Bracton* out of the Common Law thus describeth it, *Matrimonium est conjunctio viri & mulieris individuam vitæ consuetudinem retinens*.

Britton 246. *Britton* thus: *Matrimonie est assemblie de home & de feme, a lour deux volunts, per joyntyre de St. Eglise, per demurrer ensemble come un chaire à touts lour vies sans espoier de departure.*

Institu. de Patria: Potest. The Civill Law hath it in this manner: *Matrimonium est divini & humani juris communicatio, inter*

ter virum & fœminam, individuam vitæ consuetudinem continens.

The definition of Mariage which *Strigellius* so much commendeth, whereby all the difficulties that fall in debate concerning Mariage, maybe (as he thinketh) determined, is in this manner conceived.

Conjugium est unius maris & unius fœminæ, legitima & indissolubilis copulatio, à Deo instituta in Paradiso, ut intelligamus Deum esse castum & castitatis amantem, ut ei in castitate serviamus, & ut hoc modo & non aliter propagetur genus humanum. *Kickerm.*

A Rent may be thus described: A rent is a Revenue issuing out of lands or other manuall hereditaments, and wherewith the same is charged for a time of continuance. *Rent, quid?*

So that the *genus* is Revenue, and the materiall subject that supporteth the charge, is manuall hereditaments, as land and such like, for out of no other hereditament can a rent bee properly reserved or granted: and the peculiar difference is wherewith the same is charged, for a Rent is a charge, and wheresoever the land be conveyed, *transit cum suo onere*, it goeth with his charge.

So that a certaine summe of money, or other things valuable (for a rent may bee reserved or granted of other things than money) are the matter *de qua*; Land, or other manuall hereditaments the matter *ex qua*, or *extra quam*: The reservation or the grant, the *efficient cause*: The finall cause might also have beene expressed, but when the definition is otherwise plaine, it needeth not.

Le.5.§. non possim. ff. de rebus eorum. The Civill Law by this word *Redditus*, or *Reditus*, understandeth generally *Quicquid ex re aliqua obvenit aut redit*.

And because a Rent service hath his originall by way of reservation, let us here see what a Reservation is.

Reservation quid? A Reservation is an agreement betweene the Lord and Tenant, or the Lessor and Lessee, that the Lord or Lessor shall receive at times appointed a certaine summe of money or other thing appointed to bee payd for the thing demised or granted. *Com. Browning 140.b. 35.H.8.57.a*

Reliefe quid? A Reliefe, called in Latine *Releviū*; The *Feudists* describe or define thus: *Releviū dicitur honorariū, quod novus vassallus Patrono introitus causa largitur, quasi morte alterius vassalli, vel alio quo casu feudum ceciderit quod jam à novo sublevetur, veteres introitum appellabant.*

Bracton.lib.2 fo.83. Of a Reliefe *Bracton* hath these words, *Oportet statim quod tenementum, quod fuit in manibus antecessorum, & hæreditas quæ jacens fuit per eorum decessum relevetur in manus hæredum, & propter talem relevationem facienda erit ab heredibus quadam præstatio quæ dicitur Relevium.* Out of which words of his, a description of a *reliefe* may thus be framed:

Relevium est quadam Præstatio, facta ab hæredibus post mortem antecessoris ad relevandam hæreditatem per eorum mortem jacentem.

Where he seemeth to use *hæreditas jacens* for land, &c. descended to the heyre before his entry, as the Civilians likewise take the same.

Iudgement quid? A Iudgement is the determination of a cause in in controversie by a person thereunto appointed.

This Description is generall, and comprehendeth all manner of Iudgements whatsoever: The Civilians doe thus render the same: *Iudicium est actus legitimus, quo Iudex de causa proposita cognoscit, & secundum aequum & bonum pronunciat.* Wherein they note to be three degrees: First, the Cognizance or power to judge. Secondly, that this Iudgement bee publike or published. Thirdly, that it bee just and right. This connexion they yeeld to be thus; *Siquidem in nullo controversiarum genere prodest causam differri ad Iudicem, nisi cognoscatur de ea, sic nihil profuerit esse cognitum nisi pronuncietur; denique, pronunciatum inutile erit nisi ex bono & aequo procedat.*

There are sundry kindes of Iudgements, sometimes diversified in respect of place, sometimes in respect of the person that judgeth, sometime in respect of the manner of proceeding. In respect of the place, as in a Court of Iustice, and then every Iudgement is said to be the Act of the Court; sometimes Iudgement given out of Court, as upon the voluntary submission of the parties in controversie, as an award or arbitriment: with the descriptions of which I will end this part of our discourse touching *Definitions* and *Descriptions*.

An Arbitriment, which is also called an award, is a Iudgement or Determination which one or more doe make at the request of two parties at the least, for or concerning debt, trespasse, or other controversie had betweene the said parties. *Arbitriment quid?*

The Civill Law yeeldeth it thus: *Arbitrium*

 est

est arbitri sententia, sive Iudicium inter controvertentes, privato concensu, non autem publica interveniente autoritate.

But to the intent the Student may know how to collect a definition or description of any legall part or title out of his bookes of Report, I will leave him here a description of an Award or Arbitriment, where every part is drawne and deduced out of sundry Law Cases here and there scattred, which I have gathered as sundry dispersed stones into one building.

An Arbitriment is a Iudgement, 8.E.4.1.*a*. 8.E.4.10.*a*. 21.E.4. 39.*a*. *given by such person or persons as are elected by the parties to the controversies*, 9.E.4.43.*b*. 16.E.4.9.*a*. *for the pacifying of the said controversie*, 8.E.4.10.*a*. 19.H.6.37.*b*. *Askew; according to the comprimise and submission*, 19.E.4.1.*a*. *and agreeable to reason and good conscience*.

All which words composing the said description, are deduced and drawne out of the bookes cited, and onely by me laid together, and what is done here concerning an Arbitriment (of which hereafter I shall make a larger discourse) may be likewise performed in sundry other Titles.

Ob. There resteth an *Objection* to be removed; it is said by the ancient *Roman Lawyer Iabolenus*, *Omnis definitio in Iure Civili periculosa est, parum est enim ut non subverti possit*: To define in Law is difficult. and the sundry circumstances of things be so many, and so full of variety, as the definition or description is happily made if it stand or remaine unimpeached.

To

To this I give answer, That all this is in a manner true; but let us remember, *Difficilia quæ pulchra*, and use so much the more care and diligence in the composition of the same. Albeit the Interpretors doe understand him to meane by a Definition in that place, no other thing than a Rule or Ground in Law, yet neverthelesse both are necessarily attempted and performed sufficiently: For otherwise the knowledge of the Law would be but an incertaine, inconstant, and tumultuary knowledge(if that may be called knowledge at all, but grounded upon wavering opinions,) but the knowledge of the Law is not such,as shall be evidently made manifest when we come to dispute, whether the Law may be reduced into a method or no. *Resp.*

Thus much of *Definitions* and *Descriptions*,there followeth in order the consideration of *Divisions.*

Some there are which to avoid confusion because they conceipt the word *Division* to containe severall significations not reducible under an univocall head, they have therefore even divided *Division* it selfe, in bringing in the consideration of the name into his sundry significations, which they call *divisio nominis.* and which they describe thus: *Divisio, quid*

Divisio nominis est oratio qua vox in sua significata distinguitur.

But because that were somewhat improper,and that more fit place will be found hereafter in the

 second

second part of this Treatise to handle the same, I will deale onely with those *Divisions* that are of the thing, *Divisionis rei*, Divisions of materiall parts.

Divisio rei, & totius per partes resolutio, and it is either *Principalis, vel minùs Principalis.*

Principalis est qua totum propriè & principaliter dividitur; & est vel generis in species, qua est divisio totius universalis, vel est totius essentialis, in suas partes essentiales, ut homo dividitur in corpus & animam; vel est divisio totius integralis, in suas partes integrales. So that of this kinde of division as you see there are three sorts.

1 *Divisio generis est qua genus dividitur in suas species:* and this kinde of division is called of some *Divisio totius subordinantis.*

And so *Ius*, as it signifieth the law, is divided by *Bracton in Publicum & Privatum*, and of this kinde of division we have examples in the Law; as *Littleton* when he divideth an estate of *Inheritance* into an estate of *Fee Simple*, and an *Estate Tayle:* when he divideth an estate of *Freehold* into an estate of *Inheritance*, or an *estate for life:* So likewise he divideth an estate for life, either for *the life of the partie, Ou pur auter vie:* an estate for *life of the party* is either by act of Law, as that of *Tenant in Dower, Tenant by the Curtesie*, and *Tenant apres possibility of issue extinct.*

2 By act of the party, as the *generall estate* for life, which hath his originall by Demise and limitation of the partie.

Of this kinde of division speaketh *Melancton.*

Divisio

Divisio, generis in species est omnium præstantissima & in omnibus artibus communissima.

And here some doe require *Cum differentiæ exactæ haberi poßint per duas tantùm dividatur, quæ* διχοτομία *dicitur.*

And of this also they have made these three observations:

1. *Placuit omnem divisionem duabus differentiis è diverso positis perfici deberi.*

2. *Vt ita repugnent istæ differentiæ ut nequaquam in idem convenire poßint.*

3. *Postremo, ut quicquid in genere continetur, id totum differentiæ explicent.*

Of this διχοτομία so much extolled by *Ramus*, and too curiously observed by his followers, occasion was taken by *Aristotle* out of *Plato* as it seemeth, and appeareth, *lib.* 1. *De partibus animalium, cap.* 2. & 3.

But as touching the same I am of his minde which affirmeth, *Nobis sicut primum esset, & voto forsitan optandum, ut legitimis duabus differentiis divideremus; ita proximum erit ut quibuscunque duabus (tamen sin minus poterimus duabus,) at quotcunque poterimus dividamus, dummodo universam ejus quod dividitur complectamur latitudinem:* And although it be true that *Peripatetici semper dicotomiam probarunt, tamen non* ἀεὶ *& absolute, sed* ὡς ἐπὶ τὸ πολύ, and therfore we may not be tyed or restrained to make our division alwaies of two parts; but where that cannot conveniently be brought to passe, we may divide into so many parts as the nature of the thing shall require. And therefore *Littleton* in in his division of Rents, divides them into three kindes; a Rent Service, a Rent Charge, à Rent Seche, which is very good and sufficient.

And so of a *Warranty*, where he divideth every *Warranty* either into a *Lineall Warranty*, a *Collaterall Warranty*, or a *Warranty commencing by disseisin*.

So likewise every estate in *Dower* is either by the Law, which is the generall Custome of the Realme, and is of the third part; or else by the peculiar custome of the place, as of the moity in *Gavelkinde*, or more or lesse as the custome of the place shall warrant: or else thirdly, by assignation of the party, and that is twofold, either by the husband himselfe, *ad ostium Ecclesiæ*, or else by the Ancestor, as *Ex assensu patris*; or, *De la pluis beale, &c.*

So likewise we divide the Materiall Church or Temple, the place appointed for divine Service into three kindes; a Church Cathedrall, which is the seat of the Bishop, and his Chaire: secondly, a Church Collegiate or Conventuall: and thirdly, a Church Parochiall.

So likewise we divide Tithes in this manner: all Tithes are either *Prædiall*, *Personall*, or *Mixt*.

So a division of foure or more parts is to bee admitted, if the nature of the thing divided doe so require: as *Littleton* importeth in this division of Actions.

All Actions are either reall Actions, Personall actions or mixt actions; and this Division is ordinary and almost every where in our Bookes. *Littleton*

tleton seemeth to adde a fourth member, when he saith, that when a man releaseth all actions, Reall, Personall, and mixt, that this is no Barre in an Appeale, and yet a release of all actions sufficeth; he intimateth thereby that there is an Action, neither Reall, Personall or Mixt, and yet an Action, as the Appeale, an Action of Revenge.

And herein I would not wish; That for *Dicotumy* sake, the Student should frame Divisions of his owne head, and labour to reduce them *ad bimembrem Divisionem*, as some have done; But accept rather those that are approved of Authors, and generally received in that Art. And herein let me observe by the way that *Dicotumia* or the twofold division, *Si pariat multas subdivisiones, intellectui & memoriæ aggerendas est vitiosa.*

Likewise διχοτομία *ubi alterum membrum est positivum, alterum negativum, non est bona.*

In hac divisionis specie observandum est, ne id quod secundum magis & minus dividitur, in species dividi arbitremur.

And thus much *de divisione totius universalis.*

Divisio totius essentialis est qua totum essentiale in suas partes dividitur, ut in materiam & formam, & dicitur divisio totius coordinati.

Divisio totius integri est qua aliquid in sua membra, seu partes integrales dividitur, & dicitur Partitio; Et est nihil aliud quam membrorum quæ ad integritatem totius requiruntur, enumeratio: As when we doe divide a house into the soyle whereon it standeth, and the edifice and structure thereof.

So the Author of the Dialogues betweene the

Doctor and the Student divideth the Law in generall into the Law of Nature, the Law of Nations, the Law of God, the Law of particular Kingdomes, as the Civill Law, the Law of this Land.

So also have the Civiliãs divided their law thus; *Ius Civile est quod legibus Plebiscitis, Senatus consultis, Principum placitis, Magistratuum Edict is Responsisq;, Prudentium constat.*

So doe we likewise divide the Law of *England* into the Common Law, and Statute Law.

So we distinguish and divide a Mannor into Demesnes and services.

And a Rectory into Glebe and Tithes.

We are now come to the second Principall Branch which is of the lesse principall Divisions.

Divisio minus Principalis, est qua dividitur totum impropriè dictum, ut 1. *Causa per suos effectus,* 2. *Effectus per suas causas,* 3. *Subjectum per sua accidentia,* 4. *Accidentia per sua subjecta,* 5. *accidentia per accidentia,* 6. *res per sua objecta, adjuncta,* 7. *quando, per circumstantias loci, temporis.*

Common. Wee often make Divisions in the Law by the causes, as *Bracton* doth divide a Common thus by the causes: First materiall, as of those profits whereof Common may be had; as Common of *Estovers*, to burne in their houses; Common of Pasture, for feed for their Cattle; Common to digge in the soile of another; *scilicet, fodiendo, ut lapides, cretam, arenam, turbam, id est,* Common of Turbary and such like; and likewise there is a Common

Common of fishing called Common of Piscary.

In respect of the forme and manner, how a Common is divided, thus; Every Common is either, Common appendant, Common appertenant, Common *per case de vicinage*, or Common in grosse.

In respect of the efficient cause, a Common is divided thus, as all Commons are either by prescription, or else by grant: Commons by prescription are such as Antiquity of time, and long continuance have produced, as Common Appendant, Common *per case de vicinage*.

Commons that have had their originall by the grant of the Parties are either so granted as that the same is restrained to the beasts pasturing such lands; And so it may be called a Common appertenant, although improperly by Grant; or else a Common in grosse, and that in such liberty or manner of restraint of benefit as pleaseth the Grantor to bestow.

In respect of the circumstance of time, some Comons are for all times of the yeere, some others for a certaine time onely.

In respect of the place, some Commons are in the Waste of the Lord, or by especiall grant through all his Land, or in his severall, or *ubicunq; averia sua iverint*.

In Common of Pasture *Bracton* considereth these things; either the word pasture is taken largely, *de omni quod edi poterit, vel pasci, largè sumpto vocabulo, ut si quis habeat in alicujus terra communiam pasturæ, scilicet, herbagij, Pessonij, sive glandis, aut nucum, aut quicquid sue nomine Pessonȳ continetur, item foliorum & frondium.*

So I may divide Conditions annexed to Contracts, or to estates in this manner.

Conditions. All Conditions are either conditions in fact, or in Law; Conditions in fact are either expressed in words, and so created by words conditionall, or else they are implyed, namely, conditions by implication.

Conditions expressed are either possible or impossible to be performed, and then are those conditions void in Law, for, *nemo tenetur ad impossibilia*; All possible conditions are such as may be either against the Law, and that either against the Common Law, and then not onely the Condition, but the whole Contract is voyd; But if it bee onely contrary to a Statute Law which may bee dispensed wiathll, then the Condition standeth good; and the partie bound thereby is likewise bound to procure a dispensation, and make himselfe able to performe the same.

A Condition lawfull is either subsequent, or precedent; subsequent Conditions annexed to estates, doe either upon performance enlarge the same, or upon breach diminish or make voyd the same.

Conditions repugnant are such as are limited, repugnant to the premises, as land given in Feesimple by a common person upon a condition that he, nor his heires should alien. This is a repugnant Condition to the amplenesse of the estate, and therefore voyd.

In

In like manner I might divide a Custome by the causes, as the internall causes are the matter and forme; The materiall parts may be the persons whom the custome concerneth; The place and proceedings in Courts of Iustice; For every Court of Iustice hath his Customes and courses of proceedings sometime different from others. Customes

In respect of their forme, they are either generall throughout all the Realme, and so doe they constitute that part of the Common Law which is grounded upon the generall Custome of the Realme.

Or else they are particular Customes to certaine places, of the which *Bracton* saith thus; *Habent Anglici plurima de consuetudine, quæ non habent ex lege, sicut in diversis Comitatibus, Civitatibus, Burgis & Villis, ubi semper erit inquirendum, quæ sit loci illius consuetudo, & qualiter utantur consuetudine.*

Every speciall Custome, as touching the forme thereof, because it bindeth as a Law, and is as a peculiar Law of the place, hath two things considerable, First, the place; secondly, the manner and use of it. As concerning the place, every particular custome ought to bee bounded within the compasse of particular places, as sometime through a whole County or the greatest part thereof, as *Gavell kinde* in *Kent*: or within a Citie, Borough or Towne, as *Borough English*: For a particular custome cannot be at large in places uplandish.

Secondly, as touching the forme and manner of use of it, it ought to bee reasonable and agree-

Littl. l c. able to common right without absurdity, for the
14. E. 3. f. which a particular reason may bee yeelded and
Barr. 277. given.
42. E. 3. f. Hence ensueth, That it ought to bee without
avowry 66. prejudice to any, and not to bee injust in it selfe,
14. H. 4. f. *42. E. 3. f. avow. 66. 35. H. 6. 29. b. Fitzh. Cu-*
avow. 60. *stome 2.*
2. H. 4. 24. b.
5. H. 7. 9. Secondly, it ought to be certaine, *13. E. 3. f. dum fuit infra ætatem. 3. 22. H. 6. 46. 47.*

Thirdly, it ought to be alleaged in the affirmative; for a negative Allegation is not perfect, *8. H. 6. 4. a.*

Efficient causes of a Custome are two; *longe vi temporis usus*, That is, commencement without notice of the originall when it begun, which they utter in these words; *Temps dont Memorie ne court* as *Littleton* speaketh; and secondly, continuance without notable interruption: *8. H. 6. 4. b. 22. E. 4. 8. b. 35. H. 6. f. Custome 2. 13. E. 3. f. Prascript, 40. 21. H. 7. 20. a. b.*

The finall cause is the effect, that it binds like a Law, for, in things of this nature, the finall cause and the effect are all one: hereof *Bracton* speaketh, *Consuetudo quando pro lege observatur in partibus ubi fuerit more utentium approbata est vicem legis obtinet.* And againe, *Longævi temporis usus, non est vilis autheritas, Bracton lib. 1. cap. 3. f. 2.* Hence is it said, That a custome ought to be compullsary, *42. E. 3. f. Avow. 665. 5. H 7. 9.*

I will here adde something out of the Civill and Cannon Lawes touching a Custome, wherby the Student may observe the conformity of both

both studies, and conjoyne them if he list together; that one of them may assist, give light, and ornament unto the other.

First, where it was said, That a Generall Custome is a parcell of the Lawes of the Realme; They likewise affirme, that *Consuetudo generalis facit jus commune; Clem. Fin. de atate & qualita:* And againe, *Consuetudo tanti temporis cujus initium non continetur in hominum memoria, habet vim Privilegij Imperialis Le: ℘: ductus aqua de aqua quotidiana.*

Againe, *Consuetudo est jus moribus (id est) assiduis actibus introductum. C. Consue. i. Distinctio, voluntas Populi rebus ipsis & factis declarata. Tacitus concensus omnium. Le. de quibus: ff. de legibus. Tacita civium Conventio. Ius scripto non comprehensum.*

For the effect thereof, *Consuetudo legem imitatur ℘ ex non scriptis Institutis, de Iure naturali gentium & Civili: Legem imitari dixit, id est, tantundem praestare & quasi legem repraesentare Aldobe: ibid.*

Consuetudinis vero officium est primo ut confirmet, deinde ut interpretetur scriptam legem si obscura sit: in Le: minimè Paulus, & Calistratus in leg. de interpretatione, ff. de legibus: with divers like, too long here to make repetition.

Sundry other examples of division might bee produced out of the Lawes of this Reame, which argue the necessary and frequent use of Division; but to omit them lest I should bee too tedious, and to leave the student to his owne industrious Collection, I will commemorate and insert here some few precepts to be observed in the making of an useful division, and after shew the benefit of

this

this knowledge,and ſo relinquiſh the ſame.

The precepts therefore may bee drawne into two heads; The firſt in reſpect of the thing to be divided, namely,*diviſum* or *dividendum*; The ſecond in reſpect of *membra dividentia* the parts dividing.

As touching the things to be divided, it is to be obſerved, that Diviſion is not alwayes neceſſary; for ſome things are ſo entire as they cannot be divided, as *unitas*, for if it bee divided,it is no more unity, but multiplicity.

So inſtance which is neither time paſt,nor time to come, but onely the moment of time preſent, unto the which the parts of time paſt and future, are conjoyned.

Many things in their nature are intire in the conſideration of our Lawes, for Entierty is that *quod in partes dividi non poteſt*, I meane the diviſion of *totius integralis*,not *totius univerſalis*. And therefore Entierties are of two kinds; Firſt, ſome are ſuch as by nature ſuffer no diviſion, as the things before ſpoken of, Vnity, Inſtance, Corporall ſervice,of which it is ſaid, *ea quæ in partes dividi non poſſunt, ſolida à ſingulis hæredibus debentur*, as fealty and ſuch like ſervices, of which neverthele ſſe ſome certaine ones are appointed by Sta- 2.E.2.f.avo. 179.
tute,to avoyd trouble,to bee performed by the eldeſt coheire,for the reſt as Homage.

Other things are ſaid to bee entire, which although they may bee divided into parts by their nature, that is, their nature and eſſence is not repugnant to a *Diviſion*, yet the Law will permit

no

no division of them by the act of the party, although by act in Law they doe abide Division, and such is a *Rent Charge*, a *Warranty*, a *Condition*, *&c.*

As touching the parts dividing, or *membra dividentia*, the first rule is, that *Membra dividentia conveniunt cum toto & sunt toti adaquata, ita ut omnia membra simul sumpta sunt suo diviso aqualia, & quod nihil contineatur sub diviso quod non sub aliquo membro, nec aliquod membrum quod non sit sub diviso.* *Reg.* 1.

The second rule is, *Quod membra dividentia sunt à se invicèm disjuncta, diversa, contradivisa & non subalterna, id est, quod unum in altero non contineatur.* 2

The third precept is, *Quod singula membra per se sumpta sunt inferiora diviso*, contained within the amplitude of the thing divided, the parts being taken singularly and alone. 3

The fourth rule is, That the parts and members dividing be *proxima & immediata*, next and immediate under that which is divided, and not fetched afarre off, which precept is taken out of *Aristotle*, 2. *Post.ca.*5. *&* 14. 4 *Arist.*2. *Post. cap.*5. *&* 14.

The fift rule is, that *Divisio instruatur membris quam per naturam fieri potest paucissimis*: The reason whereof is assigned thus, *Cum divisio rei manifestanda gratia inventa sit, si multa contineret membra fastidium potius & obscuritatem quàm cognitionem pararet*. And therefore it is *Plato* his Precept in his *Politico*, *Non est tutum, ô amice, in minutissima redigere*. And therefore *Seneca* said well, *Simile est confuso quicquid in pulverem usque sectum fuerit, nam* 5 *ut maxima comprehendere, ita in minima deducere difficile est.*

6 The sixt and last precept is, *Quod membra dividentia quendam ordinem inter se habeant, & quod divisio omni ambiguitate & obscuritate vacet.*

And thus much concerning the Precepts of artificiall Division may suffice.

As touching the use of Division, *Plato* in his *Dialogues, Phedrus* and *Sophista*, falleth into a large praise thereof, and in the person of *Socrates* affirmeth, *Si nactus fuerit Ducem qui recte partiri sciat se ipsius tanquam Dei vestigia sequuturũ esse.* Whereof also *Quintilian* hath these words, *Vt vascula oris angusti respuunt superfluam humoris copiam, tamen paulatim instillando replentur, sic distributio si in partes, accipiuntur facilius, ut cibus mansus, citiùs ac faciliùs digeritur.*

Boetius in his book which he wrote *de divisione*, thus speaketh, *Scientia dividendi omnibus studiosis magnum fructum adfert, ut quæ facit ut res clarè à nobis tractari queat.*

In a word, the utilities thereof may be reduced

Arist.2.Post. Com.74. thus, *Primò, quòd faciat ad rei cognitionem distinctam & evolatam: Secundò, quòd prosit ad prædicata essentialia vananda, id est, ad investigandum genus & differentiam: Tertio, ad recte ordinandas & methodice disponendas disciplinas.*

Another hath these words, *Divisio perfecta est principium intelligendi & constituendi rerum & disciplinarum methodos.*

But

But to leave these Philosophers, and to behold what the Civill Lawyers affirme thereof, and amongst much this may suffice, *Per divisionem materia melius intelligitur & facilius capitur: Le. 1. juncta gloss. ff. de dolo malo.* And againe, *Est autem divisio innumerabilis quasi materia brevis compositio qua ad multa facit: Gloss. Instit oblig. §. Olim autem in verbo divisio.*

But to let these also to passe, I will conclude with that of *Bracton*, although mentioned before, *Lib. 1. cap. 1. Divisio sive partitio animum legentis incitat, mentem intelligentia praeparat, & memoriam artificiosè reformat.*

Thus having in this manner ended with Definition or Description, and with Division in such a summary fashion as I conceived most convenient for the capacity of the Student, and especially how to informe him to make use of these parts as well in the study of the Law, as in any other his studies, leaving the exact knowledge thereof unto the Logicke Schoole: I thought it good here to advertise you, that there may be neverthelesse observed of this which hath beene said concerning the premises, That the knowledge of Definition, Description, and Division, doe presuppose the knowledge of the five Predicables handled by *Porphyries Institution* to *Aristotles Organon*, for whatsoever is properly defined, described, or divided, is *species*, as hath beene already said. And the true parts of every perfect Definition are *genus* and *differentia*; and of Description, *Genus vel aliquod loco generis, Differentia vel aliquod loco differentia, Proprium & Accidens tanquam partes descriptionis dicuntur.*

Likewise is presupposed the knowledge of the *Antepredicaments*: for *Æquivocum* or *Analogon* denoting words of many significations, cannot bee defined or described so standing, but must first be distinguished into their sundry significations, *Vt certum sit id quod definiatur aut describatur*: For nothing indeed may bee defined or described, but that which is *univocum*.

Also by the knowledge had *de nominativis*, the thing is knowne in *concreto* as well as in *abstracto*: which is very necessary in Descriptions, and many times in use: As *Littleton* in the first Chapter of his Booke, in his Treatise of Fee simple. But because he writeth a booke of Tenures, which is the chiefe drift of that booke, he thought it better to tell you who was a Tenant in Fee simple, than to describe the state alone; for in so doing it was more sutable and answerable to his Treatise in hand, namely, of Tenures and their incidents rather to deale with the Tenant than the estate, yet so as that thereby the estate is likewise sufficiently knowne. The like he performed in the rest of his Chapters, as of Tenant in Taile, Tenant in Dower, Tenant for Life, and the rest. Also the knowledge of the Predicaments and Post-predicaments is likewise presupposed. And as touching the Predicaments it is evident that the *genus* or *differentia* of every thing defined, described or divided, are to be sought in their proper and peculiar Predicaments.

As

As concerning the Poſt-predicaments, how many they are in number, and how many are needfull for this knowledge, may well bee made manifeſt by ſome examples, and the uſe of them in the Lawes.

Ariſtotle maketh foure kindes of *Oppoſites*; firſt, thoſe that are *relativè oppoſita*, as the huſband and the wife, the father and the ſonne, the maſter and the ſervant, of which conſiſteth the eſtate *Oeconomicall* of every family and houſhold. 32.H.8.3. Dyer. So likewiſe the King and his Subjects, the Magiſtrate and the People, of which conſiſteth the eſtate *Politicall* of the Kingdome and Common-wealth. 4.El.2.22.1. Dyer. So alſo the Lord and his Tenant, in whom anciently ſtood the ſtrength of the Eſtate: the Leſſor and Leſſee, Grauntor and Grauntee, Feoffor and Feoffee, Bargainor and Bargainee, Coniſor and Coniſee, Recoveror and Tenant againſt whom the recovery was had, and ſuch like, in whom and betweene whom all Conveyances and Contracts have their being. So likewiſe in ſuits reall the Demaundant and the Tenant, in ſuits perſonall and mixt the Plaintiſe and the Defendant, in an Aſſize the Plaintiſe and Tenant; Actor and *Reus* in criminall cauſes: betweene which perſons all ſuits and proceedings in Law are determined.

Theſe are all *relativè oppoſita*, and have reference each to other; as one man cannot be properly Plaintiſe and Defendant in one and the ſelfe ſame action; or *Actor* and *Reus*, except in ſome ſpeciall cauſes onely, as where Interpleader may be admitted, as in a Writ of Detinue, where Gar-

 niſhment

3 H.6.18. nishment is required, there the Defendant is be-
20.H.6.28. come Actor against the Garnishee.
20.H.6.29. So in a *Quare impedit*, where the Defendant
22.H.6.45.a maketh Title to have a Writ to the Bishop, the Defendant is become as Actor.

3.H.6.18.a. In a *Replevin* upon an *Avowry* made, the *Avow-*
22.H.6.45.a *ant* is become *Actor*.

22.E.4 10.a So in a *Quod ei deforceat*, the Demandant or Plaintife shall defend his estate against such recovery as shall be pleaded against him, and become Defendant, and may vouch, *Ac si esset tenens in priori brevi*, by the Statute of *Westm*.2.

Some resemblance of this is found in the Civill Lawes, where it is said, *Actor in tribus istis judicijs, familiæ oriscundæ, communi dividendo, & finium Regundarum, intelligitur, qui ad judicium provecat. Le. 13.14.ff. de Iudicijs. li.2.§.3.& Lex.44.§.5.ff. familiæ hiercisc. l.11. in fine.ff. de Iurisdict. Le.20. finium regundarum. Le. 37. in fine.ff. de obligationibus & actionibus.*

2 The second kinde of opposites are those which are *contraria*, as right and wrong, ignorance and science; and of these some are without any *media*, and some have their *media*; and of those that have
Com.467. their *media*, some are by participation, and some
Com.247. by negation, which the Logick Schoole teacheth more at large.

3 The third kind of Opposites are those that are *privativè opposita*, as light and darknesse, sight and blindnesse, which things succeed and deprive one another, where there is a progresse from the habit to the privation; but seldome or never any re-

turne

turne from the privation to the habit: Villeine and Free are privatives; in prison and at large are *privativa.* *Com. 397.a.*

4 The fourth and last kind of Opposites are those which in Propositions and Clauses are *contradicentia,* the one Affirmative and the other Negative; of which expresse and full affirmatives the Law requireth all issues to be joyned tryable by Iurors, that they may not bee inveigled in the tryall of matters in fact.

Also the Law of England being more precise in the forme of pleading than any other forreine Law, to the intent the issue and point that commeth to be tryed in matters of fact might be evident and cleare to a Iury, doth require that all affirmative pleading in Barre or defence, to make it the more perspicuous affirmative, should bee averred, that is, an offer made of cleere proofes.

Of Negatives in the Law there are two kindes, as first, meere negations, of which we commonly say, *Negativum nihil implicat:* and there are also *Propositions negative,* which doe imply an affirmative, and those we call Negative pregnants, which we doe refuse in all issues of tryalls by Iurors, except in some cases, where the necessity of the cause doth require the same.

So moreover, *Modi prioris* and *Modi simul,* which *Aristotle* also handleth as *Post-predicaments,* are worthy consideration: For the better understanding whereof, note that *Aristotle* affirmeth that *Prius quatuor modis dicitur.*

Primò, id quod secundum tempus est prius, id est,

prius

prius tempore: So the law of Nature preceded the law of Nations, and the law of Nations preceded the law of every peculiar people, and so the Common Law of this Land preceded the Statute Law, which as occasion was offered, in every Kings reigne had his originall. So in the making of a Deed, there is writing, sealing, and delivery; the writing goeth before sealing, and the sealing before delivery.

2 *Secundò, aliquid est prius ordine Naturæ.* There are many things which are *simul tempore*, where neverthelesse there is a Priority and Posteriority in Nature. As when Tenant for Life doth surrender to the Grauntee of the Reversion, not having attorned to him before, in respect of time the included Attornament and Surrender come together, and are wrought at one instant, and yet the Attornament is first in Nature, and precedeth the Surrender: For the Attornement implyed doth first settle the Reversion in the Grauntee, before the Surrender can take place.

So if Lessee for yeares and he in the reversion in Fee doe joyne in a Feoffement to a stranger, it is first the surrender of Lessee for yeares, and after the Feoffement of him in the Reversion in Nature and operation in Law; and they both are yet performed in respect of time *simul & semel.*

If a man by his last Will and Testament in the former part thereof, devise Lands deviseable, holden in Socage to *I. S.* in Fee, and afterwards in in the latter part of the same will, deviseth a rent out of the same land to *Io: No:* in fee, and dieth, by the Devisors death, the whole Testament will take effect at one time But : the Law shall adjudge it first a devise of the rent, and after a devise of the land; for in course of nature hee that granteth rent out of land, ought to bee owner of the land, and so devise the rent, and not first devise away the land, and after devise the rent; That were no good conformity.

Tertiò, secundum ordinem Prius dicitur; This is priority according to conformity of order; So in every writ, men are by the rule of the Register in their writs to hold order in their Demands; For preposterous order is disorder, and destroyeth all; for as *Bracton* saith, there ought to be *ordinata dispositio*, and this is *Bonum ordinis*, the good of order; *Ordo est cujuslibet rei suo loco concinna digestio.* 3 Bract. 188. 35. H. 6. 13. b. Bract. 316. f. 400.

Fourthly and lastly, *aliquid dicitur prius honore, quod melius est & honorabilius est, id prius est*, and this is called *Prius dignitate*, as a mesuage precedeth in dignity land arable, and land arable pasture; the whole is more worthy then the parts, the husband precedeth the wife, and so must be placed in all Writs and pleadings. 4 3. H. 6. 33. 4. H. 6. 3.

Aristotle according to the opinion of former Philosophers, having set downe these foure kinds of Priorities, addeth of his owne invention a fift, *Quæ convertuntur secundum essendi consequentiam, & quod alteri quomodo libet causa est prius natura possit.* But this seemeth to be but a *species* of *Prius natura* spoken of before.

Q So

So also is it *de modis simul*, for it appeareth by that which hath beene said, that *quædam* are *simul tempore, quorum generatio est in eodem tempore*, *neutrum enim eorum neque prius, neque posterius est tempore.*

Quædam sunt simul natura, as are all *Relativa* and *Correlativa*, all those that are *relativè opposita*. Againe, they are thirdly also *simul natura*, which are *species ejusdem generis*; But of this I will surcease, and speake onely of some few things that remaine, which further the knowledge of Definition and Division.

For as much as Division is *totius in partes distributio*, it shall bee necessary to consider the nature of the whole, *totum est quod ex partibus constat*. And some there are which have divided the consideration of the whole into these parts; There is

Coke lib. 11. 50. a. *totum universale, totum essentiale, totum integrale, totum in quantitate, totum in modo, totum in loco, totum in tempore.*

But for these latter foure, since they doe undergoe *nomen totius* improperly, and are used to draw reasons in Topicall inventions, and not usefull to Divisions, I let them passe, and shall therefore retaine onely the usuall consideration of the three former.

1 *Totum universale* is that *quod in species subjectivas dividi potest*, as when a *Rent* is divided into a Rent-service, a rent Charge, and a rent Secke.

An estate of Inheritance divided into an estate of Fee simple, and an estate in Taile; so that Inheritance is *totum universale.*

Totum

Totum essentiale is when the whole is divided into the matter and forme, *Sic itaque materia & forma hic induunt rationem partium*; As Man is divided into these essentiall parts, the body and soule, and of this kinde we have no great use in the Law. 2

The third is *totum integrale*, whereof we have more frequent use, when the whole is divided into the integrall parts, whereof it consisteth, as a Mannor into Demesnes and services; a Rectory is divided into Glebe and Tithes; a house into soyle and structure as hath appeared before. The Division of *totum universale in suas species* is Logicall or Metaphysicall: The Division of *totum essentiale in suas partes essentiales* is Naturall; The Division of *totum integrale in suas partes* is in manner Artificiall or Mechanicall; And this difference there is betweene *totum essentiale*, and *totum integrale, ut si una pars essentialis desit, totum non potest dici mutilum, sed planè abolitum: Et ut priores duæ Divisiones sumuntur ex substantia; Ita hæc Divisio totius integralis sumitur ex quantitate*: And therefore *totum integrale* is twofold, the one I may call *totum integrale continuum*, and the other *totum integrale discretum*, even as quantity it selfe is divided. 3

Totum continuum est perfectè dictum, Quia ex partibus substantialibus & quantis per se unitis constat; estque vel homogeneum, vel heterogeneum; homogeneum est quod ex partibus idem nomen cum toto habentibus constat, as all parts of water are water, all parts of bone are bone, all parts of flesh is flesh,

1.R.3.fo. 3. every yeard of a peece of cloth is cloth.

Heterogeneum est quod constat ex partibus diversi nominis à toto, ut corpus humanum constans ex capite, thorace, corde, pedibus &c. & ex his partibus quædam sunt Principales, sine quibus totum non potest manere incolume, ita partes humani corporis constituuntur a 2.R.3.2.b. *medicis cerebrum, cor & jecur: minùs Principales quæ abesse possunt sine totius interitu, ut manus, pes, &c.*

Totum discretum est totum imperfectè dictum, & constat ex aggregatione partium, vel substantialium, vel accidentaliũ, ex qua aggregatione non oritur totum per se unum, ut in substãtialibus, acervus lapidum, grex ovium, &c. And of these wee have some few examples in the Law, as the Cart and Oxen or Horses drawing the same, may all bee distrained, and 8.H.4.16. the distresse not excessive, because they all make Brooke distr. but one totall: And so in a Deodand may all be 55. forfeit, because they make but one totall, moving to the death. So likewise a Corporation may be called *totum integrale discretum* or *aggregatum, quod ex multis personis aggregatis constat.* 20.E.4.3.*Broo. distr.* 89.12.*H*.8.13.*b*.

Totum discretum accidentale, sive ex partibus accidentalibus constans, est quod impropriè & planè accidentalitèr totum dicitur; & est cum 1, *causatum ex suis causis dividitur:* 2, *cum subjectum per sua accidentia;* 3. *cum accidens per sua subjecta;* 4, *cum accidens per sua accidentia dividitur.* And here I leave, for I shun to be over tedious or curious in these things, for that my indeavour is rather diligently to try the use, then curiously to enquire the Art.

Because wee have formerly both defined and divided

divided by the causes, it shall be necessary to say something of them.

There be foure causes of every thing, the materiall, the formall, and the efficient, and fourthly, the finall cause, whereof two are essentiall as it were, and enter into the composition, as the materiall and formall, and the two other are the externall, the efficient, and the finall cause.

The materiall cause they have divided into three kinds, although improperly, yet for use sufficiently, as *materia ex qua, materia in qua*, and *materia circa quam*. *Materialis causa.*

Materia ex qua may be thus defined, *materia est qua cum forma constituit rem*, & this regarded as well in things substantiall, as accidentall, and then hath it also two kinds, *materia permanens*, which remaineth in the thing constituted, as an house made 1
of stones, timber, earth, &c. A garment made of cloth, wollen, linnen or silke; A Potters vessell made of earth, all which as substances do remaine in the thing composed.

Or *materia transiens*, which is changed in the 2
mixture or composition, as meale and water are the materiall causes of bread, but transient and changed in the composition.

In accidentall things such as are most Titles or matters of the Law, there is the like composition of matter and forme, as by examples hereafter in many particular things will bee made manifest, as in all your Inheritances or hereditaments, corporall, compound.

And of this kinde of materiall cause, *Materia*

 ex

ex qua, there is another Division; for it is either *materia remota* or *propinqua*, remote, as a garment of wollen cloth hath woll to be the remote or mediate cause, and wollen cloth for the propinque and immediate cause.

Materia in qua, and *materia circa quam*, are causes improper and seene in accidentall things; as *materia in qua est subjectum*, and *materia circa quam est objectum*.

Formalis. Forme or the formall cause is said to be *causa unde formatum pendet*, and is either substantiall, as the soule of man, whereby hee consisteth, is the forme of man, for as *Plato* said *Anima cujusque est quisq;*, and this cause is thus described, *forma est qua dat esse rei*, and it is also *remota* or *propinqua*.

The accidentall forme in substances is the outer shape and figure of things, which for want of the true knowledge of the inward, wee be often compelled to use.

The accidentall forme in accidents is *Essentia*, as *forma Reip: est ordo & unio inter Magistratum & subditos certis legibus sancita*, whereof result the sundry kindes of Common Wealths.

There resteth the consideration of the efficient and finall causes.

Causa efficiens est, à qua primò incepit motus & operatio; of these efficient causes some doe precede the worke, and some doe effect the worke; Causes efficient which doe precede the worke, are impulsive causes; the first instigation which move the undertaking of the worke: So *Cicero pro Milone*, *Maxima illecebra peccandi impunitatis spes*,

ſpes; A great impulſive cauſe of offence is the hope to eſcape unpuniſhed.

So *Saluſt* maketh the immoderate deſire of rule and vaine glory to be oftentimes the impulſive cauſe of warre, *libidinem dominandi cauſam belli habent, & maximam gloriam in maximo imperio ponunt*. Theſe be internall impulſive cauſes; there are alſo externall; ſo liberality and beneficence is a great externall impulſive cauſe of benevolence; *Qui liberalitate utuntur benevolentiam ſibi conciliant:* *Cic. lib. 2. de*
So truth ſpeaking is ſometimes an impulſive *Finibus.*
cauſe of hatred, flattery of friends, *veritas odium parit, obſequium amicos*.

Cauſes that effect the worke, are thoſe that are active to performe the worke; Thoſe that are agents in the worke are, 1, the neceſſary or ſole cauſe, 2, the ſufficient cauſe, which alſo may be ſole, but not of neceſſity required; 3, the coadjuvant cauſe, and fourthly, the inſtrumentall cauſe.

Neceſſaria cauſa ea vocatur à qua ita procedit effe- 1
ctus, ut non poßit poſita cauſa non procedere effectus, nec ab alia cauſa talis effectus poßit provenire.

So God was the efficient cauſe, and ſole cauſe in creating of the world; And ſo the Sunne is the ſole efficient neceſſary cauſe of the day by his light in our Hemiſphere effecting the ſame.

The efficient cauſe which is called the ſufficient 2
is that cauſe which is able alone to produce the work; but it is not the ſole and onely cauſe to produce that effect, for that that effect may as well be produced by another cauſe as ſufficient as the

for-

former. As fire is the cause of heat, and sufficient alone to produce heat; and yet heat doth not alwayes proceed from the fire, but from the Sun, from exercise, and sundry other meanes, so that fire is not necessary and alone required to bring forth heat.

3 *Coadjuvant* causes are those that worke to the producing of the effect, but together with some other cause, which is more principall in the operation; So in the obtaining of a victorie by battell, the Generall is not the sole cause, but there doe concurre the Captaines, Centurions, Souldiers, and such like; as *Cicero* in his Oration *pro Marcello, in societatem victoriæ cum Cæsare venisse Duces, Centuriones, Milites.* So *Afranius* the Poet speaketh of Wisedome, *usus me genuit, Mater peperit Memoria.*

4 The instrumentall causes are the instruments used in the worke, *Instrumentales causæ* (saith one) *sunt organa per quæ est efficax causa Principalis,* as Bookes are the instrumentall causes of learning *& militum instrumenta sunt arma,* to which may be adjoyned that cause which they call *causa sine qua non,* as *Medium in visione.*

Causes that follow the worke, are called Conservant causes, *Polibius* yeeldeth this example, *Duo sunt quibus omnis Resp: servatur, in hostes fortitudo & domi concordia.* So in another example, *Seneca, Melius beneficijs Imperium custoditur quam armis.*

Sent. de brevit. vita.

And of all these efficient causes as touching the manner of the working, some are causes mediate, or or removed, and ſome are immediate and propinque.

This may ſuffice briefly for the knowledge of the nature of the efficient cauſe, if we adde a word of the accidentall cauſe, namely, an accident that happeneth not intended, but caſually intervenient, and yeeldeth furtherance to the effect: *Sic piſcatio fuit cauſa fortuita, & per accidens, piſcatoribus Mileſiis, aurei tripodis inveniendi*. And ſo *Cicero lib. 3. de natura Deorum: Phædro Iaſoni profuit hoſtis, qui gladio quo eum petere volebat, vomicam ejus apperuit, quam Medici ſanare non poterant*. And ſo wee ſee that in the Law a caſuall chance is the cauſe of the death of man, although perpetrated by the act of another. *Cic. l. 3. de natura Deorum.*

There followeth the laſt and finall cauſe, and it is that cauſe *Cujus gratia efficiens agit*, and it is the fruition of the work, and therefore *finis eſt ipſe uſus rei*, and oftentimes differeth not from the effect it ſelfe, *re vera, ſed ratione finis. Finis*, ſaith *Ariſtotle, eſt primus in intentione, & ultimus in executione:* The firſt thing intended, and the laſt thing effected. *Finalis.*

The power of the end or finall cauſe is twofold, it is firſt impulſive to the worke; ſecondly, directive to the meanes, and therefore it is often called *Cauſa cauſarum*.

In reſpect of his impulſive power it may be one *re* with the efficient, impulſive, inward cauſe; and it is the ſame which directeth the meanes, and giveth name to the action, as *Bracton* ſpeaketh; *Intentio tua, & affectio tua nomen imponit operi tuo*. And

 againe,

againe, *Tolle voluntatem, & omnis actus erit indifferens.* And therefore in as much as the finall cause directeth the meanes, *Non faciamus malum, ut inde eveniat bonum.*

Cicero most excellently, *lib. 2. de natura Deorum,* expresseth notably the finall causes of all things: *Omnia aliorum sunt causa generata, ut fruges atque fructus quos terra gignit, animantium causa; animantes autem hominum, ut Equus vehendi causa, Bos arandi, venandi & custodiendi Canis, ipse autem Homo ortus est ad mundum contemplandum & imitandum.*
1. *Offic.* And againe the same Author; *Homines hominum causa generati, ut ipsi inter se alij alijs prodesse poßint.* Likewise the same Author doth excellently expresse the end of government: *Moderatori Reip. beata Civium vita proposita est, ut ea nimirum opibus firma, copijs locuples, gloria ampla, virtute honesta sit.* Of one and the selfe same thing there may be many finall causes, *Vnde quidam sunt Principales & ultimi, & alij intermedij, qui quodam modo ad ultimum conducunt.*

Thus much may suffice in the consideration of the causes, and of these things that have beene affirmed, The Student may be instructed sufficiently to undergoe the first Logicall Exercise, which is *Tractatio simplicis Thematis,* an exercise of wonderfull use in the true obtaining of the knowledge of the Law, and is able to furnish him with copy of matter for *Argument* in every Case, and upon every sudden occasion, and wherein those things which we have spoken of the causes may be abundantly exemplified.

There

There resteth then nothing but to shew the manner how it may be performed, and to set forth some examples in the Law of the same: But before I depart from this discourse of the causes, for the better explanation of that which hath been said touching the same, we will adde some examples and instances drawne out of the Volumes of the Lawes, and out of the Arguments of Cases debated, that thereby our Student may the better understand the use thereof.

Therefore first of all touching that materiall cause, *Ex qua res constituitur*, wee may observe in the Law, That in things corporall compound this kinde of matter resulteth to be one with the integrall parts; as the matter whereof an house is composed are these materialls of Stone, Timber, Earth, Lime, and such like, whereof it is framed, and which are the integrall parts of this whole. 1

So a Mannor which is *Quiddam totum compositum corporale*, consisteth of Demesnes and Services; and the Demesnes doe containe, land, meadowe, pasture, wood, &c. and the services doe import not onely the rent payable, but the corporall service and attendancy of the Tenants thereof. *A Mannor.*

So a Monastery, site, house, and also the lands & possessions belonging thereunto, is included in the generall name Monastery, because those import the matter *ex qua consistit*. *Monastery.* 38.*E.*3.21.*a* *Com.* 168.*b.*

So the matter of a Parke is land inclosed, and the Deere; for the Deere are held as parcell of the Parke. 5.*E.*4.28. *a.* *Ardun.* 10. *H.*7.6.*a.* 10 *H.*7.30.*a*

Of corporall things the matter is alſo corporall and viſible, and are ſubject to manuall tradi-
Rent. tion and delivery; as the matter of a Rent is a ſumme of money, or other corporall thing payable, reſerved or granted, as Rent-Corne, and ſuch like.

Tithes. The matter of Tithes are things annually produced by way of increaſe.

Herriot. The matter of an Herriot or Mortuary is the beſt beaſt of the owner.

Corporation. The matter of a Corporation conſiſteth in the bodies naturall of the perſon or perſons of which
Vide 21. E.4 56.a 63.a. 68.a. it is combined; who although they be framed into a politike conſideration of perdurance and ſucceſſion, yet is there in that conſideration a reſpect alſo had of the body naturall.

Of things incorporeall conſidered by the Law, the matter or materiall cauſe is that which is put into the definition *loco generis*, in lieu of the generall: for true it is that *Genus in definitione vel deſcriptione ſupplet vicem materia, differentia vero forma.*

Fee. So we may ſay that the materiall of a Fee Simple, and alſo of an Eſtate Taile, is an inheritance, becauſe inheritance is the *genus* in the definition or deſcription of both of them.

Homage. The matter of Homage is a corporall ſervice.

Warranty. The matter of Warranty is a Covenant reall, whereby the party which made it ſtandeth bound to defend the thing warranted by him, or to yeeld in value.

The Law. The matter of the Law of England generally taken,

taken, *ex qua constituitur*, is the law of Nature, the law of God, the generall Customes of the Realm, Maximes drawne out of the Law of Nature, as the Principles of Reason, primarily or secondarily deduced, Constitutions and Acts of Parliament. *Materia circa quam*, on which it worketh, are *lites & contentiones*, cases of debate daily comming into question touching persons, possessions, and injuries done by word or act.

In a contract of Sale, the materiall causes are the things sold, and the price agreed upon; the forme is the manner of the contract, absolute or conditionall, perpetuall or temporary; the efficient causes, the parties contracting, the buyer and the seller; the end or finall cause is to transferre property from the one to the other, to supply each others indigence: the matter *ex qua*, is either permament or transient, as hath beene said: The consideration whereof yeeldeth in the Law this fruitfull distinction: For if a man take wrongfully the materiall which was mine, and is permanent, not adding any other thing thereunto, than the forme onely by alteration thereof, such thing so newly formed by an exterior forme, notwithstanding still remaineth mine, (as some have held opinion) and may be seised againe by me, and I may take it out of his possession as mine owne: But they say, if he adde some other matter thereunto, as of another mans leather doth make shooes or boots, or of my cloth maketh garments, adding to the accomplishment thereof of his owne, he hath thereby altered the property, so *Sale.*

that the first owner cannot seize the thing so composed, but is driven to his action to recover his remedy; howbeit by the judgement of the Court in a case of that nature depending, it hath beene determined that the first owner might seize the same, notwithstanding such addition. But if the thing be transitory in his nature by the change, as if one take my corne or meale, and maketh therof bread, I cannot in that case seize the bread, because as the Civill Law speaketh, *Hac species facta ex materia aliena, in pristinam formam reduci non potest, ergo ei à quo est facta cedit.*

So some have said, that if a man take my barly, and make thereof malt, because it is changed into another nature the barly cannot be seised by me.

Regula. But the sure Rule is, That where the materiall wrongfully taken away could not at first before any alteration be seised, for that it could not bee distinguished from other things of that kinde, as corne, money, and such like; there those things cannot be seised by the former owner, because the property of those things cannot be distinguished. For if my money be wrongfully taken away, and he that taketh it doe make plate thereof, or doe convert my plate into money, I cannot seize the same, for that money is undistinguishable from other money of that coyne.

If a Butcher take wrongfully my Oxe, and doth kill it, and bring it into the Market to bee sold, I may not seize upon the flesh, for it cannot bee
12.H.8.9.b. knowne from others of that kinde: Bur if it bee
10.a. found hanging in the skin, where the marke may ap-

appeare, I may seize the same, although when it was taken from me it had life, and now is dead.

So if a man cut downe my Tree, and square it into a beame of timber, I may seize the same, for he hath neither altered the nature thereof, nor added any thing but exterior forme thereunto. But if he lay the beame of timber into the building of a house, I may not seize the same, for being so set it is become parcell of the house, and so in supposition of Law after a sort altered in his nature.

Againe, by consideration of the nature of the matter or materiall causes of things, the law doth frame sundry differences; as if I deliver unto one a piece of cloth of twenty yards together to keep, and restore it unto me when it shall be demanded, and the party will cut it into severall yards and pieces of cloth, hee hath not altered the matter thereof, nor diminished the quantity, and yet if he tender the same unto me I am not bound to accept thereof, but may recover my damages for that wrong so offered unto me; for although in matter and substance it be the same, yet it is altered in forme, and impaired in the use.

So if he take my piece of plate, and breake it into pieces, &c. 18.*E*.4.23. *a*.*b*.

Likewise the Statute made in the time of King *Edward* the first concerning Wrecks, hath ordained that if a Ship be wrecked, if any living thing therein escape alive, it shall not be adjudged; but that the Merchandize therein be viewed and preserved for the owner, if he come to challenge the *Wrecke*.

same

same within a yeare and a day. But what if in such case the Merchandize be victuall, as fresh fish; or fruit, as Orenges and such like, as will not last uncorrupt by the space of a yeare, if the Sherife in such case should sell those goods within the year, and be ready to yeeld the money to the owner, hath he offended that law? Certainly no: for the consideration of the nature and matter of those things in such case causeth the said law to be interpreted contrary to the letter of the law: For the letter of the law commandeth a preservation, and
Pl.Com.465 466.a. in this case the Sherife hath done contrary, for he hath sold, and yet neverthelesse hath justly executed that law.

Thus you see that the consideration of the matter or materiall causes whereof the things controverted doe consist, hath great use in the decision of law.

Materia in qua is onely *subjectum accidentium*, and therefore considerable in accidents onely, which subsist in their proper subjects, as Knowledge in the Vnderstanding; the Vertues morall in the Will of man; health, strength, and agility in the Body: And as *Materia in qua* is said to be *subjectum*, so is *Materia circa quam*, *objectum*, both which are somewhat improperly attributed to the materiall cause, and are both so evident as I passe them over.

Monastery. In consideration of a Monastery, the matter *in qua*, or subject of that Title, is the persons whereof that Corporation consisteth; as the Abbot and his Monkes, that is, his Covent; The Prior and

and his Cosreers; The matter *circa quam* is comprised in their possessions.

In an Arbitrement (of which I shall speake more hereafter) the matter *in qua* are the parties at strife, *circa quam* the thing whereof the controversie riseth, reall or personall : The materiall cause *ex qua* is most eminent, and most eminent to be found in things corporeall, having of themselves substance; and in things incorporate, that which is *loco generis in descriptione*, in both which as there is *genus propinquum*, and *genus remotum*, so is there *materia remota, & materia propinqua*. *Arbitrement.*

As a Fine whereby lands or hereditaments are conveyed, is said to bee a concord, for the entry thereof is, *Est concordia talis* ; but this is *genus remotum*, or *materia remota* : for an Arbitrement is also a Concord, a Contract is a Concord : but to say it is a concord of Record, is to adde *genus propinquum*. And thus much touching the materiall cause. *Fine.*

As touching the formal cause, it is either as hath beene said, substantiall or accidentall : The formall substantiall cause in things of life, is that which is the fountaine of life and motion : In things which are without life, that are simple and uncompound; it limiteth their bounds, and is the cause of their being : In things that are compoũd it is the convenient knitting and union of the parts. The formall cause entreth the definition or description *loco differentiæ*, bringing and adding particularity unto the generall, untill it doth fulfill a perfect definition or description, and there- *The formall cause exemplified.*

fore as one saith well, *dicitur forma à formando : Differentia verò quia differre facit*. The forme is said to bee *Modus quidam materiæ, quo sibi contingat, ut hujus vel illius speciei capiat nomen :* And *forma dat esse rei*, and that *esse* is nothing else but *existentia formæ in materia, eaq; plus affert ad essentiam rei quàm materia, est enim ipsamet essentia aut certè præcipua pars essentiæ*.

Claime. In the Cōmentaries of Mr. *Plowden* in the Lord *Zouches* case, a claime is thus described; A Claime is a Challenge by a man made of the property or ownership of a thing which he hath not in possession, but is detained from him, where the *genus* is Challenge, but to expresse what manner of Challenge, there is added this difference, namely, of the property and ownership of a thing detained, which is *loco formæ :* So three of the causes are comprehended in that definition or description : The materiall cause *de qua, viz.* a Challenge, *circa quam*, of things detained : The formall cause the property or ownership, the efficient cause by a man wronged, onely there wanteth the finall cause which is twofold, 1, to manifest that property, 2, to reduce the same propertie backe againe to him for whom the claime is made.

Cond. of Oblig. In 28. *H*. 8. 17. *a. Dyer*. The Condition of an Obligation is thus described : The Condition of an Obligation is an assent of the obligee in defeasance of an obligation made for the advantage of the obligor, where the matter thereof is an assent, the forme a defeasance, the efficient cause the obligor and obligee, the finall cause the advantage of the Obligor.

A

A Contract is an agreement betweene parties concerning goods or lands for mony or other recompence, where the generall matter *ex qua* is the agreement, which is chiefly respected in contracts: the matter *circa quam*, concerning goods or lands: the forme or difference, for money or other recompence, for that maketh it a contract; for the want of recompence causeth it to bee but *nudum pactum, unde non oritur actio*. The causes efficient, the parties contracting; The finall cause *Bracton* doth notably expresse, *Inventa sunt hujusmodi stipulationes & obligationes ad hoc, ut unusquisq; habeat, & sibi acquirat quod suum interest*.

Contract. Dr. Stu. c. 24. *fo.* 103. *a.* Com Browning & Beston. 141. *a.* Com. 141. *Bract. lib.* 3. 8. 2. *f.* 100.

In the Reports of my Lord *Dyer*, 16. *El.* 336. *b. n.* 34. *a.* A Consideration is thus described. A Consideration is a cause or occasion meritorious requiring mutuall recompence in fact or in Law: where the matter is an occasion meritorious, the forme mutuall recompence, &c. not to trouble our selves over long in this kinde.

Consideration

Secondly, in consideration of the formall cause there is to be observed, That when division or distribution is made *ex causis*, those divisions which doe proceed of the formall cause are most essentiall, whereof I shall shew some few instances or examples.

Commons being divided according to their materiall causes, are either Commons of pasture, Commons Estovers, Common of Turbary, &c. But being divided according to their formall causes, all Commons are either Appendant, Appurtenant, or in grosse.

Commons.

If

Conditions. If you distribute Conditions according to their materiall causes, or things whereof they are, then we say they are conditions reall, which are annexed to the estates; There are also conditions personall, annexed to personall contracts, as to Obligations of all kinds, promises, covenants, and other contracts: But being divided according to their forme, There we may say, that all conditions are either possible or impossible: and impossible conditions are voyd in Law: All possible conditions are either lawfull or unlawfull; and unlawfull conditions doe make the contract also voyd, whereas impossible conditions are onely voyd themselves, but the contract standeth single: all lawfull conditions are either precedent or subsequent, and all those conditions which are annexed to estates, are either by way of encrease of estates, or by way of defeasance of estates.

Consider. All considerations are either executed with a recompence past, or else executory with a recompence after to bee made and performed; And this Division is *ex causa formali*.

In as much as the forme giveth the essence, it was said of *Vlpian* the *Romane Lawyer*, out of the rules of Logicke, That *mutata forma propè interimitur substantia rei*: For so in the former examples wee see, that if a man take my Barley and make Malt thereof, it cannot be seised by the former Owner; and yet neither matter, quantity nor outward forme is lost, but it is become a thing of another nature and vse, because the inward forme (to speake as Morall Philosophers) whereof dependeth the use, is changed; for Morall Philosophy doth not so curiously observe the naturall causes as Naturall Philosophy; but according as to the information of manners: So if a man of any peece of cloth which he had to keepe containing 20. yards in one whole peece, will cut the same into 20. severall yards and peeces, The matter nor the quantity is not changed, and yet if hee will restore the same peeces, it is no lawfull restitution, neither am I bound to receive it.

If a man possessed of 20. packes of Wool, by his last will and Testament devise and bequeath all the said Wooll unto *I. Stile*, and after the Testator coverteth the same wooll into cloth and dieth possessed of the same cloth. *I: Stile* the Devisee of the Wooll shall not have by Law the cloth made of that Woll, for that the forme of the Wooll is changed, notwithstanding the matter doth remaine, and it is turned to a thing of another nature; and the making of the said Wooll into cloth by the Testator himselfe is a countermand of the said last will and Testament. So it is also of things incident, as if the principall thing whereunto another thing is incident, appendant or belonging, be changed in nature, the incident is lost and altered: As if a man have a dwelling house whereunto there is a Common of Estovers belonging (which is wood for firing to be burnt in that house) if this house by casualty of fire or tempest be burned or blowne downe, or taken downe, and a new be built in another place neere, or in another forme, the Common of Estovers is lost, and not to be used in this new house, for this is not the former houſe, but another houſe unto which the ſaid Eſtovers cannot belong; but if the ſaid firſt houſe were not wholly pulled downe but repaired, or if another new houſe be built upon the ſame foundation, and in the ſame forme with the former; The Common of Eſtovers remaineth with the new houſe, for that in judgement of Law is the ſame houſe: and ſuch building being upon the former foundation is but a reparation.

But here a difference is to be obſerved, that if the thing incident doe not belong to the principal thing, as it is in nature a ſpeciall thing, but in the generall; then although the ſaid principall thing be altered in *ſpecie*, the generall remaining, the thing incident ſhall remaine to ſuch generall: As if a man have a water-corn-mill, unto the wch hee hath a Mill-leat or water-courſe belonging comming thorough the land of another man unto the ſaid Mill. Now if hee change the nature of the ſaid Corne-mill, unto a fulling-mill, or *è converſo*, wherein both forme and finall cauſe, namely the uſe is altered; it hath beene much diſputed in our time, whether the ſaid water-courſe did lawfully belong unto the ſaid fulling-mill, as it did when it was a Corne-mill? for the owner of the land where thorough the ſaid ſtreame did runne, had diverted the ſaid water-courſe, pretending that he might lawfully do the ſame, for that the owner of the Mill had changed the nature of the Mill; and the preſcription to have the ſayd water-courſe is thereby altered: But it was adjudged

judged that the ſaid water-courſe did ſtill belong and remaine, and ſo ought unto the fulling-mill, as it had formerly done unto the Corne-mill, for that it did not belong unto the Corne-mill, as ſpecially unto a Corne-mill, but it did belong unto it generally as unto a mill going or driven with water, and not otherwiſe.

And thus much may ſuffice for the conſideration of the formall cauſe, as it is the eſſentiall and ſubſtantiall cauſe.

The Law alſo conſidereth accidentall formes, for the Law preſcribeth a forme in all abjurations; ſo likewiſe the Law preſcribeth a forme how homage ſhall bee made by the Tenant unto the Lord: And ſo likewiſe of Fealty, both which *Littleton* doth expreſſe: The Law preſcribeth the forme how Battaile in a writ of right, and in an Appeale ſhall be waged and performed: So likewiſe the Eccleſiaſticall Lawes preſcribe formes of Conſecrations of Churches, Chappells, &c. of Parſons, Orders, Inſtitutions, Inductions, and ſuch like.

All Lawes doe retaine ſome formalities which may not be altered, as in the Common Lawes of this Realme, we have our formes of Writs, Pleadings, Entries of judgements, and ſundry other formes and ceremonies ordayned, which without great and urgent cauſes cannot be altered.

Theſe outward formes are nothing elſe, as one deſcribeth, then *modi quidam rebus agendis præſcripti*, or as another deſcribeth, *Ordinata ſeries rem ad ſubſtantiam deducentes*: And concerning theſe out-

outward formes and solemnities, these rules are observed and prescribed; 1, *formæ præfinitæ omissio reddit actum invallidum : Procurator, Cod: de Procuratore. Le: diligenter in Princip. ff. de mandatis.* And againe, *Qui formam prætermittit jam aliud facere videtur :* And thus much concerning the formall cause.

The efficient cause exemplified. As touching the efficient cause; the impulsive inward causes of all crimes are commonly these, *spes lucri, impunitatis, vindictæ, malitiæ, odij, &c.* The outward, the accessary before the fact, which is the abettor and instigator thereunto.

Contract. The sufficient and necessary cause of a Contract is consent of parties, for in Contracts the consent is chiefly to bee regarded, as hath beene said.

Mariage. And in Mariage *Consensus, & non Concubitus matrimonium facit: C: Nuptias, de Regulis Iuris.* And as *Bracton, lib. 1. ca. 5. ff. 7.* alleageth, *fit per mutuam utriusq; voluntatem.*

Appropriatiō. In the worke there are both principall and coadjuvant causes: In an Appropriation of a Church the efficient causes are, The Ordinary, the Patron, and the King, and they ought to agree in the act, *& sunt Actores hujus fabulæ :* The Ordinary, inferiour or supreme, for hee is the principall Agent therein, because he hath the spirituall jurisdiction; And the Act of the Appropriation is a thing spirituall : And the Ordinary saith, *appropriamus, consolidamus, & unimus*, as the principall Actor in the cause : The Ordinary may bee termed therefore the principall efficient cause, and the other

Com.498.

the

the coadjuvant cause. These the Pope in ancient times as supreme *Ordinary* then permitted, used to doe; and these as supreme *Ordinary* may the King doe, but alwayes with the consent of the Patrone, who is a coadjuvant efficient cause: the formall cause is the consolidation of the *Incumbency* and *Patronage* into one *person* capable of spirituall charge: and the finall cause to make a perpetuall Incumbency.

The efficient causes of an Act of Parliament, are the assent of the three Estates; namely, first of the *King*; secondly, of the *Lords Spirituall and Temporall*; and thirdly, of the *Commons*; and each without the other cannot perfit this worke; and yet untill the Royall assent it is but as an *Embrio in ventre matris, 4.H.7.9.b. Com. 79.a.* and by the Royall Assent comming last, it taketh life and vigour. *Act of Parliament.*

Writing, sealing, and delivery, are the efficient causes of a Deed, all must concurre, and each without other is fruitlesse; but the complementall act which commeth last of all is the delivery, and thereby the Deed receiveth his perfection. *Deed. Com.*.108.*b.* 22.*H.*6.45.*b* 1.*H.*6.4.*b.* 2.*E.*4.3.*b.*

If divers come together to doe a murther, although one alone doe give the wound whereby death ensueth, yet are they all which are present and consenting to the act, Principals and efficient causes of this murther; he that striketh is the principall agent, and the rest coadjuvant: and yet although one gave the stroke, yet shall it be adjudged in law the stroke of every of them, given by him which gave it, as for himselfe, and given of the *Murther.*

others by him as their minister and instrument, and yet all equall in degree as principals, and not accessaries: and yet as you see not equall in degree as efficient causes.

Com. 98.a.

Ravishment. If a man and a woman be present, with purpose that the man shall by violence carnally know the body of another woman there also present, against her will, and the man doth the fact in the presence of the other woman, she that was so present, as well as the man, shall be a Principall Ravisher; the one, *viz.* the man, the cause agent, and the other coadjuvant: and so one woman may be a principall to the ravishment of another.

Livery. Livery and seisin is the instrumentall efficient cause of the conveyance of a Freehold estate in land, and sufficient alone to performe the same, and yet is it not the sole cause, for it may be conveyed by other meanes, as by fine, bargaine and sale, by devise, and otherwise.

Casuall. There is also an efficient cause casuall: As if a man intend to doe an unlawfull act, and in doing thereof another hurt ensueth, not intended, but by chance, cleane beyond all expectation or desire, yet shall he be said the author of that act not intended, so happening by chance, that did the first act.

The finall cause exemplified. This may suffice to exemplifie the cause efficient: There resteth the finall cause, of the which I will shew some examples, as I have done in the rest. Many arguments are drawne from the finall cause, and of much use in the law.

The end and finall cause of the law generally taken,

taken, as *Bracton* well affirmeth, is this, *Finis legis est ut sopiantur jurgia, & vitia propulsentur, & ut in regno conservetur pax & justitia. Bracton li. 2. cap. 2.*

The finall cause of an action is, as likewise the same *Bracton* affirmeth, *Vt non liceat unicuique se sine Iudicio vindicare, & quod sibi ablatum est per Iudicem reposcat.*

The finall cause why also the same ought to be by writ, is, *Quòd sine brevi non debet quis experire in Iudicio, nec mutari potest petentis intentio vel modus petendi.* *Brac. 102. A.*

The end why Attorneyes are permitted in Court, or a man to answer by Baily in an Assize, or to pursue or defend by Guardian, is, *Vt qui rebus suis superesse vel nolunt vel non possunt, per alios possint vel agere vel convenire.* *Le. de Procura. Attorney.*

The finall cause why an Attorney is required to a Grant, is that the Tenant may know to whom he ought to be attendant to pay his rent, or to do his service, so that where there is no attendancy required, there needeth no attornement. *31. H. 8. b Atturnem. 60 2. E. 6. d. Att. 45.*

The finall scope and end of the Averment of a Pleading, is to reduce matter traversable to a cleere and certain issue: and therefore if the matter pleadable be not answerable or issuable, there needeth no Averment. *36. H. 6. 17. b.* *Averment.*

The finall cause why Wardship was ordained, is, *Vt qui per ætatem se ipsos defendere nequeant, ab aliis defendantur.* §. *Est autem. Institu. de tutela.* Agreeably saith *Bracton, Quosdam oportet esse sub tutela & cura aliorum, eò quòd se ipsos regere non norunt.* *Wardship.*

The end why writings were made betweene men in their contracts, was as the same *Bracton* alledgeth, *Fiunt aliquando donationes in scriptis, sicut in chartis ob perpetuam memoriam, propter brevem hominum vitam, & ut facilius probari posit donatio.*

Bract. lib. 2. cap. 16. b. Le. 4. ff. de pignatoribus. Livery.

So the cause why Livery and Seisin was ordained in the Law, and first invented, was because it is a thing notorious, that the people might take knowledge of the passing of estate of most accompt, and be the more able to try the same when they should happen to be impanneled on a Iury for that purpose.

It would be over tedious to heape up more examples, which almost are evident in every Title concerning this matter.

As we doe consider the end of things at the Common Law, so also in Statute Lawes the end and scope that the makers of such Lawes aymed at, is of speciall regard in the interpretation of those Lawes, and often considered by the Iudges, unto whom power of interpretation and exposition of those Lawes is given; as upon perusall of sundry cases grounded upon Statute learning will most evidently appeare.

It often happeneth that the finall causes of things are more than one, and sometimes many, and some of them subalterne each to other, and sometimes distinct, whereof ensueth this exception to the generall rule, *Sublata causa tollitur effectus:* For if there be divers finall causes, although the one be taken away, yet the effect remaineth,

maineth, if one of the causes doe remaine: As for example, The finall causes of mariage are three, *Generatio Prolis, Conservatio Domus, Solatio Vitæ:* and although hope of issue be taken away, yet the mariage subsisteth firme. *Mariage.*

The finall causes of Arbitriments and Awards are alledged principally to bee two; first, every Arbitriment is ordained to make a finall determination, and to appease the variances, strifes, and debates betweene the parties referred unto them. *Arbitriment* 19.H.6.37.b *Nedham.* 8.E.4.10.a. *Laken.* 8.E.4.12.a. *Yelverton.*

Secondly, every Arbitriment is ordained to reduce that which was uncertaine, by the divers allegations of the parties, to certainty: and every of these ought to concur in every good award. 2 6.H.4.6.a. *Hanford.* 4.H.9.17.b. *Weston.*

So likewise our Bookes doe generally affirme, That in Actions where Ayde is grantable to the Tenant or Defendant, that the same is done for two causes; the one for feeblenesse of estate of him that prayeth Ayde; secondly, for the losse or detriment that may come to him of whom the Ayd is prayed. 10.H.7.4.a *Ayde.* 17.E.3.47.a 21.H.6.37.b

So the finall causes why ayd is granted of the King upon prayer thereof, are these, *Quisque auxilium petit à Rege, oportet quod sit per cartam Regis, de dono aut concessione rei petitæ, juxta effectum Statuti de Bigamis. Secundò, Vel aliter propter salvationem reversionis Regis, vel alicujus tituli sui. Tertiò, Vel aliter propter debilitatem status sui. Quartò, Vel ubi Rex habere possit detrimentum:* And any of these suffice to grant the Ayd. 2.H.7.8.a. 4.H.6.18.b. 9.H.6.2.a.3. 22.E.4.21.a

The finall causes wherefore a confirmation is *Confirmation* behoovfull, are ſet out by *Bracton* to bee theſe:

Bract.l.2.fol. 58. *Quando donatio ſit tantum bona pro tempore, & poteſt confirmari ab hæredibus, vel aliјs qui jus poſtea habent. Secundò, Vel quando nunquam abſolutè fuit ſtatus bonus, ſed talis qui potuit evacuari. Tertiò, Vel cum quis rem alienam dederit, confirmatio requirenda fuit veri Poſſeſſoris ſeu Domini.*

Warranty. There are three finall cauſes of a Warranty of lands, &c. Firſt, *Voucher* to recover in value, when the Tenant of the Land is impleaded by a ſtranger: ſecondly, *Rebutter*, to repreſſe the party and his heyres that made the Warranty, if they ſhould chance to ſue: and the third, *Warrantia Chartæ*, by the Iudgement; in which Writ the lands ſhall be bound to a Recovery in value, *pro loco & tempore*.

As it was ſaid at the beginning, that the end is alwayes the firſt thing in intention, and the laſt in execution, ſo are there things deſtinated to their end, and once being applyed thereunto doe alter their nature and become of another conſideration: As in a former propoſed example; If a man cut downe my Timber Tree, and ſquare it of purpoſe to make a beame for a houſe, I that am the true owner may ſeize the ſame, notwithſtanding it be framed for the building. But if it bee laid in the building, it may not bee ſeized by the owner, although the building be not perfected: for now it becommeth parcell of the houſe or building, as hath appeared in the former example. But if a man prepare all materialls for building upon his land, and is ready to build therewith, but dyeth before

before it be erected, those materialls shall goe unto the Executor or Administrator, and not unto the Heyre, who should have had them had they beene laid in the building, because they were *destinata tantum, quæ pro factis non habentur.*

The finall cause in all humane actions is of singular regard, for that all things attempted by men have their end; and the utility of the thing is measured by the end thereof; wherefore it is said well by one, *Vtile ex fine colligimus; quicquid enim utile est, id alicujus rei consequendæ causa utile oportet esse. In laude etiam & vituperatione finem respicimus, cum multis in rebus non tam referat quid facias, quam ob causam facias, ita ut factum ex fine laudetur vel vituperetur, & homo rectè dicitur potissimam causarum omnium esse finem:* And whereof we say vulgarly,

Exitus acta probat, finis non pugna coronat.

And many times the name and denomination of a thing is drawne from the finall cause; as a *Fine* used for the assurance of land, *dicitur finis, quia finem litibus imponit.* *Fine.*

Sometimes the Lawes regard the beginning of an act, *Origo rerum attendenda est*; sometimes the *media* or meanes to attaining it; and sometimes the end for which it is atchieved: To enter into discourse whereof in this place would be impertinent: and therefore by way of Law-examples thus much to have said of the causes shall suffice.

And thus much touching the reasons drawne from sundry parts of the Art of Logicke, proving the

the necessity, or at least the utility thereof in the studies of the Lawes of this Realme. Now resteth that we propound some places out of the bookes of our Reports of our Common Law decisions and determinations of Cases, where the use of Logicke hath either beene required or admitted and practised. And although this bee evident in the most notable arguments at large in the books of the Law, where sundry reasons drawne from Logicall invention and Topicke places doe abundantly appeare to every one which will or can observe the same; yet in this place I will produce those instances wherein the same are either named and expressed, or admitted and apparantly practised.

Where it is discoursed in the Reports of Sir *Edward Coke*, which Acts of Parliament are generall, which are speciall; I finde observed these words, *Statuta generalia, & generale dicitur à genere, speciale dicitur à specie*; And which are *genus, species*, and *individuum*; know ye that *Spiritualty* is *genus*, a Bishopricke or Deanary, &c. are *species*, and the Bishopricke of *Norwich*, the Deanary of *Norwich*, &c. are *individua*; *sic dicta, quia in partes dividi nequeant*: And out of that deduceth hee to your understanding what Acts of Parliament are generall, and which are speciall. So there you see two of the most eminent Predicables remembred, *Genus & Species*, and unto them annexed the *Individuum*, whereof the *Species* is affirmed.

Debt per Obligat. In 11.*H*.7.23.*a*. An Action of debt was brought upon an obligation, where the obligation was endorsed,

dorsed, upon this condition, that if the defendant did make such estate to the plaintiffe of certaine lands before such a Feast, as the counsell of the plaintife should advise, then the Obligation should be voyd, the defendant pleaded, *quod consilium querentis, non dedit ei advisamentum*, before the said Feast; now whether this plea is sufficient or no, or whether he should say, *nullum consilium dedit advisamentum*, or that *consilium nullum dedit advisamentum*; for it seemed that those words *consilium non dedit advisamentum*, were not generall enough, of which opinion there was *Bryan*; so that admit that the plaintife had foure men of his counsell, and two of them gave counsell, and two of them not; here *consilium non dedit advisamentum* is true, *eò quod duo non dederunt*, but that *nullum consilium dedit advisamentum*, is false apparantly, In that case when two of them had given their advise; where hee sheweth that *universalis negativa*, and *particularis negativa* may stand together, for proofe whereof he citeth the Sophisters verse,

Præ contradic, præ contrar, præ postq; subalter:

Accidents may bee considered *in abstracto*, as they are without subject, and in their owne nature of themselves; And also they may bee considered *in concreto*, as they reside and subsist in their proper subject, and these are Logicall tearmes, and yet used in the Law. *Coke lib. 10. fo. 31.*

Although the Common Lawyers of this Realm using a continued speech, *& non concisis argumentis*,

tis, yet doe they obſerve very oft the formes of Arguments uſed in the Schooles, as Sillogiſmes, Enthimemes, Inductions, Examples, Sorites, Dilemata, &c. as may be proved by ſundry inſtances: And firſt of Sillogiſmes.

In *Shellies* caſe the third point or queſtion of the caſe on the part of the plaintife, was reduced by them that argued of that ſide into a Sillogiſme thus;

That which originally veſted in the heyre and was not in the Anceſtor veſted in the heire by purchaſe,

But the uſe (ſpoken of in that caſe) veſted in *Richard Shelly* (who was brother and heire and was never veſted in *Edward Shelly* the Anceſtor,

Ergo,

The uſe veſted in *Richard Shelly* by purchaſe.

20.H.7.b. A man brought an action of treſpaſſe againſt the Executors of his Anceſtors, for taking up and carying away of a Fornace which was fixed and annexed to the Freehold with morter, and it was held by three of the Iudges, *Read, Fiſher*, and *Kingſmill*, that the Action would lye, and that the taking away thereof was wrongfull, and their reaſon is there by the Reporter reduced to a Sillogiſme; in this manner:

Thoſe

Thoſe things which cannot bee forfeited by Outlawry in a perſonall Action, nor bee attached in an Aſſiſe, nor diſtreyned for rent, thoſe things the Executor cannot have, *Major.*

But a Fornace fixed, a table fixed in the ground with poaſts, or a pale ſet in the ground, or bedſted of timber fixed to the ground, doores or windowes, or ſuch like fixed to the ground or freehold, cannot be forfeited, nor attached, nor diſtreyned; *Minor.*

Ergo,

The Executors ſhall not have ſuch things. *Con:*

Many reaſons are propoſed in the caſe of the *Poſtnati*, and Arguments framed and compoſed Sillogiſtically in *Calvins* caſe, as thus;

Every one that is an Alien by birth, may be or might have been an enemy by accident, but *Calvin* could never have beene at any time an enemy by any accident, *ergo*, he cannot be an Alien by birth. 1

Whoſoever are borne under one naturall legiance, due by the law of nature to one Soveraigne, are naturall borne ſubjects, but *Calvin* was borne under one naturall legiance, and obedience due by the law of Nature to one Soveraigne, *Ergo*, He is a naturall borne ſubject. 2

Whoſoever is borne under the Kings power and protection is no Alien; but *Calvin* was borne under the Kings power and protection, *Ergo*; 3

4 Every ſtranger borne muſt at the time of his birth be *amicus*, or *inimicus*, but *Calvin* at his birth could not be *inimicus*, becauſe he was *ſubditus* (and *amicus* properly he cannot bee called, for that is proper to an Alien freind that is in league; So *Scotia* where hee was borne cannot properly bee called *ſolum amici, Ergo,*

5 *Calvin* is no Stranger borne.

Whatſoever is due by the law of Nature cannot be altered; but legiance and obedience of the ſubject to the Soveraigne is due by the law of nature, *ergo*, it cannot be altered.

6 Whoſoever at his birth cannot be an Alien to the King of *England* cannot be an Alien to any of his Subjects of *England*: But *Calvin* at his birth could not bee an Alien to the King of *England, Ergo,* He could bee no Alien to any of the ſubjects of *England. Coke li.7. 24.b. 25.a.*

And thus much may ſuffice for example onely to point out the continuall and frequent uſe of Sillogiſticall diſpute in our pleadings and Law-Arguments.

I will next proceed to treat of the choice and election of Propoſitions and Principles; and likewiſe to exemplifie the ſame by ſundry examples out of the bookes of the Common Law, whereby our Student may be the better furniſhed and adapted with matter fit for Argumentation.

Methodus

Methodus studendi.

A*Ristotle* in the first booke of his Topickes, expressing the meanes whereby in every faculty or science intellectuall resting upon discourse of reason, men might abound in matter apt for argumentation, and might be furnished with copie of reason fit for the proofe or disproofe of things called into debate, in such the sciences by them professed, expresseth a fourefold observation.

1. *Quarum una* (as he saith) *est in propositionibus eligendis.* *Arist. Top. li. 1. cap. 12, 13, 14.*

2 *Altera, in distinguendo quot modis quicquid dicatur.*

3 *Tertia, in differentijs inveniendis.*

4 *Quarta, in similitudinis cognitione & scientia.*

All which are notable instruments of knowledge, greatly profitable, yea necessary for the obtaining of all such sciences as doe depend upon reason: and so consequently much availeable to to be obſerved in the ſtudy of the Lawes of this Land, which are grounded upon the depth of reaſon, and inveſted oftentimes by the name of reaſon in our Reported Caſes, and ruled Authorities of the ſame. 11. *H*. 7. 24. *b*. 13. *H*. 7. 23. *b*. *Com*. *Colth*. 270. *b*. *Com*. *Brown*. 140. *b*. 27. *H*. 8. 10. *a*. *Montague*.

Of which foure principles purpoſing (for direction of ſtudy) to ſay ſomewhat in order as they are afore propoſed, it is to be conſidered, that the firſt of them being *propoſitionum electio*, containeth the election, choice, obſervation, and collection of all received principles, propoſitions, ſentences, aſſertions, axiomes, and reaſons, importing either certainty of truth, or likelihood of probabilitie. Wherein firſt *Ariſtotle* giveth precepts to collect them, & then after giveth counſel ſo to digeſt them, as that they may at all times bee ready for our uſe: Wherefore hereof intending an ample diſcourſe, it ſhall be requiſite to follow the ordinary and beſt method by definition, diviſion, and the due ſpeculation of their cauſes, whereby may be manifeſted what they are, of how many kinds they are, the divers manner of collection of them; and laſtly, the end, ſcope, and uſe whereunto they tend, & the profit enſuing by obſervation of thē.

That firſt therefore the names by which in our Law they have uſually beene called might bee made manifeſt before their nature be diſcovered; (*primò enim de nomine conveniat*) it may with little labour eaſily appeare, that ſundry are the titles or names given in the Volumes of Reports, and other Writings of the Law unto ſuch propoſiti-

ons

ons, as doe remaine as reasons of resolved cases.

Sometimes they have beene called grounds; So in the 30. *H*. 8. 44. *Dyer n*. 30. it is said, *est une auter grounde in tenure in Chief. s. Il doet este immediate del Roy; et il convient commencer, et prend son original creation per le Roy mesme, et per nul de ses subjects.* So likewise speakes *Rede*. 5. *Hen*. 7. 23. *b. Est bone Ground in Trespas, discontinuance vers un est discontinuance vers touts,* with infinite such other.

Grounds.

Vide 12. *H*. 7. 13 *a. Davers. Com*. 121. *b. Stamford.*

Sometimes they have beene called *Maximes*, for so saith *Fortescue* in the 34. *Hen*. 6. 33. *a. Est un Maxime en nostre Ley, Que in chescun action personal, le Nonsute del un sera le Nonsute de ambideux, forprise in tiels cases que sont except per statute.*

Maximes.

Likewise saith *Knightley*, 29. *Hen*. 8. 38. *a. Dyer numero* 51. *Est une Maxime, Que un action sera touts faits conceive ou le plus meliour trial, et notice del fait poit este conus; et specialment lou de tort est personal,* with divers such like.

Sometimes they are called *Principles*, for so in the 8. *Hen*. 7. 4. *a*. it is said, that it is *un Common Principle, que Terre (s. Estate de frank tenant) ne pas sans Livery de seisin.*

Principles.

Likewise saith *Sanders* in the *Com. Colthurets Case*, 28. *b. Il ad este tenus come Principle, Que quand un fait Livery de seisin que son Livery sera pris plus fort vers luy.*

Vide Com. 345. *a*.

Sometimes they have beene called *Eruditions*. In such sort saith *Keble*, in 11. *Hen* 7. 15. *a. Ceo ad este un erudition, Que le partie navera Capias ad satisfaciendum, mes ou Capias gist in l'original.* And some in

Eruditions.

Vide 14 *H*. 8 28. *a. Pollard* 24. *H*. 8. 40. *Dyer. nu*. 66.

3.E.4.7.a. Lit. in 29.*Hen*.8.40.*a*. *Dyer numero 66.* saith *Iustices Il*
Vide 33. *H.* *est une Common Erudition, Que in cel Countie lou le*
6.54. *a.* 44. *tort commence, l'action sera porte.*
E.3.34.*b*. Moreover, sometimes for their firmnesse they
Lawes positive. have beene called *Lawes Positive*, for so speaketh *Belknap*, 2.*Rich*. 2.*Fitzh*. *Accompt* 45. *Il est ley positive, Que home navera damages in breve d'accompt.*

Lawes. Sometimes they are invested by the title of Law it selfe; for in such manner it is said, *Tempore Ed.* 1.*Fitzh*. *Grant*.41. *Lex est, cuicunque aliquis quid concedit, concedere videtur, & id sine quo res esse non potuit*. And so *Bracton* saith, 9. *Hen*. 6. 59.*b*. *Iay prise pur ley, Que si home plede un plee & preigne un protestation; et puis son plee est trove en-*
Vide 9. *H*.4. 59.*b*. *Paston*. *counter luy, il naver unque advantage de son protestation*. Of which manner speech there are manifold examples.

So that be they named *Grounds*, *Maximes*, *Principles*, *Eruditions*, *Lawes Positive*, *Lawes*, *Rules* or *Propositions*, or by whatsoever other name they be called, let us now seek the nature of them by their Definitions.

Li.1.*F*. *de Reg*. *Iuris*. *Paulus* the ancient Romane Lawyer thus defines a *Principle* or Rule of Law: *Regula Iuris, rem quae est, breviter enarrat, &c.*

Com. *Colth*. 27. If we doe respect the originall thereof together with the effect it yeeldeth; *Morgan* in the Commẽtaries of *Plowden*, thus defineth it: A maxime is the foundation of Law, and the conclusion of reason: for reason is the efficient cause thereof, and Law is the effect that floweth therefrom.

Such

Such of the Civilians as in the deſcription of a rule of Law, doe onely reſpect the manner of the collecting of them from particular caſes or circumſtances, doe thus affirme; *Regula juris eſt multorum ſpecialium per generalem concluſionem brevis comprehenſio.* Or as *Ioachimus Hopperus* in his firſt booke *De juris arte*, though diſagreeing in words, yet one in ſenſe with the forme; *Regulæ juris ſunt quædam conjectiones tantum, & breviaria ex pluribus ſpeciebus in unum per commune aliquod collecta.* Another of them, in this manner; *Regula eſt ſententia generalis, quæ ex plurium legum mente à juriſconſultis notata atque animadverſa, paucis verbis ſummam earum conſentionem & tanquam harmoniam complectitur.*

Prateus de Reg. Iuris. lib. 6.

Ioach. Hopp. de Iuris arte. 371. a.

Sim. Shard. Lexic. Iuris Regul.

Matth. Gribaldus in his firſt booke *de ratione ſtudij, cap. 7.* ſaith, *Regulæ juris nihil aliud ſunt quam breves & compendioſæ ſententiæ, ex pervagatis definitionibus perſtrictæ, quo & minori labore diſcantur, & faciliùs diutiuſq; memoriâ teneantur.*

Matth. Gribald. l. 1. c. 7. de ratione ſtudy Iuris.

But binding our ſelves to no preſcript rules of Art, for the better underſtanding of the ſame, we may deſcribe a rule or ground of Law thus:

A Rule or Principle of the Law of England, is a Concluſion either of the Law of Nature, or derived from ſome generall cuſtome uſed within the Realme, containing in a ſhort ſumme the reaſon and direction of many particular and ſpeciall occurrences. Definition.

Notes collected out of Authors.

Paulus lib. ff. de reg. Iuris.

Regula juris est plurium compendiosa narratio, & quasi causa conjectio.

Nec absimile est quod Grammatici dicunt, eam esse multorum similium collectionem.

Ant. Masa de exercitio Iurispr. lib. 1.

In summa autem est, ac si quis, prædictis cum verbis Archid. dist. 3. & Reg. conjunctis, ita diceret, Quod Regula sit compendiosa definitio; seu cum Quintiliano, Universale vel perpetuale præceptum diversarum rerum, quasi sub unâ eademq; causâ cadentium universalitatem complectens.

Joach. Hopp. de Iuris arte. l. 2. fo. 469. a.

Est Regula nihil aliud quàm plurium rerum & specierum in unam quasi summam conjectio.

As touching the Division thereof, wee shall better observe how many principles and grounds there be by the due consideration of their causes from whence they spring.

All causes of every thing are either internall or externall.

Internall are, the causes { Materiall, or Formall.

Externall are, the causes { Efficient and Finall.

Dt

De Causis.

Non solum ea quæ insita sunt causa dicuntur, sed etiam ea quæ extrinsecus sumuntur, ut id quod motum affert & efficiens est. Arist.11. Met.c.4. To.23.

Causarum quatuor sunt genera. Arist.l.2.

Unum est forma atque essentia rei. Dem.c.11. To.11.

Alterum est in quo inest necessitudo non absoluta, sed ex adjunctione; si alia quædam sint, hæc esse necesse est.

Tertium genus est id in quo inest rei efficiendæ vis primaria.

Quartum est finis cujus causa aliquid fit.

Nam ad interrogationem factam per verba, propter quid sit aliquid, nihil aliud unquam respondetur, quam aliqua ex dictis quatuor causis: Inter quas tamen, finis est potissima, & quasi aliarum causa: Materia enim non esset causa, nisi haberet formam; & forma itidem nisi ab agente introduceretur; Agens quoque non ageret nisi moveretur à fine; finis autem ipse immobilis permanet: Est ergo primum movens, & prima causa, &c. Ant. Ma de exercitio Iurisperitorum l.1.p.38.b.

Materiall cause.

As touching the Materiall cause, matter, or subject wherein these grounds are conversant, the same are all those things whereof debate may rise betweene parties judicially: which are as well divine as humane. Insomuch as *Iuris prudentia*, or the knowledge of the Law, is *Divinarum humanarumq; rerum scientia*. And hence proceedeth it, that all Grounds or Rules of the Law of England Bract.lib.1. cap.4.§.4.

 in

in respect of their matter which they do concerne are either such as are not restrained to any on-proper or peculiar title of the Law, but as occasi, on serveth, are applyable unto every part, title, or tractate of the Law, as by the view and due consideration of examples following may bee made manifest; All which, being either conclusions of naturall Reason, or drawne and derived from the same, doe not onely serve as directions and Principles of the Law, but are likewise as Positions and Axiomes to be observed throughout all mans life and conversation; having their originall from those Arts that are necessary and behoovfull for maintenance of humane society.

Grounds borrowed out of Logicke.

And first of all concerning the Art of Logick; from thence the learned of our Lawes have received many principles, as wel out of that part which concerneth the Invention of Arguments, as of that which teacheth the disposing, framing, and the judgement of the same.

From the first part these may serve for example.

14 H.8.31.b *Idem non potest esse agens & patiens.*
28.H.8.10.b *Omne majus continet in se suum minus.*
n.37.Dyer. *Magis dignum trahit ad se minus dignum.*
Com.213.b. *In praesentia majoris cessat minus.*
Com.323.b. *Frustra fit per plura quod fieri potest per pauciora.*
9 H.7.24.a. *Turpis est pars quae cum toto non convenit.*
Com.161.a. With many other such like, &c.

From

From the Iudiciall parts of Logicke, these and divers others.

Qui negat confusè, negat confusè & distributivè. 2.R.3.7.a.

But how that saying may be understood, and in what sense it may be intended true, and in what not, peruse the case of 4.*H*.7.8.*a*. touching the travers of a suggestion of breach of the peace: where although the said Rule be not mentioned, yet the meaning thereof, by the case there debated is partly made manifest. Moreover, *Brian* borroweth the Sophisters verse, and maketh it a Ground to try whether an issue tendered be an expresse Negative or no, in 11.*H*.7.23.*a*.

Præ contradic: post contra. Præ postque subalter.

This likewise is derived thence, *Negativum nihil implicat.*

Out of Naturall Philosophy, these, with divers others, are deducted, that follow.

VIs unita fortior. Com. 307. a.

Est naturæ vis maxima. Com. 72. b.

Vltra posse non est esse. Com. 268. a.

Sublata causa tollitur effectus. Com. 294. a.

Vltra scire non est posse. With many other of like quality. 8.E.4. 10. a.

Grounds borrowed out of Morall Philosophie;

FRom whence, as from a Fountaine, all Lawes doe flow; we doe observe these few following for an example; as,

Com.244.a. *Qui sentit commodum, sentire debet & onus.*

14.H.8.6.a. *Volenti non fit injuria.*

Com.501.a. *Sit utere tuo, ut alienum non ladas.*

13 H.8.16.a *Fraus & dolus nemini patrocinatur.*

14 H.8.16.a *Agentes & consentientes pari pœna plectuntur.*

14.H.8.8.a. *Summum Ius summa Injuria.*

Com.160.b.

Com.370.b. *Vix ulla lex fieri potest quæ omnibus commoda sit sed si majori parti prospiciat, utilis est.*

Com.48.b. *A vero non delinabit Iustus.*

Quod tibi fieri non vis, alteri ne feceris. With many more such like.

Grounds borrowed out of the Civill Law.

OVt of the Civill Lawes there are also very many Axiomes and Rules, which are likewise borrowed and usually frequented in our Law. For sith all Lawes are derived from the law of Nature, and doe concur and agree in the principles of Nature and Reason: And sith the Civill Lawes, being the Lawes of the Empire, doe bewray the great wisedome whereby the Romane estate, in the time it most flourished, was gover-

ned:

ned: Sith likewise the Law of this Land hath alwayes followed best and most approved Reason (which is also a type of humane wisdome) it doth ensue of necessity, that great conformity must be betweene them. Which conformity may be made apparant partly by these (among some thousand Axioms and Conclusions of Reason) following.

Qui tacit consentire videtur. Com. 357.b

Vigilantibus & non dormientibus Iura subveniunt. 5.H.3.222.

Quod initio non valet, tractu temporis non convalescit.

Quando duo Iura in uno concurrunt, æquum est ac si esset in duobus. Com.168.a.

In æquali jure, melior est conditio possidentis. Com. 296.b.

Optima Legum Interpres est Consuetudo. Com. 336.b.

Frustra Legis auxilium petet, qui in Legem peccat.

Ignorantia facti excusat. 14.H.1.27.b.

Modus Legem dat donationi. Com. 251.a.

Non est regula quin fallat. Com. 162.b.

Modus & conventio vincunt Legem. 1.H.3.33.b.

With others in manner infinite, written and published in the Latine tongue.

In the French also many other grounds there are in our Law, to be found agreeable in sense and meaning to such as are frequent and usuall in the Civill Lawes, and there published in the Latine tongue, whereof also these following may serve for example. *L. verum §. tempus: ff. pro hoc. L. sedes de rescript.*

Nul prendra benefit de son tort demesne.

Nemo ex dolo suo proprio relevetur aut auxiliũ capiet. *L. bona fides ff. de Reg. Iuris.*

Home ne sera double charge pro une mesme duetie.

Bona fides non patitur idem ab eodem bis exigi.

Auxy

Auxy mult auctorities & voies que home ad a faire un fait, auxy mult auctorities & voies ad cesty a qui le fait est fait a ceo dessolver. 1. Hen. 7. 16. a.

L. nihil: ff. de Regul. Iuris. *Nihil est magis rationi consentaneum quam eodem modo unum quodque dissolvere quo conflatum est.*

13. H. 8. 16. a in fine. *Le Common wealth sera prefer devant private wealth.*

Vtilitas publica privatorum commodis ante-ferenda. L. 1. §. fin. & cap. tol.

Com. 260. a. Halls case. *Le ley in chescun act adrespect al comencement.*

Origo rerum attendenda.

Com. 259. b. Halls case. *Imagination de mente de faire tort, sans le act fait, nest punishable in nostre Ley.*

Com. 160. b. Throgm. case. *Affectus non punitur nisi sequatur effectus. Prateus lib. 3. c. 4.*

Intent direct done plus tost quam parols.

Proferentis intentio & voluntas, magis quam verborum locutio examinetur. Prat. lib. 3. cap. 3.

Com. 504. b. *Quant divers choses sont fait a un mesme instant, & l'un ne poet prender effect sans l'auter; le common ley adjudger ceo de preceder & ensuer, que aptment doet preceder & ensuer in feasant l'entent des parties de prender effect.*

Vbi in Instrumento reperitur plures actus successive fuisse celebratos, semper fingitur ille actus praecessisse qui reddit actum validum. Nicholai Everard Topica Iuris loco 1.

Non attento ordine verborum, talis ordo presumitur qualis debet esse.

With many others to like purpose, if place did permit, or cause did require to observe the same: Yea many times when as no Ground or Rule is expres-

expressed in our Law, but that we may onely collect Cases concurrent upon some Conformity of Reason: We shall find in the Civill Lawes a proposition or rule which shall most aptly and most fitly expresse the same Reason in such shortnesse of speech, as nothing shall seeme more sufficient in that respect. And unto the which Propositions such as are or may be framed by us in the French, cannot in excellency be worthily compared.

Grounds borrowed out of the Canon Law.

As touching the Canon Law. Forasmuch as the studies both of the same and of the Civill Law, are in sort conjoyned by the professors of both, what may be said of the one, in this respect, may be verified of the other: Which as well by veiw of the title *De Regulis Iuris in Sexto Decretalium*, as also in divers other titles of the same Law, especially in such as are most usuall for matters of debate in this Realme, as are those of Excommunication, Mariage, Divorce, Legacies, Tythes, and such like, will at large appeare.

Grounds derived from Use, Custome, and Conversation of Men.

Finally, many Grounds and Rules of the Lawes of this Realme are derived from Common use, Custome, and Conversation among men, Collected out of the generall disposition, nature, and condition of humane kinde: Which Grounds are of two natures; The one observed out of humane actions, the other out of usuall and ordinarie speech.

Principia externa propriè vocamus ea quæ in Communi hominum vita versantur & ab experientibus & prudentibus animadvertuntur. Ioh. Hopper : de Iuris arte.

Hæc non tam ex ipsa hominis natura quam foris adveniunt, debentq; non ex mente hominis aut animo, sed ex Communibus vitæ moribus longo usu & tractatione colligi. Ibidem. Hæc sunt igitur illa quæ dico externa Principia, quæ ex communibus vitæ usibus & moribus diligenter in historia observatis decerpuntur, quæq; non tam orninc describi, & Literis mandari, quam longa tractatione colligi, & per manus tradi possunt. Ibidem.

Of the first sort are these, and such like following.

Com. 545.a. Paramour. *Home est tenus destre prochein a soy mesme.*
Manxel. 6. a. b. *Le inclination de touts homes est de faire ou parler choses pour leur gaine, & nient pour leur perde : Et de*
Com. 261. a. *ceuxque violent gabber, de gabber pur advantage.*
Halls case. *Est le propertie de nature de preserver luy mesme.*
8.H.6.19.b. *Quant home est partie, il ne poet esse Iudge indif-*
Per Martin. *ferent a luy mesme.*

With many other of like qualitie, which the intendment of the Law deriveth and collecteth out of the usuall condition, nature, and qualitie of things upon the probabilitie and likelihood of occurrences often or for the most part hapning and falling out.

Axiomes.

Axiomes or *Propositions* of the second sort, are drawne from the phrase of speech, and deduced from the ordinary manner of Conference by talk among men most usuall in all places, As are the common and ordinarie Proverbs and proverbiall Assertions, and such like; the which, as well by reason of their ordinary and often use in talke; as also for their probabilitie and likelihood of truth have been sometime used as Axiomes, Principles, and Grounds of the Law; and are to bee found confirmed with many Cases, having beene used as reasons in the same: Whereof these few ensuing may serve for example.

Da tua dum tua sunt; post mortem, tunc tua non sunt.

Qui ambulat in tenebris, nescit quò vadit.

Necessitas non habet Legem.

As good never the whit, as never the better.

Let him that is cold blow the coale.

One to beat the bush, and another to take the birds.

With many other such like speeches, which although they are of small moment, being every where ordinarie; yet neverthelesse for the perspicuity and plainness, they have heretofore, at some times, in Law arguments beene used, and fitly applyed in debate of Cases (although not *ad probandum*, yet *ad illustrandum*) and so likewise may at any time hereafter, upon like occasion offered, without blame be frequented.

Although these generall Positions, Maximes & Rules proposed, and such like, cannot be properly reduced (as aforesaid) under any one peculiar title

Proverbiall Grounds.

Proverbium vulgò interpretatur probatum verbum, cum dicatur quasi Commune omnium verbum. Proverbia verò citata, instar jurium haberi traditum est. L. solent. ff. de officio Procurat. Sim. Shardus Lexicon Iuris.

Com. 280.*a.*
Com. 173.*a.*
Com. 18.*b.*
29. *Eliz.* 356.*a.*
14 *H.* 8.23 *a*

of the Law, extant in any Abridgement, Table, or directorie; yet neverthelesse may they be brought under generall titles or common places, to bee framed of purpose, as hereafter in place more convenient shall be declared.

And thus much therefore of generall Grounds or Maximes.

Maximes appliable onely to one title.

Now followeth to speake of such as are to bee reduced under one particular title, tractate, or matter of the Law, serving to no other use, but onely doe concerne the said speciall matter, and cannot bee transferred thence, neither may properly serve any other then their native place, unto the which they are wholly and alonely to bee referred: As for example,

Vnder Grants these.

T.E.1.Fitz. Grants. 36. Aff. p.3.

Quando aliquis quid concedit, & id etiam concedere videtur, sine quo res concessa esse non potest.

Grant sera prise plus fort vers le Grauntour, &c.

Vnder Contracts these and such like.

Ex nudo pacto non oritur actio. Com. 5. a. Com. 302. a. Com. 305. a. Com. 321. a.

17. Ed. 4. 1. a.

Contract ne poit estre, si ne soit que chescun partie soit agree.

Vnder Prerogative, these and such others.

Nullum tempus occurrit Regi. Com. 243. a. 261. a. 321. a.

Le

Le Roy ad auxy un Prerogative en le forme de brefs port per luy, different de ceaux que common person ad, &c. Vide 18.Ed. 3.2.a.

Vnder Deeds these.

Fiunt aliquando Donationes in scriptis, sicut in chartis, ad perpetuam memoriam, propter brevem hominum vitam, & ut faciliùs probari possit Donatio. Bract. li.2.c. 16.f.33.b. 14.H.8.22.b

Choses incident que per lour mesme ne poient estre grant sans fait, uncore ils passeront oue le principal a qui sont incident sans fait. With divers other in every title of the Law of like effect. Brudnel. Vid.Lit.183 21.H.7.37.b.

These speciall Grounds are of divers sorts: for some concerne the very nature and essence of the title: some the consequents and incidents annexed thereunto. Those which doe concerne the nature of the thing, doe flow from some of the causes thereof, as the Materiall, the Formall, the Efficient, or the Finall. Some from the generall notion; others from the special difference; and some doe proceed from the effect. Those which doe proceed of the consequents, concerne either the Incidents inherent and inseparable, or the adjuncts, and such like. The divers kinds of Grounds which doe concerne one title.

Which grounds so drawne, if they be orderly disposed with al their subdivisions, and particular Rules, and the same furnished with apt cases, will make a perfect and exact treatise of such matter as concerneth that title, resembling those treatises compiled, by *Littleton*, *Parkins*, *Stanford*, of the Pleas of the Crowne, and others of like forme.

Arbitrement.

But in this place not intending to combine any ſuch Grounds as do concerne one title or matter, or thereof to endeavour to draw a type of any perfect treatiſe, it ſhall be ſufficient at this preſent, for example onely, to expreſſe that which is here meant, by the diſpoſing of ſome few Grounds of the title of Arbitrement, according to the obſervation above mentioned, that thereby might bee conceived, how ſuch like Grounds concerning one title or matter doe flow from the cauſes and conſequents of that title, whereunto they are applied; and that a coherency of them might be both found and orderly framed for the more certaine obtaining of knowledge in obſerving this, or the like courſe to this hereafter following.

Firſt although we find not an Arbitrement to be defined in any report of our Lawes; yet nevertheleſſe *Raſtall* in the ſmall treatiſe of the Termes of the Law, thereof yeeldeth this deſcription,

Arbitremēt, *quid?* *Arbitrement eſt un award, determination, ou judgement, quel pleuſieurs font al requeſt de deux parties al meins, pur, & ſur aſcun dett, treſpas, ou auter controverſie ewe perenter les dits parties.* But more artificially it may be deſcribed out of the Civill Law thus:

Arbitrium eſt Arbitri ſententia ſive Iudicium inter controvertentes; privato conſenſu, non autem publica interveniente authoritate, datum.

Out of the bookes of Reports of the Lawes of this

this Land this full deſcription may be drawne.

An Award is a judgement 8. *E*.4.1. 8.*Ed*.4. 10.*a*. 21.*Ed*.4.39.*a*. given by ſuch perſon or perſons as are elected by the parties unto the controverſie, 9.*Ed*.4.43.*b*.*Fairfax*. 16.*Ed*.4.9.*a*.for the ending and pacifying the ſaid controverſie. 8.*Ed*. 4.10.*a* 19.*Hen*.6.37.*b*. *Askewe*. according to the comprimiſe and ſubmiſſion.19.*Edw*.4.1.*a*. and agreeable to reaſon and good conſcience. 19.*Hen*. 6.37.*a*.

Touching the Etymology or notation of the names thereof,it ſeemeth to be called an Arbitrement,becauſe the Iudges elected therein,may determine the controverſie, not according to the Law, but *Ex boni viri Arbitrio*. Or elſe perhaps because the parties to the controverſie have ſubmitted themſelves to the Iudgement of the Arbitrators,not by compulſary meanes, and coertion of the Law, but *Ex libero Arbritrio ſuo*, of his own accord. It is called an Award of the French word *Agarder*,which ſignifies to decide or judge.It is in the Saxon or old Engliſh ſometime called a *Loveday*,for the quiet and tranquility that ſhould enſue thereof,and for the ending of the cauſe which is wrought thereby.

The Etymologie. 1 2 3 4

The Materiall cauſe whereabout it is converſant,is the controverſie,which

The Materiall cauſe.

1, Firſt,may be either action,ſuit, quarrell, or demand; and the

2 Second that,concerning dutie or demand, either perſonall,reall or mixt, or every of them.

The Formall cauſe is, the forme and manner of

the

The formall cause. the Award, or the yeelding up of their judgement, according to reason, intent and good meaning.

The efficiẽt cause. The Immediate efficient cause, is the Arbitrator or Arbitrators.

The Mediate efficient cause, is the comprimise or submission, and the parties at variance, being also parties to the submission. Wherefore for the more brevitie we will discourse of every of these last recited, when we shall discover the power of the Arbitrator.

The finall cause. The finall cause, is both to appease

1, First, the debate and variance so risen betweene the parties, and compromitted; and also to reduce

2, Secondly, that which was before uncertain, unto a certaintie.

So that by these you see, that those five things which are found to be incident to every Award, *viz.*

1 First, *matter de controversie.*

2 *Submission.*

3 *Parties al submission.*

4 *Arbitrators*, and

5 *Render sur del Iudgement*, spoken of in 4 *Eliz. Dyer* 217. *a.* are here reduced into a methodicall consideration of the causes of every Award, seeing indeed, they and no other are the very causes of the same.

Genus. The *genus* or generall notion of the former description, is, that it is a Iudgement.

Differentia. The speciall difference whereby it is distinguished

shed from other Iudgements, and expressed in the said description, is, that it is given by Iudges elected by the parties, and not by coertion of the Law.

The effect is, when it concerneth any payment of money, to alter, change, and make the controversie *transire in rem judicatam*, and thereupon to give action for the summe awarded. The effect. 1

If it doe determine any collaterall or other matter than payment of money to bee made or done, then it is not compulsary to constraine the parties to performe it; but every of them is restored to his former action. Except the compromise or submission be by deed; and so therein it resteth wholly upon that security by bond, covenant, statute, or recognizance, by the which the parties compromitted themselves. 2

The Adjunct, is the performance thereof and the manner how, which whether the Award bee performed or not, it maketh nothing to the nature and substance of the Award it selfe. But neverthelesse such performance of the Award is a requisite consequent annexed to the consideration of the nature of an Award. The Adjunct.

These, the generall causes of an Award, thus considered; next followeth the consideration of the grounds that flow from every of them.

From the Materiall cause which is the controversie, these Grounds or Rules are deduced. Materiall cause.

In Reall matters, *que concerne franke tenement, Arbitrement ne lia, le title, ne done ceo. 14. Henr. 4. 19. a.* Reall Matters

In matters of Realty, which concerne freehold, an Arbitrement doth neither give title, nor binde the right.

Reall Actions. *In Reall Actions, un Arbitrement nest plee.*

Mixt Actions. *In Mixt Actions, Arbitrement nest plee: Si non que le Comprimise soit per fait.* 19. *Hen.* 6. 37. *b. Newton.*

Personall Actions. *In Personall Actions sur personall torts, Arbitrement est plee, coment que le submission ne soit per fait.* 14. *H.* 4. 24. *b. Rauish gard.*

Reall Chattels *In controversie concernant le propertie de Reall chattels, un Arbitrement transfer propertie de ceo accordant al agard.* 21. *H.* 7. 29. *b.*

Personall Chattells. *In Chattels personall, Arbitrement transfer propertie.*

Personall dutie. *In Personall dutie grounde sur specialtie, Arbitrement nest availeable.* 3. *H.* 4. 1. *b.* 8. *H.* 5. 3. *b.*

Matters de Record. *In Controversie grounde sur matter de Record, Arbitrement ne sera regard.* 6. *H.* 4. 6. *a.* 8. *Hen.* 5. 3. *b* 4. *H.* 6. 17. *b.*

Dutie in certaine. *Arbitrement doet este de dutie nient certaine.* 6. *Hen.* 4. 6. *a.* 2. *Hen.* 5. *Fitzh.* 23. 4. *Hen.* 6. 17. *b.* 10 *Hen.* 7. 4. *a.*

Controversie de dett solement, ne poet este mise en Arbitrement. 45. *E.* 3. 16. *a.* 2. *H.* 5. *Fitzh. Arbitrement* 23. 8. *H.* 5. 3. *b.* 4. *H.* 6. 17. *b.* 10. *H.* 7. 4. *a.*

Dett. *In Contract de dett oue auter chose mise en comprimise Arbitrement sera bone.* 2. *H.* 6. *Fitzh. Arbitrement* 23. 4. *H.* 6. 17. *b.* 10. *H.* 7. 4. *a.*

Dett. *Dett sur Contract sans specialtie, per le resolution de ascuns liure poet este mise en Arbitrement.* 45. *E.* 3. 16. *a.* 6. *H.* 4. 6. *a.* 4. *H.* 6. 18. *a.*

These

These with divers other grounds, doe proceed, as we have said, from the Materiall Cause or controversie.

There resteth now to speake of such as do proceed from the Formall Cause. Formall Cause.

Every Award, as touching the forme thereof, ought to have these foure qualities.

1. First, that it be not a thing impossible to be performed by the parties.

2. Secondly, that it doe not ordaine matter unlawfull to be done.

3. Thirdly, that the same Award agree with reason and good meaning.

4. Fourthly, that it be sensible, full, and perfect in understanding.

As touching the first.

1. *Arbitrement ne doet este de chose ou matter impossible.* 8.*E*.4.1.*b*. *Moyle*. 8.*E*.4.10.*a*. *Yelverton*. 19.*E*.4.1.*a*. *Neele*. 9.*H*.7.16.*b*.*Keble*. Impossible.

2. *Arbitrement ne doit este de chose encounter ley*. 19.*Edw*.4.1.*a*.*Neele*. 21.*Ed*.4.*b*.*Bridg*. 9.*Hen*.7.16.*a*.*b*.*Keble*. Encounter Ley.

3. *Arbitrement ne doet estre unreasonable*.46.*E*.3.16.*a*. 43.*E*.3.17.*b*. 2.*H*.5.2.*a*. 17.*E*.4.5.*b*.9.*H*.7 10.*b*.*Keble*. 46.*E*.3.17.*b*. 21.*E*.4.40.*a*. 10.*H*.4. *Fitzh*.*Arbitrement*. Vnreasonable.

This Ground last remembred, being generall, containeth therein many speciall Rules under it; whereof some doe follow.

Arbitrement doet este tiel que les parties poient performer

Satisfaction *sans assistance des auters.* *former sans le assistance de ascunes auters queux ils ne poient compel a ceo faire & performer.* 8.*Edw*.4.2.*a*. *Illingworth*. 17.*Edw*.4.15.*b*. 18.*Edw*.4.23.*a*.*Catesby*. 19.*E*.4.1.*b*. *Brian*.

Assistance *des auters.* *Mes si les parties ont mean per le ley a compeller tiels estrangers a ceo performer, le Agard est assetts bone.* 17.*E*.4.5.*b*.

Iudiciall Act. *Arbitrement que le party faire un judiciall Act est bone, coment que il ne poiet ceo performe sans assistance del Court*.19.*H*.6.38.*a*. *Past*.*Nonsuite*. 19.*E*.4 1.*b*. *Brian*.*fine*. 12.*E*.4.8.*a*. *Retraxit*. 22.*E*.4.38.*a*. *Retraxit*. 5.*H*.7.22.*a*.*b*.*Discon*.*&c*.

Satisfaction. *Chascun Arbitrement q̃ ne import satisfaction del tort que est mise in comprimise, nest bone*. 43.*E*.3.28. *b*. *Finchd*.46.*E*.3.17.*b*. 2.*H*.5.2.*a*. 45.*E*.3.16.*a*. 19.*H*.6.38.*a*. *Past*. 22.*H*.6.39.*a*. *Port*. 30.*Hen*.6. *Fitzherbert Arbitrement*.27.9.*E*.4.44.*a*.*Chock*.9.*H*. 7.16.*b*. 12.*H*.7.15.*a*.

This Ground is also generall: Wherefore it shall be expedient to divide it by the particular circumstances of cases unto more especiall propositions, together with their severall exceptions to be set downe in manner following.

Redeliuerie *des biens.* *Arbitrement in tiel maner, que pur ceo que un des parties ad les chattels del auter, que il eux redelivera, ceo nest satisfaction*. 45.*E*.3.16.*a*. *Kirton*. 2.*Hen*.5. 2.*a*. 12.*H*.7.15.*a*.

Redeliuerie *des biens.* *Mes si sur le delivery des biens, cesty a que sont deliver poet aver ascun benefit, per tiel delivery in satisfaction del tort, donque est le Arbitrement bone*. 2.*H*. 5.2.*a*. 14.*H*.4.14.*b*. 12.*H*.7.15.*a*.

Parte del Chose. *Arbitrement que un partie avera un partie del chose com-*

comprimise, & sur que le controversie fait, & l'auter partie est void. 45. E.3. 16. a. 10. Hen.4. Fitzh. *Arbitrement* 19.

Arbitrement que le partie payera part de sa dett, est void. 45.E.3.16.a. *Part del Chose.*

Arbitrement sur matter de dett, sils agard que les parties endebted payera plus que il doit in recompence del dit dett ceo est void. 9.H.7.16.b.*Keble.* *Plus que il doit.*

Arbitrement que cesty que est suppose daver fait trespas, faira de ceo son Ley, & sur ceo sera discharge, nest satisfaction al auter, & pur ceo nest bone. 46.Ed. 3.17.b. *Gager de Ley*

Arbitrement que in satisfaction del tort que les parties entermariont, ceo nest bone agard; car nest satisfaction. 9.E.4.44.a.*Chock.* Entermariage.

Arbitrement que un des parties que est in arrerages in accompt accomptera al auter, ceo nest satisfaction. 30.H.6. *Fitzh. Arbitrement* 27. *Accomptera*

Arbitrement que les parties fera act a tiel jour, & devant que le agard est perfect, le jour est passe tiel agard nest bone. 8.E.4.11.a. 8.E.4.22.a. *Iour passe.*

Arbitrement que refer le feasance del chose ou auter matter a tiel chose q̃ nest in Rerum natura; tiel arbitrement est void. 21.E.4.40.a. 9.Ed.4.44.a. 39.H. 6.10.a. *Non in Rerum Natura.*

Having thus shewed the Circumstances of certaine Arbitrements, which have beene taken to be against reason, sounding to no satisfaction, and therefore voyd: Now resteth to be shewed certaine circumstances, in Arbitrements agreeable unto reason, and imparting satisfaction, and therefore deemed good. Reasonable.

Equall. *Arbitrement doet este equal in respect d'ambideux parties, & l'un come l'auter sera lie a ceo. 7.H.6. 41.a. Strange. 19.H.6.38.a. Newton. 20.H.6.19.a. Newton. 39.H.6.12.a. Moyle.*

Enter ascuns des Parties. *Lou divers d'une parties & d'auter eux submit al agard, & le Arbitrement est, que l'une de l'une partie payera a un auter de l'auter partie tant, sans rien parler des auters; ceo est bone agard, pur ceo que poet este que le auters naveront cause daver ascun chose. 22.E. 4.25.b.*

Quitt. *Arbitrement pur ceo que les torts fait per les parties chescun al auter sont equal que ils seront quit chescun vers lauter; ceo est bone agard. 19.H.7.37.b. Newton. 20.H.6.19.a. Newton. 21.H.6. Fitz. Arbit. 9.*

Quitt. *Arbitrement que une des parties sera quit vers lauter, & que cesty auter payera ou faira tant pur ceo que son trespas fut le greinder, est bon agard. 10.H.6.4.a. 20.H.6.19.a. Newton.*

Petit Recompence. *Arbitrement que l'une done al auter quart de vine, ou tiel petit recompence pur satisfaction del tort, est bone agard, 43.E.3.33.a. 45.E.3.19.b Belknap. 9.E 4.44.a. Nedham.*

Greinder value que le tort. *Si le Arbitrement soit, que un des parties payera greinder sum in value que le tort est que il ad fait, uncore le agard est bone, & ceo gist in discretion des Arbitrators, 8,E,4,21, Chock.*

Release. *Arbitrement, que chescun release al auter, est bone, 9,E,4,44,b, Danby.*

Release. *Arbitrement que l'une release tout son droit in tiel terre, est bone satisfaction: Si cesty a que le release sera fait soit in possession del terre, &c. Et ceo appiert per le agard, 9,E,4,44,b. 21,E,4,40,b.*

Ar-

Arbitrement q̃s l'une partie done al auter tiel chose, coment q̃s le partie nad tiel chose, uncore est le agard bone, & il doit provide ceo, 19, *E*, 4, 1, *a*, *Neele*. 9, *Henr*: 7, 16, *a*. *Doner ceo que il nad.*

Arbitrement bone in part, & void in part, 19, *E*, 4, 1, *a*. *Bone in part.*

Arbitrators poient ordaine act deste fait in lour agard pur le melieur securitie del performance de ceo, come obligation, 8, *H*, 6, 18, *b*, *Newton*. 19, *H*, 4, 1, *a*, *Chock*. *Security del Agard.*

Chescune Arbitrement doet este plaine & certaine en sence, 8, *E*, 4, 11, *a*, *Pigot*. Certaine.

Arbitrement est chose entier, 18, *E*, 4, 23, *a*, *Brian*. Entier.

Thus much touching the Matter and Forme of Arbitrements and the Axiomes, Grounds and Rules deduced from the same: Wherein we have not expressed every Rule that might be found in the books, or collected thence, tending hereunto: Neither are those Axiomes or Propositions here put downe, furnished with all those cases that might be thereunto applyed: For, not intending to expresse the type of any treatise of this title, but onely a methodicall Abstract or Directory, that which is here exemplified in part may be sufficient to expresse our meaning before declared. But to proceed.

The Efficient Causes, and the Rules drawne from the same come next to consideration. Efficient Cause.

The first whereof is the Arbitrator: Of whom the Authour of the Institutions of the Canon Law giveth this description: *Arbitri dicuntur proprie, qui (nullam potestatem habentes ex Lege,)* con- *Iohannes Paulus Lancelottus. Arbitrator quid.*

consensu Litigantium in Iudices eliguntur: in quos compromittitur, ut eorum sententiæ stetur.

Out of the bookes of the Common law, a description of an Arbitrator may be thus collected.

Vne Arbitratour est Iudge private, eslew per les parties. 9. *Edw.* 4. 43. *b. Fairefax.* 16. *Edw.* 4. 9. *a. Feneux.* 19. *Hen.* 6. 37. *b. Askew. pur appeaser les debates enter eux.* 8. *Edw.* 4. 10. *a. Billinge. Et de arbitrate & adjudge selonque lour bone intent.* 19. *H.* 6. 37. *a. Paston.*

Sithence in the Award it selfe, the Law requireth such qualities, there hath not beene made many nor scarce any question, who may be an Arbitrator, and who not: Neither (considering what hath beene said touching the forme of an Award) should it be greatly necessary. Therefore we wil proceed, respecting in the Arbitrator these three things.

1. First his Ordinance, from whom it is.

2. His Authority, what it is.

3. His Duty, wherein it consisteth.

Ordinance. Touching his Ordinance, hee is ordained by these two things:

1. First, by the election of the parties. 20. *H.* 6. 41. *a.*

2. By his owne undertaking of the charge. 8. *E.* 4. 10. *a. Billinge.*

Authoritie. Touching his Authority, what it is.

1. First it is derived from the submission, and extendeth no further.

2. Thereby hee is a Iudge betweene the parties.

3. And

3, And therefore he cannot transferre his authority over to any other.

Touching his Duty, it consisteth in these three. Duty.

1, First to heare the griefe of the partie.

2, To judge according to equitie.

3, To notifie their Award.

First therefore concerning the election of the Arbitrators by the parties to the Controversie (which ought likewise to bee parties to the Submission) there is first of all to be considered, what persons may by the Law submit themselves to an award made by others, and what persons cannot. Election of the Arbitratour.

And therefore, *Queux persons poient eux submitter al agarde.*

Si l'une des parties submit luy a une Arbitrement d'une parte, et Depute del auter parte in nosme del dit auter party: Arbitrement sur ceo fait per enter eux semble bon. 4. Eliz. 217. a. 60. *Deputy.*

Le Baron poet luy mesme submit al agard pur luy et sa feme pur chattels des queux il ad le disposition in droit, et per reason de sa fem, et ceo Liera la feme. 21. Hen. 7. 29. b. *Baron & feme.*

Si enfant submit luy al une agard, il sera lye de ceo performer cy bien come home de plein age. 13. Hen. 4. 12. a. 10 Hen. 6. 14. a. *Enfant.*

Si divers d'une parte ont fait tort a un auter, & cesti a qui le tort est fait, et un de les auters submit eux al agard, de cest agard fait les auters nient parties al submission averon advantage in extinguishment del tort. 7. Hen. 4. 31. b. 20. H. 6. 12. a. 20. H. 6. 41. a. *Ascuns des parties.*

Si divers del une parte submit eux mesmes al agard de certaine persons, & divers del auter parte: Les Arbitratours ont power de faire agarde pur matters *Ioynt & severall.*

enter eux joyntment, & ißint pur matter enter eux severalment, 2. Rich.3.18.b. vide 21.Hen.7.29.b. Com.Dalton.289.b.

Ascunes des parties. *Si divers del une parte & de auter submit eux al agard del une, que fait agard perenter ascunes d'une party, & ascunes del auter party & nemy perenter eux touts, & ne parle rien en son agard des auters, uncore tiel agard est bone, 22.Edw.4.25.b.*

Thus much touching the parties that doe submit themselves unto an Award, and which make an election of the Arbitratours. Now followeth that somewhat be also said as touching the undertaking of the charge of the said Award.

vndertaking the award.

Del parcel. *Si le Arbritratour protest, que il ne voile meddle ave tout ceo que est commit a luy, ou conteyne en le submißion, ou s'il fait agard tantum del parcel, le agard est bone, 19.Hen.6.6.b. 39.Hen.6.11.b. Prisot, cont. 4. Eliz.217.60.7.8.Eliz.243.b.52.*

Parcel. *Mes si le submißion soit per fait conditionalment que le dit agard soit deliver devant tiel jour: une Arbitrement de parcel nest bone, 4.Eliz.217.60.7.8.Eliz. 243.b.52.*

Parcel. *Mes uncore, si le submißion soit que ils estoieront al agard des Arbitratours de tout le chose comprimit ou fait pur ascun parcel de ceo: donque le Arbitrement est bone pur parcel, 39.Hen.6.11.b.*

And thus much hath beene said of the taking upon them of the charge of the Arbitrement.

Now resteth it likewise to speake of the Authoritie of the Arbitrators themselves: which is, as before is declared, grounded upon the submission.

The

The ſubmiſſion or comprimiſe therfore out of the Civill Law, is thus defined;

Compromiſſum eſt ſimultanea illa partium promiſſio, qua ſua ſponte, ad alicujus boni viri Arbitrium ſuam remittunt controverſiam. *Compromiſe ou ſubmiſſion.*

Submiſſions are in two manners, either by writing, or by word.

Thoſe that are by writing, are either by obligation, or by covenant.

Which obligation is either of Record, as a recognizance, or by deed betweene the parties.

And this ſubmiſſion by writing, or by word, is either abſolute, or conditionall, ſo that the award be delivered by a certaine day, or ſuch like.

Wherefore in as much as the authority of the Arbitrator is deduced from the ſubmiſſion, it followeth that,

Le Arbitrement que eſt fait de choſe nient containe in le ſubmiſſion, eſt voide, 7. Hen. 6. 40. b. 19. Hen. 6. 39. b. Fort. 9. Ed. 4. 44. a. Chock. 19. E. 4. 1. a. Neele. 7. 8. Eliz. 242. b. 52. *Nient containe in ſubmiſſion.*

Mes ſi le ſubmiſſion eſt de choſe perſonal, les Arbitrators poient agard, que un des parties fera act que eſt de choſe real in ſatisfaction der perſonal tort, 9. Ed. 4. 44. a. Brian. *Nient containe in le ſubmiſſion.*

Si le ſubmiſſion ſoit de choſe real, les Arbitratours poient agard ſatisfaction deſte fait de choſe perſonal, 9. E. 4. 44. a. Brian. *Real.*

Si les arbitratours agard, que un des parties fera act al eſtranger, come feofment, ou tiels ſembles, tel arbitrement eſt void, 22. Hen. 6. 46. b. 17. Ed. 4. 23. a. Catesby, 19. Ed. 4. 1. b. Brian. 5 Hen. 7. 22. b. *Eſtranger.*

Incident. *Si le submißion soit d'une chose, le Arbitrement poit esse fait de chose incident a ceo.8 Hen.6.18.b. 19.Ed. 4.1.a. Chock.ver.9.Hen.7.15.b.16.a.*

Vpon this authority given to the Arbitrators by the submission,to deale in manner as aforesaid, in things touching the same submission.

Iudge. It ensueth also secondarily,that

Le Arbitrator est un Iudge perenter les parties, 19. Hen.6.37.b.Ascongh, 9.Ed.4.43.b.Fairf.16.Ed.4. 9.a.Iency.Com.Fogasta.6.a.

Wherefore likewise it ensueth that the Arbitrator being a Iudge cannot transferre that his Iudiciall authority to any other.

And therfore,

Estranger. *Si le Arbitrement soit, que les parties estoicra al arbitrement d'un estranger;ceo nest bone agard,47.Ed. 3.21.a.Cont. 8.Ed.4.10,11.a.*

Estranger. *Mes si l'estranger ad fait un Arbitrement devant perenter les dits parties, le Agard pur estoier a tiel Arbitrement del estranger est bone, 39.Hen. 6,10.a. 11.a.*

Estranger. *Mes si le Arbitrement soit que les parties performera le Agard d'une auter devant fait perenter mesmes les parties, lou in verity nest ascun tel agard: uncore cest Arbitrement est bone prima facie tanque soit monstre que nest tiel agard,39.Hen.6.12.a.Prisot.*

Advice. *Mes uncore si le Arbitrement soit, que une act limit per le Agard sera fait per le advise & counseil d'une auter person; tiel Agard est bone, 8.Ed. 4.11.a. 14.Ed.4.1. a.Chock.*

Advice. *Mes si le Agard soit, que le act sera fait per le Advise del Arbitratour mesme apres le Agard rendu*

sur

sur tel Agard nest bone, 19. *Ed.*4.1.*a. Chock.*

Si les parties eux submit al Agard de certaine persons, & s'ils ne poient agree, donque al ordinance d'un auter come umpier: si les Arbitratours font Agard de parcel, le umpier ne fera agard del auter parcel remnant, 39.*Hen.*6.10.*a.b.* *Vmpier.*

Mes si le submission soit tiel que le umpier fera Agard del tout ou parte, donque il poit faire Agard de cest parte, ovesque que les Arbitrators navont meddle, 39.*Hen.*6. 11.*b. Prisot.*

Now as touching the duty of the Arbitratours. First *Duty.*

Les duties des parties est a vener devant les Arbitratours & monstre lour grieves.

1 *Et le Arbitratour doit eux oir.*

2 *Et solonque ceo adjudge, ou auterment il nest bone Iudge,* 8.*Ed.*4.10.*a. Billinge.*

Those which affect the Method of *Ramus* (that is, to begin with the efficient cause, as here, with Arbitratour) rather then that which is usually prosecuted by the Interpretors of *Aristotle* (namely, to begin first with the matter and forme, which we hitherunto have endeavoured to follow) may here adde to, the second part of the duty of an Arbitrator (that is, to that which hath beene here said of this Iudiciall Authority and Iudgement) as much as hath beene before, first of all, shewed by us, touching the Materiall and Formall causes, and the Grounds and Rules incident thereupon.

But neverthelesse, to proceed with our intended enterprise; touching the third part of the dutie of an Arbitrator, *viz.* the publishing or notifying

fying of his Award; It is to be considered that the publishing or notifying of an Award is either provided for and ordained by the submission it selfe; or else it is left and permitted to the discretion of the Arbitrator.

If it be provided for, by the submission; for the most part it is in this manner, that either the same Award made, be notified to the parties, or some of them; & that, either by a certaine day or time, or else without limitation of any time.

As concerning therefore the delivery of the Award, there is to be noted; that where such provision is made of notification by the submission, that then;

Pronounce. *Arbitrement nest Arbitrement devant que il soit pronounce*, 8.*Ed*.4.21.*b*.*Chock*.

Delivery de Agard. *Lou per le submission est ordaine ou provide condicionalment, que le agard soit deliver, ceo nest ascun arbitrement in ley devant que il soit deliver in fait*, 8.*Ed*.4.11 *Yelverton*.8.*Ed*.4.21.*a*.*Chock*. *vide* 1.*Hen*.7.5.*a*.37.*Hen*.8.*Browne*, *Conditions*, 46.

Delivery. *Mes si le submission soit que le agard sera delivere al parties, &c. devant un jour hoc petentibus, mes nul certaine jour limit quand doit este deliver, les parties doient prender notice del agard a lour perill*, 8.*Edw*.4.1.*b*.21, *&c*.

Delivery. *Si divers d'un partie & divers de auter party submit eux al Arbitrement de un auter, provise, que il soit deliver al parties, ou a un de eux : ne besoign al Arbitrator a deliver ceo a ambideux del un partie ou a un de chacuns partie : mes suffist si soit deliver al ascun des dits parties*, 4.5.*Eliz*.218.*b*.5.

Si

Si le submißion soit que le Arbitrement sera deliver devant tiel jour, il poet cy bien este deliver per parol come per fait : si non q̃ le submißion soit q̃ il sera per fait,4.5. Eliz.218.b.5. Delivery.

Si le submißion soit q̃ le Arbitrement sera deliver ceo poet este fait in un County, & deliver in auter County,5.Hen.7.7.a. County & lieu del delivery.

Si le submißion soit per fait, & le temps pas in q̃ le Arbitrement doet este fait, les parties ne poient proroge le temps ouster pur faire le agard sans novel submißion a tel entent,49.Ed.3.9.a. Temps.

Mes si le submißion soit sans fait, les parties poient proroge le temps q̃ fut done pur faire le agard, 49.Ed. 3.9.Fitzh.agard, 22. Temps.

Si les Arbitrators font lour agard perenter les parties un jour, ils ne poient faire auter agard perenter les parties un auter jour, coment q̃ le temps don per le submißion ne soit expire,22.Hen.6.52.a. vide 33.H. 6.28.b. Temps.

Arbitrement ne poet este fait parte a un temps, & parte al auter, coment q̃ soit deins le temps del submißion,39.H.6.12.a.Danby,8.Ed.4.10.b.Fairfax, 19. Ed.4.1.a.Chock, vide 3.Hen.4.1.b. Temps.

Mes les Arbitrators poient Common enter eux mesmes,& agree sur un chose un jour,& de auter chose auter jour, & in le fine faire une entire agard de tout : Et ceo est bone, 47. Edw.3.21.a. 39.Hen.6.12.a. Danby. Temps.

Si Arbitratours agard un chose de une parte, & devant q̃ ils poient agree de lour agard del remnant, le temps done per le submißion expire; tout lour agard est voide,39.Hen.6.12.a.Prisot. Temps.

But

But if there be by the submission no order taken for the Delivery or Publication of the Award; Then

Notice. *In honesty & Conscience le Arbitratour est tenus de faire notice al parties de ceo. vide 8. Edw. 4. 10. a. Billinge, vide 8. Edw. 4. 2. a b. Markham.*

Notice. *Mes in rigore Iuris l'arbitrement mesme est intend chose Notorious, 8. Ed. 4. 1. b. Chock. 8. Edw. 4. 21. b. Chock.*

Et pur ceo.

Notice. *Parties al Arbitrement sont tenus de prender notice del agard a lour peril, 8. Edw. 4. 18. 21. 18. Edw. 4. 18. a. 1. Hen. 7. 5. a.*

Notice. *Coment que les Parties ne sont daver Notice done a eux de L'arbitrement, uncore si les Arbitratours agard que un des parties fera act que depend sur auter primes destre fait del auter partie, de ceo il aver notice, 8. Edw. 4. 21. b. 20. Edw. 4. 8. b. Sulliard.*

Hitherto hath beene said of such matters where the Arbitrators have executed their Authoritie without controll of the parties: But if, before any Award made, their Authority shall be lawfully countermanded; Then doth there remaine in this place to be considered,

1, Whether such Countermands be permitted by the Law.

2, And in what Cases not.

3, And also in what manner the same is to be done.

Wherefore

Countermād. *Si le submission soit sans fait, chescun des parties poit Countermand & discharge les Arbitratours,*

49. Edw.

49. Ed. 3. vide Fitzherbert Arbitrement 22. 21. Hen.6. 30.a. 28.Hen.6.6.b.5.Edw.4.3.b.8.Edw.4. 10.b.

Mes donq; les parties doient doner Notice al Arbitratours del dit discharge, 8.Edw.4.10.b. Markham, 8.Edw.4.12.a.Lakyn. *Countermãd.*

Mes si divers d'un part & diverse d'auter part eux submit al Arbitrement sans fait, un del une parte ne poet discharge le Arbitratour sans les auters son Compagnons de mesme le partie, 28.Hen.6.b. *Countermãd.*

Mes si le submission soit per fait un des parties ne poit Countremaund les Arbitratours, 49. Edw. 3. Fitzh. Arbitrement 22. nient in le liver a large. 5. Edw.4.3.b.8.Ed.4. 11.b.Pigott. *Countermãd.*

The last cause of the foure before remembred being the Finall Cause (that is) the end and scope wherefore men doe submit themselves unto the Arbitrement and Award of any person, consisteth upon two things. *Regula à sansa finali.*

1 *Chacun Arbitrement est a faire final determination & de appeaser le strifes, debates & variances enter les parties. 19 .Hen.6.37.b.Newton, 8.Edw.4.10. a. Lakyn. 8.Edw.4.12.b.Yelverton.* *Final determination.*

2 *Chacun Arbitrement est a reducer chose incertaine a une certainty, & nemy a reducer un certainty in auter certainty, 6.Hen.4.6.a. Hankford.4.Hen.6.17. b.Weston. 10.Hen.7.4.a.* *A reducer incertaintie al certaintie.*

Thus much hath beene sayd as touching the Causes.

Now as concerning the Genus or Generall Notion: In the former definition of an Arbitrement, It is to be considered, That

Iudgement. *Chescun Arbitrement est un Iudgement, 8.Ed.4.1.b.Fairefax.8.Edw.4,10.a.Ieney. 21.Ed.4. 39.a. Vavasour.*

Because the speciall difference used in the sayd former definition of an Award, was this, That it was given by Iudges elected by the parties, and not by compulsary Iurisdiction of the Court, thereof ensueth, That

Intent del Arbitrator. *Il est diversitie ou home est Iudge per authoritie del ley, & per Election del partie mesme : Car Iudge de Record ne doner Iudgement vers les parties, si non q. ils sont appells devant eux per processe del ley : Mes autrement est dun Arbitratour q. est Iudge per enter les parties, 8.Ed.4.2.a.Illingsworth.*

Of this also ensueth, that whereas every Iudgement of Record shall be executed literally, according to the warrant issuing out of the Record, upon and for the executing of the said Iudgment; Yet neverthelesse.

Intent. *Chescun Arbitrement doit estre expound et intend accordant al intent des Arbitratours, & nemy Literalment.17.Edw.4.3.Brian. 21.Edw.4.39.a.b. vide 19.Hen.6.36.b.Markham.*

Intent, *Mes si l'intent des Arbitratours ne estoit ove la ley: donq. les parties ceo performera accordant eux parolls in tiel sence que agree ove le ley. 21.Edw.4.39.b. Fairefax.*

The Causes of an Arbitrement being thus deciphered there followeth next the consideration of the effects thereof.

The Effects of an Arbitrement are these which doe ensue.

Per

Per Arbitrement le Controverſie tranſit in rem Iudicatam.49.Edw.3.3.a.Hanmer.20.Hen.6.41.a. Paſton. 9.Edw.4.51.a.Danby. 6.Hen.11.b.Huſſey. Com.Fogoſſa,6.a. *Tranſition in rem judicatã.*

Et pur ceo

Lou le party port action pur le tort a luy fait, est bone Plea que il eux ſubmit al Arbitrement de tiels, qui agard que il pajera tant &c. mes le jour de payment de ceo neſt uncore venu, 6.Hen.7.11.b.Huſſey. 9.Edw.4.51.a.Chock.20.Hen.6.12.b.Newton. 20. Hen.6.40.a.b.Paſton. 28.Hen.6.12. 5.Ed.4.7.a. *Iour de nint venus.pur pay le mony.*

Mes ſi le jour de payment ſoit paſſe, il doit monſtre que il tender les deniers al jour, & que il eſt uncore priſt.8.Hen.6.25.b. Martin. 16.Edw.4.8.b. Pigot. *Iour de payment.* *Vncore priſt.*

Car,

Arbitrement per que les Arbitratours agard, que un des parties pajera money, done action. 5.Edw.4. 7.a.Chock. 16.Edw.4.9.a.Pigot. 17.Edw.4.2.b. Townſend. 17.Edw.4. 8.a. Pigot. Fitzh. Natura brevium121.g.6.Hen. 7.11.b.Huſſey. 9.E.4.51. Danby. *Done action.*

Et ſi les parties ne performe L'arbitrement, le parte eſt reſtore a ſon primer action, 49.Ed.3.3.a. *Reſtore al primer actiõ.*

Mes uncore eſt a ſon Election de aver Briefe de debt ſur le agard, ou le primer Action, 49.Ed.3.3.a. 33. Hen.6.2.b. *Reſtore al primer actiõ.*

Mes ſi le payment ſoit fait, le primer tort eſt tout ouſterment determine per le agard, 4.Hen.6.1.a.8.Hen. 6.25.b.21.Hen.7.28.b. *Determine.*

Ex que enſuit auxy.

Si les Arbitratours agardant, que un des parties pajera tant des deniers, Et cheſcun de eux eſt oblige al *Double Action.*

 auter

auter pur estoier al agard le party avera action sur le agard, & auxy sur le fait si agard ne soit performe. 21.E.4.41.b. 33.Hen.6.2.b.

Collaterall matter.

Si le submißion soit par paroll, & Arbitrement soit que un des parties fairont un collateral act, auter q̃ payment des deniers, ceo ne done action, & si ne soit execute in fait et satisfie, le Arbitrement nad ascun effect; Et tel Arbitrement ne determine le primer tort, 19.Hen. 6.38.a.Newton. 20.Hen.6.19.a.Markham. 5.Edw. 4.7.a.Chock. Com.Fogoss. 11.b.

Collaterall matter.

Vncore si le submißion soit per obligation, si un Collaterall act soit agard deste fait; si ceo ne soit performe, le obligation sera forfeit, 9.Ed.4.44.a.

Thus much touching the effects of an Award.

A Consequent thereof is, the Performance; wherein we are to consider, That

Performance.

Les parties doient faire tout ceo que in eux est a ceo performe, 21.Ed.4.39.b.Fairefax.

Assistance.

Si per le Arbitrement soit agard que un act sera fait le quel home poit performer, in deux manners lun voy per luy mesme, et per l'auter voy il doit aver l'aide d'un auter person: le party doit ceo performer per tel meane, que il solement poit faire sans aid de l'auter, 21.Ed.4.40.b.Hussey.

Parte.

Arbitrement ne doit este fait in part, et in part ne my, 6.Hen.7.10.b.

Parte.

Mes coment que Arbitrement ne poet este fait per les Arbitratours, part a une temps, et part a auter temps: uncore ceo poit este performe part a un temps et parte al auter, ? Ed.4.10.b.Fairefax.

Temps.

Les parties averant reasonable temps a eux allowe pur le performer d'un agard, si nul temps soit limitt,

20.

20.Edw.4.8.b. 21.Ed.4.41.a.b.&c.

Si le act que les Arbitratours agard que l'un party performera, ne poit este performe devant auter Act primes fait per l'auter partie, si cest partie ne fait le primer act, l'auter est excuse, 5.Edw.4.7.a. *Primer Act.*

Arbitrement que l'un partie pajera mony, & l'auter fera Releas; ceo sera fait a un mesme temps, si ne soit obligation de performer le Agard. 21. H.7.28.b. Knightly, & Reede. *Tout a un temps.*

Mes si soit Obligation a performer le agard, donq; chacun doit performe son parte de soubs le peril de L'Obligation, 21.Hen.7.28.b. Reede. *Chacun performe son parte.*

Si Obligation soit fait pur estoier al Arbitrement coment q; le Arbitrement soit void in Ley, uncore ceo doit este performe, auterment le Obligation sera forfeit 22.Hen.6.46.b.Port, per Cur. *Voide award Quare.*

Mes si action soit port sur tel void Agard, le Action ne sera maintaine, 22.Hen.6.46.b.Port. *Void agard.*

Si le matter contenus in le agard, & le matter contenus in le submission de que les Arbitratours doient agarder, differt in parolls, ou in circumstance, les parties al Arbitrement ne seront receive in sute sur ceo de avererrer que tout est une, 7.8.Eliz.242.b.52. *Averment.*

Thus much hath been spoken concerning Arbitrements, their Causes, Effects, and Consequents.

There resteth to accomplish our intended methode, that wee adde somewhat touching that wherewith an Arbitrement is compared, matched and resembled in the Booke Cases.

Wherefore know you that,

Chacun Accord resemble un Arbitrement. *Paria.*

Vncore chacun Accord doit este satisfie ou Recom- *Differentia.*

 pence;

pence; et Accord ne done Action; lou del auter parte Arbitrement pur que les parties sont adjudge de paier deniers, done action; & ne besoigne deste plede, execute come devant ad apparus, 6.Hen.7.11.b. 5.Ed.4.7.a. 17.Ed.4.2.b.17.Ed.4.8.a.Com.6.a.Fogossa.

And thus farre forth for example sake, have we set out these Grounds & Rules of Arbitrements: Whereunto if there were added, in their due places, the residue of the Rules & grounds which may bee collected out of the bookes of the Law concerning the same, and furnishing both these and them with as many Cases as might be applyed thereunto; the same Cases being put at large under every of their Rules, to demonstrate that in particular, which the Rule includeth in generall, the enterprise would prove (as I think) some shew of a Treatise, concerning this Title.

Which being no hard thing to accomplish, thereby would appeare that it were neither unpossible neither unprofitable, nor altogether unpleasant, to reduce every title of the Law particularly to a Methode; and so consequently, the whole body thereof into a perfect shape, which now seemeth wholly without Conformitie, and altogether dismembred.

Wherefore now, as touching the Materiall Cause of Rules and Grounds, thus much said, may suffice.

Formall

Formall Causes and Grounds of the Law.

THE divisions of grounds of the law, as touching and concerning the forme, are in two sorts to be considered. 1, First, the Coherence of the words and the Matter. 2, Secondly, the manner of the Manifestation thereof.

For the Coherence of the matter and words, there are to be regarded these two qualities.

1. First, Verity, and

2. Secondly, Amplitude or Generality.

Verity of Propositions or Grounds consisteth of two sorts: For they import either a necessary or knowne truth which cannot be impugned: Or Contingent Veritie or Probability, which may sometimes notwithstanding their shew of truth, be impeached of falshood, and so be subject unto many exceptions.

The former of these are called Primarie Conclusions of Reason. And the latter Secondarie Principles.

1, Those of the first sort are such generall assertions of the Law, as are imprinted in the mind of every Man, and discerned by the light of very Nature it selfe: which, as most certaine and undoubted, need no confirmation or fortification, but of themselves are most sufficiently known to be true and not impugnable: which the Philosophers doe call, *Prima & per se cognita*; *Communes animi Conceptiones & Notitiæ*, familiar to the conceit of every person.

Notes

Notes Collected touching the Veritie of Principles.

Arist lib.1. Dem.cap.25 T.43.

PRincipiorum, Alia sunt necessaria, Alia in rebus contingentibus cernuntur. Axioma verum, est, quando pronunciat vt Res est.

Peter Ramus li.2.dial.c.3.

Axioma verum est, aut { *Contingens.* / *Necessitans.* }

Peter Ramus ibidem. Arist. Top. lib.1.cap.1.

Necessarium Axioma, quando semper verum est; nec falsum esse potest. Vnde Aristoteles, Vera quidem sunt & perspicua ea, quæ non ab alijs sed à seipsis fidem habent.

De primis Principijs.

PRincipia nihil aliud sunt quam Propositiones immediatæ.

Arist.lib.1. dem.cap.8. T.24.

Ego propria cujusq; generis Principia appello, quæ, quod sint, Demonstratione probari non possunt: (Nam, quæ sit verborum vis & significatio, tum Principiorum, tum eorum quæ ex Principijs efficiuntur, intelligendum est) Quod verò ipsa sint Principia, citra demonstrationem ponitur; Reliqua autem Demonstratione concluduntur.

Arist lib.1. dem.c.2.T.5

Prima et principia pro eodem sumo. Est autem Principium demonstrationis Propositio, quæ ob id immediata dicitur, quoniam nulla est alia prior per quam ipsa confirmari possit.

Primaria

Primaria principia dicuntur universalia quædam Iuris pronunciata, quæ omnibus hominibus ita sunt impressa naturaliter & infixa, ut, velut indubitata & notißima, non alia egeant Demonstratione, aut certè levi aliqua probatione Confirmentur. Io.Coras.de Arte juris. lib. cap.24.

Vnde et Communes animi Conceptiones et Notitiæ appellantur quod suapte vi & perspicua sit & evidens horum Principiorum veritas & Natura, quasi sine aliqua Dubitatione & Contradictione veluti ab omnibus Concessa, in disputatione sumantur. Ibidem.

Of which sort for Example are some of them before mentioned, and here againe to be remembred in this behalfe, in manner following.

Volenti non fit injuria.

Omne majus continet in se minus.

Qui sentit Commodum sentire debet & onus.

Fraus & dolus nemini patrocinantur.

With infinite other in universall manner proposed, and with not a few in speciall set forth; As in Grants, as afore hath beene declared.

Quando aliquis quid concedit, & id etiam concedit sine quo res concessa esse non potest.

In Testaments.

Testamentum est morte confirmatum. Com.Griesbr. 280.b.

In Rents.

Chacun Rent est issuant hors de terre.

With exceeding many other of like nature to be found in every title or tractate of the Law. The manifest truth and great Reason of which said Grounds is evident to every person of any Iudgement, and need no proofe for demonstration and establishing of them.

2 Secondary Principles, are certaine Axiomes, Rules, and Grounds of the Law, which are not so well knowne by the light of Nature, as by other meanes: and which although they need no great proofe to be confirmed; because they comprehẽd great probabilitie; yet many times are they, at the first shew, not yeelded unto without due consideration: and are peculiarly knowne, for the most part, to such onely as professe the study and speculation of Lawes.

Probabilia sunt quæ probant, aut õibus, aut plurimis, aut certe sapientibus atque ijs vel omnibus vel plurimis vel ijs quorum spectata est & perspecta sapientia. Arist. Top. lib.2.c.1.

Probable they are said to be, because, although the manifest truth of them be unknown, yet neverthelesse they appeare to many, and especially to wise men, to be true.

And of this sort in the Lawes of the Realme there are so many found, that some men have affirmed, that all the Law of the Realme is the Law of Reason: because they are derived out of the generall Customes, and Maximes, or Principles of the Law of Nature or Primary conclusions.

And for the knowledge of these Propositions there is a greater difficulty; and therefore therein dependeth much the manner and forme of Arguments in the Lawes of *England*.

Doctor and Student *l.* 1. c.5.*f.*10.*a.*

Notes

Notes collected touching the difference betweene Primarie and Secondarie Prinples.

PRincipia immediata quæ in demonstrationibus accipiuntur, in duo genera distribui possunt. *Arist. l. 1. c. 2 T. 5.*

Vnum eorum quæ quanquam demonstrari non possunt, non tamen ita aperta, & per se manifesta sunt, ut necesse sit ante cognita esse ei qui artem aliquam discere velit, quas nos Positiones appellamus.

Altero genere continentur ea, quæ ita sunt per se perspicua, ut non possint non esse, omnibus multo ante cognita, & perspecta quam quicquam doceatur; quæ Pronunciata dicuntur.

To like effect speaketh *Aristotle* in another place, *Ea pro initio & proposito sumenda sunt.*

1 *Quæ in omnibus.*

2 *Vel certe in plurimis rebus inesse videntur.*

The former sort *Aristotle* seemeth to call, as afore shewed, *Pronunciata*, the other *Propositiones.*

And although in the Law of the Realme, they are indifferently called, without distinction, Rules, Principles, Grounds, Maximes, Eruditions, and such like: yet the judgement of *Massæus* herein is worthy observation.

Accursius videtur non parum aberravisse à vero, cùm idem significare voluerit Principa, Maximas, & Regulas; cùm (Aristotele auctore) icuiusque scientiæ principia sunt quædam propria, quæ quod vera sint non contingit demonstari, & quæ per se, & non *Ant. Massæus l. 1. de exercitio Iuris peritorum.*

non per alia fidem habent, quoniam nihil prius ſuperiuſque in ea ſcientia eſt per quod confirmari explicarique poſſint.

Talium autem Principiorum, nonnulla ſunt poſitiones, alia dignitates, ſic dicta, ob id quod jure illis fides habenda ſit, cùm ea unuſquiſque audita ſtatim admittit : quale eſt iſtud : Totum unumquodlibet majus eſt aliqua ſua parte. Hæ rurſus appellantur Maxima, Propoſitiones, & Communes animi conceptiones ; quod multorum ſcilicet intellectu facile percipiantur. Tales autem non ſunt Regulæ ; quæ licet ſint univerſalia Præcepta, indigent tamen probatione, & probari poſſunt : Nec tamen audita admittuntur.

He ſeemeth to attribute the name of Principles, Axiomes, and Maximes to the firſt ſort, and the name of Rules to the ſecond.

Of the ſecondary Principles or Rules there are two kindes. Some deduced and drawne from the uſuall and ordinary diſpoſition of things (as hath been before declared) and by the obſervatiō of humane nature diſperſed in the minds of men, collected by long obſervation : Whereof ſome are altogether upheld in the Law upon common preſumption, and intendment : Others doe reſt upon diſcourſe of Reaſon deducted in Argument. But of the former, ſome are ſuch, as although they are but probable, and import no certaine truth, and therefore may notwithſtanding bee ſometimes untrue : yet nevertheleſſe for the great likelihood of them in humane actions, and the better to frame a conformitie, through the whole

body

body of the Law, the said Lawes permit no allegation to impugne them, or any speech or averment to impeach their credit.

The first sort of Secondary Rules grounded upon entendment.

Others there are also that depend upon entendment: But of the former kinde, this is one, grounded upon naturall affection.

La ley ne voit presume que ascun voit lede son heire, ou auter que est prochein de son sanck, mes que il voit plus tost advance luy. *Com. Sharington & Pledal.*

Which Ground, upon the presumption of naturall affection, is not such, as that it foundeth alwaies true; (for in divers persons nature worketh diversly) Wherefore although this assertion shew how every man should be affected, notwithstanding it is no proofe that all men are so affected. And yet neverthelesse this strong entendment of Law, doth not permit any thing to impeach the same; and will not suffer any person bound by collaterall warranty (the reason whereof floweth herehence) to traverse such affection, although there be never so pregnant proofe to encounter the same.

Notes touching the Definition, Division, and necessary Consequents of Secondarie Principles.

Johannes Corasius de juris arte cap. 26. lib. 1. *IVris Præcepta secundaria sunt certa quædam Axiomata & Definitiones seu Regulæ, quæ non tam naturâ quàm civili aliquâ ratione & authoritate, aut communi mortalium usu per hominum animos diffunduntur.*

Quæ etsi plerumque vera sunt, nec valdè egeant demonstratione; non tamen ita, priusquam pressius considerentur ab illis cognoscuntur qui nostræ scientiæ dant operam. Quapropter, levi aliqua & verisimili ratione, ut ijs assentiantur, opus est.

Doctor and Student *l. 1. c. 5. fol. 10.* See the manner and meanes how they are inferred by discourse out of the generall Customes or Principles of Reason, and the example thereof used by the Author of the Dialogues of the Doctor and Student.

Presumption or Entendment of Law, whereupon certaine of the secondary Rules are grounded (as before is shewed) are in two sorts: for *species præsumptionum sunt duæ: una, quæ legitimis probationibus regulariter refutari potest, quam communem licebit appellare: altera, quæ reprobari non potest, quæ & specialis rectè fortasse dicetur. Certè magno Reip. bono constituuntur hujusmodi præsumptiones: nec potest fieri ut sine præsumptionibus ulla certa jura, aut ullæ certæ leges describantur.* *Ioach. Hopp. de juris arte lib. 2. fo. 466.*

Ibidem. Secondary Principles are grounded either upon

Entend-

Entendment of Law,of which ſort ſome are ſuch as doe admit of no proofe to encounter them,and reſt upon Entendment, but yet admit proofe to the contrary. Or diſcourſe of reaſon.

So likewiſe the Law upon like common preſumption conceived of the acts and behaviour of men, intendeth this Principle.

Nul home ſans cauſe voile faire act a prejudice ſoy meſme. Com.Manxel.6.a.

And hereupon the Law preſumeth that every aſſertion and allegation proceeding from any perſon which ſoundeth to his prejudice and hurt,is ſo undoubtedly true, as that there ſhall not be ſuffered any travers or deniall of the ſame. Wherefore if in a *Pracipe quod reddat* brought of twenty acres of Land againſt one,and he,before the Statute of *Conjunctim feoffatis,* had pleaded Ioyntenancy with another of deed; or ſithence the ſaid Statute, if he had pleaded Ioyntenancy by Fine with another; although the Plea be utterly falſe, yet ſhall not the demaundant have any anſwer or travers thereunto; becauſe that when the demandant by his Writ hath admitted him Tenant of the whole; and hee ſaith that he was Ioyntenant with another; this other, if he be falſe, may ſtop the Tenant by this Record; To ſay the contrary of his affirmation,and thereby may gaine the Moity of the land, againſt him that hath ſo pleaded: And therefore, for that, that men are not wont to tel untruths in diſadvantage of themſelves;and that the ſaying hereof if it were not true, will greatly be to the prejudice and hurt of him that affirmed

affirmed it; thereupon the Law presumeth, that it was true indeed; and will in no wise admit the travers against the same; or give the demaundant ability to impugne it; but hereupon presently, the Writ shall abate, and no maintenance of the writ for the cause aforesaid, shall be allowed.

In like manner also unto matters of Record the entendment of law doth give an impeachable credit; And hereof also this rule of Law is drawne.

Com. Ludford. 491.b. *Matters de Record import in eux (per presumption del ley, pur leur hautnesse) credit.*

And therefore none shall bee permitted to say that the Kings Patent under the great Seale was made or delivered at any other time then that wherein it beareth date; No more then a man may say, That a Recognizance or Statute Marchant or Staple, was acknowledged, or any Writ was purchased at any other time, then that wherein it beareth Date. For an averment that it was antedated, or that it was delivered or acknowledged after the date, is an averment tending to the discredit of the great Seale, or of the Iustice or Officer of Record which recorded the Recognizance, or the Statute Marchant, or such like.

Lambert's Iustice of Peace lib.1.cap.13. In the dealings and affaires of Men, one Man may affirme a thing which another may deny. But if a Record once say the word, no man shall be received to aver; speake against it; or impugne the same. No though such Record containe manifest and knowne falshood, tending to the mischiefe and overthrow of any person.

38. Ass. 21. And therefore whereas certaine persons were

Out-

Outlawed in the Kings bench, in the time of *Shard* Iustice, and their goods forfeit, and their names likewise certified into the Exchequer with an abstract of their goods, It hapned so that the name of one (by misprision of the Clerke) was, among the rest certified likewise into the Exchequer, as outlawed, and that hee had goods to the value of sixe pounds, whereas indeede the same man was not outlawed. And thereupon a writ issued to the Sheriffe of that County, where the said good s were supposed to be, to seize the same to the use of the King, who returned that a Nobleman had seized the same goods; And thereupon issued forth another Writ out of the Exchequer, to cause him to answer the same goods so seized by him, who upon the Returne of the second Writ, alleaged, that the partie whose goods he had seized, was not outlawed: And *Greene*, one of the Iustices of the Kings bench came into the Exchequer with the person who was supposed out-lawed, and there testified that hee was not outlawed; but shewed, that that which was certified, was done altogether by the misprision of the Clerke: Where *Skipwith* returned him this answer; That although all the Iustices would now record the contrary, that they could not be permitted, nor any credit might be given therunto, when as there was a Record extant, and not Reversed, testifying the same Out-lawry: yea, the Law so mightily upholdeth the intended Credit of a Record, that it preferreth the same before the oathes of men, founding to the contrary, and in respect thereof, will not permit a verdit to bee received, which might impeach the same.

9.Hen.6.56. b And therefore whereas one brought a Writ of waste, and assigned the wast in divers particular things, & moreover in a Messuage & Tenemēts in Wood-Church; where among other wasts assigned, the Plaintife shewed, that the Defendant had done and permitted waste in the Hall of the sayd Messuage, &c. The Defendant pleaded in this Action, that Woodchurch was a Hamlet of A. and no Towne of it selfe. Which plea includeth a Confession of the waste to have beene done in such manner as was declared. And upon this plea, the parties were at issue: with the which the Iurie were charged : And further it was given them in charge, that if they found that Woodchurch was a Towne of it selfe, and no Hamlet of A: as the Plantife had supposed, that then they should assigne damages severally for every waste committed. The Iurie at length found, that Woodchurch was a Hamlet of it selfe, and assessed damages for certaine of the particular wastes supposed severally, as they ought. And as touching the wast supposed to be done in the said Hall, they said there was no such Messuage. The Iudges rejected their verdit, because it was contrary to that which was implyed by the Plea of the Defendant of Record: and so inforced the Iury to give damages for a wast: which (indeed) was not done contrary to the Conscience of the Iurie ; notwithstanding that some of them made protestation, that in so doing they might bee perjured: Which

Which wholly was done onely to uphold the credit of the Record;and that the verdit (of Record) might not be contrary to that which was implyed by the Plea of the parties.

Moreover, there is a Rule of Law wholly grounded upon Entendment, which is this;

Livery del fait sera intendin le lieu ou le date fuit.

The delivery of a Deede shall bee intended to be where it beareth date.

Which Rule the Law upholdeth for certaine truth, (although in very deed it may bee at sometimes untrue) And therefore will not permit any proofe which may impeach the intended truth of the said proposition. For confirmation whereof, a notable case cited in the 31. *Hen.* 6. and by way of Argument alleadged in *Fogassa* his Case, may be produced; which was in this manner. An Action of Debt was brought upon a Deed; The Defendant denyed the same; whereupon the parties were at issue; and the witnesses produced to prove the Deed were examined, where the Deed was delivered: who answered; At *Yorke*, which was in another County then where the said Deede bare Date; And hereupon the Defendant demurred: And after upon consideration, Iudgement was given against the Plaintife in overthrow of the Action founded upon that Deed; which cannot be intended to be delivered else where then at the place where it beareth Date.

31.*H.*6. *Co.* *Fogassa.* 7.*b.*

Many Examples may bee further produced to like effect, to prove that divers Rules there are received in the Law which upon presumption and common Entendment, to eschew some notable mischiefe or inconvenience, are so holden for Truth, that in no wise they shall bee incountred; although indeed, as occasion may fall out, they do containe manifest and apparent falshood. But these already in that respect alleadged may abundantly suffice for example.

The second sort of Secondary rules grounded upon entendment

Of like nature also there are in the Law other kind of Rules or principles; which although, they doe concerne contingent matters; and therefore may sometimes be impeached, and found untrue; Yet doe they cary a kind of Credit also upon presumption or Entendment of Law, although not so vehement as the former.

Wherefore although the Law doth receive them *Prima facie*, and at the first shew, as likely, and giveth credit unto the Assertion contained in them, yet neverthelesse doth it admit proofe to the contrary, and so suffereth such presumption or Entendment, which upholdeth such Rules, to bee impeached, and controlled by a contrarie tryall by pregnant proofe, and so doth permit any averment to be made against the same. For Example:

20.H.7.11.b Coningsby. It is a Rule in Law that a Verdict *sera intenda touts foits vray tanq; il est revers pur ceo q; il est issint trove per serement de* 12.*homes*.

A verdict shall be intended alwaies true, till it be reversed, for that it is so found by the oath of twelve men.

5.H.7.22.b. And hereupon it is agreed for Law, That if a Iudgment be given erroniously, the party grieved thereby

thereby ſhall not onely have his writ of Error to redreſſe the ſame, but alſo a *ſuperſedeas*, to Countermand execution thereupon. But if Iudgement be given upon a verdict, although the ſame verdict be untrue, and the partie grieved doe bring his writ of Attaint; Yet neverthleſſe he ſhall not in that caſe have a *ſuperſedeas* to ſtay execution, for the intended truth, which the Law ſuppoſeth in the ſaid verdict. And yet the Law permitteth the falſhood in verdicts to be laid open, & puniſheth them with great ſeveritie, 33.*Hen*.8.196. *Brookes caſe*,4.*Ed*.6.*Com*.49.

If a Writ of *Conſpiracie* be brought againſt one for that hee gave evidence before the Iuſtice of Peace at their Seſſions, concerning the ſuſpition of a Felony ſuppoſed to bee done by the Plaintife, upon which Evidence the Plaintife was indicted of the ſaid Felonie; and after found Not guilty by a Iury of twelve Men; It is no plea in this writ of *Conſpiracie* for the Defendant to ſay, that the Plaintife was guilty of the Felony, for that were to encounter the verdict; which ſhal be entended true. *20.H.7.11. b.Coninsby.*

And although the Law doe give Credit to all verdicts, yet doth it not foreclose the partie grieved thereby, but permitteth him to impugne it, and to impeach it of falſhood, if he can, by his writ of Attaint. *Com.Wrotſley.193.b.*

Alſo there is a Rule in the Law, That

Feeſimple ou auter eſtate certaine convay a un ſera intend de continuer in le perſon in q̃s il eſt repoſe, touts foits durant meſme l'eſtate.

An eſtate of inheritance or other eſtate certaine conveyed to a man, ſhal be intended to continue in the perſon wherin it was repoſed alwaies during the continuance of the ſaid eſtate.

Although this for Law be *Prima facie* intended true; yet neverthelеſſe thereunto this muſt be added, *viz.*

Si ne ſoit monſtre coment auterment ceo eſt diviſt.

If it be not ſhewed otherwiſe how it is diviſed.

By thus much ſaid, it is ſufficiently made manifeſt, that ſome propoſitions, Rules and Grounds of the Law are intended true; but yet proofe is allowed to encounter the ſame.

So hitherto hath beene ſpoken of the *Verity* of *Propoſitions*; whereof ſome are indeed and nature manifeſt true, and grounded on neceſſary reaſon; and other ſome are true alſo, but upon matter contingent.

Contingent verity, was ſaid to be of two kindes. The one grounded on common Preſumption and entendment of the Lawes, which likewiſe was ſubdivided into two branches. Some of them ſuch as doe not admit any Contradiction to impugne them; For the certaine ſuppoſed truth (though indeed not alwaies found in them, yet alwaies deemed by them) alloweth no controll; The other ſort of Rules reſting upon Entendment, are ſuch as are *Prima facie* ſuppoſed true, but yet no otherwiſe ſuppoſed true then till the contrary be proved, and they impeached of falſehood: Of both which there hath beene ſhewed ſufficient examples.

Now

Now therefore in order followeth the second principall part of *Contingent Propositions* or *grounds* framed upon observation of Nature, and disposition of things, collected and drawne by discourse of Reason, because it cannot be equally evident to every Mans capacity. And for as much as the said discourse and manner of reasoning, through the weaknesse of mans understanding, and difficultie of the matter, may faile and be oftentimes deceived in some circumstances which may and daily doe occurre through the variety of particular matter, which againe (in Reason) may offer a contrary resolution; Therefore are those *Grounds* not universally true, but subject to many and manifold exceptions: And yet neverthelesse true in all such Cases as are not comprehended under those *Restraints* or *Exceptions*. Of which kinde we mentioned some in the beginning; as namely; The second principall kind of contingent Propositions.

1, *Sublata Causa tollitur Effectus.*

2, *Qui tacet consentire videtur.*

3, *Quod initio non valet, tractu temporis non convalescit.*

4, *Quando duo Iura in uno concurrunt, æquum est ac si esset in diversis.*

Every of wch with many other of the like nature, though they be of themselves, upon the first view of great *Probability*, yet neverthelesse, being with more earnest consideration pondered, are found not so firme as they seem, but are subject to some controulment, and to be impeached with sundry instances and exceptions. Of such like the number is in manner infinite: at the least many thousands

in

in our Law, which are publiſhed in the *French.*

12.H. 8.2.b. Eliot. *Neſt Löial pur aſcun de enter in le terre del auter ſans ſon licence.*

It is not lawful to enter in another mans ground without Licenſe.

Diſcent de Eſtate d'inheritance in terr, toll le entry de ceſty q̃ droit ad.

The diſcent of an eſtate of inheritance in lands taketh away his entry which hath right.

But theſe few ſhall ſuffiice in this place for an example.

Wherefore for as much as the minde of man is beautified with two faculties or powers in quality different, though flowing from that which is in nature indiviſible: whereof the one we now call for diſtinction ſake (*Capacitie*) and the other (*Diſcourſe.*

By the former of which we apprehend, as with the inward eye, the naturall light and reſplendencie of many *Primary Propoſitions*, and knowne Notions; whoſe clearneſſe and evidence cauſeth every one to yeeld thereto their conſent.

And by the later we doe Collect, Reaſon, Argue, and inferre of thoſe former Notions and Reſolutions, certaine *Secondarie Propoſitions*, deſcended and derived from the firſt, as branches from the Roote, or Rivers from the Fountaine; which by how much the more they are drawne from their ſpring, by ſo much the more (by reaſon of the variety of interpoſed circumſtances) they are oftentimes obſcured and made leſſe cleare and evident.

And

And ſith that every Science is not of like certainty, by reaſon of the variable condition of the ſubject whereupon it is imployed; ſo that rightly of Morall Philoſophy (conſiſting wholy of mans changeable and inconſtant converſation, and frõ whence indeed, the knowledge of all Lawes are in a generality derived, and therto to bee referred) ſaid the Philoſopher *Ariſtotle* right well, in excuſe of his purpoſed Method in the delivery of the ſame, That *Doctrina diſcernens honeſta & turpia, tantis dubitationum fluctibus concutitur, ut multis lege tantum & opinione, non naturâ, conſtitutum eſſe jus videatur*. It followeth me thinketh, of neceſſitie, that it is ſcarcely poſſible to make any ſecondary Rule of Law, but that it ſhall faile in ſome particular caſe: whence ſpringeth this often uſed aſſertion, *Non eſt Regula quin fallat*: And therefore the Ordainers and Interpreters of Law, reſpect rather thoſe things which may often happen; and not every particular circumſtance, for the which though they would, they ſhould not be able by any poſitive Law to make proviſion.

Ethica verò ſupponitur quaſi moralis ſcientia, quia tractat de moribus. Bracton l. 1. c. 2. 4. b. *Ariſt. Ethic. l. 1. c. 3.*

By reaſon whereof they doe permit the Rules, Axiomes, and Propoſitions of the common Law, upon diſcourſe & diſputation of reaſon, to be reſtrained by exceptions; which are grounded upon two cauſes. The one is Equity: the other is ſome other Rule or Ground of Law, which ſeemeth to encounter the Ground or Rule propoſed: wherein, for conformities ſake, and that no abſurdity or contradiction be permitted, certaine exceptions are framed, which doe not onely knit and conjoyne one Rule in reason to another, but by meanes of their equity, temper the rigour of the Law, which upon some certaine circumstances in every of the said Rules might happen and fall

Bract.l.1.c.5 out: *Et omnia benè coaequiparat*, as saith *Bracton*.

And therefore the Author of the Dialogues

Lib.1.ca.16. betweene the Doctor and Student, describeth equity according to this the effect thereof here mentioned: which is, that it is no other thing, but an exception of the Law of God, or of Reason from the generall rules of the Law of man, when they by reason of their generality, would in any particular case, judge against the Law of God, or the Law of Reason: The which exception is secretly understood in every generall Rule of every positive Law. And a little after, in the same place affirmeth, That equity followeth the Law in all particular cases, where right and justice requireth, notwithstanding that the generall Rule of the Law be to the contrary.

And the exception so framed upon any Rule or Ground to the which it is annexed, doth not impeach the credit of the said Ground; but being included therein, as aforesaid, *Format Regulam in omnibus casibus non exceptis*.

L. qua sit. ff. de fundo instructo.

But lest some men might thinke, that whatsoever is spoken in the said Dialogues touching equity, might bee onely understood of that equitie which either enlargeth or restraineth Statute Lawes, and of which M. *Plowden* in his Appendix unto the Argument of the case of *Eston* and *Studd*, in his second Commentaries so largely out

of

of *Aristotle*, and *Bracton* discourseth. There followeth in the same place of the said Dialogues, and in the chapter next ensuing are proposed two Axiomes, Grounds, or Rules, with their exceptions, there put for example, and which doe tend to the purpose and proofe of that whereof wee now speake.

And because that those said Rules there mentioned are last of all here for example before proposed, it shall be requisite first of all to furnish every of them with examples.

But yet for the better understanding of that which is behoofefull to be knowne concerning equity in generall, we are to note that every Rule with his exceptions or (to speake otherwise in words) every received difference in the Law (being indeed nothing but a Rule or Ground and his exceptions) doth either flow from equity, or else result of the combining of two Rules together, as before hath beene declared.

The use therfore of equity is triple in our Law: For

The triple use of equitie in the Lawes.

1 Either it keepeth the common Law in conformity by meanes here mentioned.

2 Or it expoundeth the Statute Law.

3 Or thirdly giveth remedy in the Court of Conscience in cases of extremity, which otherwise by the Lawes are left unredressed.

Wherefore as all men endued with the right use of reason, and conversant in the knowledge of any Law, must of necessity confesse, that everie Law doth stand upon permanent Rules, as of Iron not to be bent or broken upon this or that occasion, or to be infringed upon this or that occurrence (for elſe there need no Court of Law, but all ſhould be one with the Court of Conſcience, and have their proceedings framed according to the Arbitrary conceipt of the Iudge.) So likewiſe neverthelesſe, upon every circumſtance of time, perſon, place, and the manner of doing, there falleth out ſuch matter of equity, that if Law ſhould bee purſued according to the ſetled Rules thereof, *Summum jus* (as *Cicero* ſaith) would prove *Summa injuria*: wherefore Law without equity were rigour. And yet againe, of the other ſide, if all Lawes ſhould change and be controlled as often in every caſe as equity would require, then ſhould there be (as aforeſaid) no Law certaine. And therefore it ſtandeth with good reaſon, that the common Law in ſome caſes, ſhould allow and follow equity, as farre forth as the conſtancy of the Law would permit, and for the better conformity of one Rule thereof with another: which common Law againe in other caſes ſhould refuſe equity for the better avoyding of confuſion.

EQuity therefore in all the use thereof, and in every of the threefold before mentioned observations hath a double Office, Effect, or Function.

Sometimes it doth amplifie.

Sometimes againe (when reason will) it doth diminish or extenuate.

A description of the former is that which *Bracton* yeeldeth, *Æquitas est rerum convenientia quæ in paribus causis paria desiderat jura, & omnia bene coæquiparat, & dicitur æquitas quasi æqualitas.* *Lib. 1. c. 4. ¶. 5.*

This enlargeth the common Law; for it teacheth to proceed in the same from one case to another like thereunto; and so to proceed, that *Si aliqua nova & inconsueta emerserint, & quæ prius usitata non fuerint in regno; si tamen similia evenerint, per simile judicentur; cum bona sit occasio à similibus procedere ad similia.* *Com. 467.* *Bracton li. 1 cap. 2. ¶. 7.*

And therefore these cases differing never so much in circumstance, so that they doe concurre in reason, should be ruled after one and the selfe same manner. For, *Vbi est eadem ratio, idem jus statuendum est.* But hereof we shall hereafter have more ample occasion to speake, when we take in hand the last of *Aristotles* before remembred observations; namely *Similitudinum collectionem,* or *cognitionem.*

This

This equitie moreover in Statutes enlargeth the letter to cases not comprehended within the words; if neverthelesse they doe stand in equall mischiefe.

Lastly, in all cases of mischiefe, for redresse whereof Positive Law or ordinary Rules of Law are defective; equity extendeth forth her hand in the Court of Conscience to helpe therein the said defect of the Lawes.

2 The second kinde of equity doth againe of the other side restraine the ample or generall rules of the common Lawes by ministring exceptions, in like manner as is before remembred.

And in Statute Law it doth also limit the overlarge letter, drawing it wholly to, and keeping it within the bounds of the intent and meaning of the makers.

In the Court of Conscience it giveth likewise comfort, considereth all the circumstances of the fact, and is as it were tempered with the sweetnesse of mercy, and mitigateth the rigour of the common Law; and leaving the inflexible stiffe Iron rule, taketh in hand the Leaden Lesbian rule: which being rightly swayed in cases of extremity, and therein, enjoyning the common Law of her strait proceeding, issueth this sentence full of comfort to the afflicted, *Nullus recedat à Cancellaria sine remedio.* *4. Hen. 7.*

Wherefore if the same equity bee used in such cases only as are of extremity (as indeed it should) it causeth the Chancellour, into whose hand the managing thereof within this Realme is commit-

ted

to be in high estimation of honour: so that *In ejus sorte juris dicendi gloriam conciliat magnitudo negotij, gratiam æquitatis largitio; in quâ sorte sapiens Prætor offensionnem vitat æquabilitate decernendi; benevolentiam adjungit lenitate audiendi.* Cicero in Orat. pro Murena.

And thus much by the way hath beene spoken of equity, upon the occasion of speech of exceptions which doe restraine Rules and Axiomes, that the originall fountaine from whence such exceptions do spring, might the better and more manifestly be conceived.

And therefore thus much thereof sufficeth, reserving the rest to his due and native place.

Now wee will proceed with the first example published in the said Dialogues of the Doctor and Student, concerning the exceptions attributed and annexed unto Maximes, Rules, and Grounds.

There is (saith he) a generall prohibition in the Lawes of *England*; That

It is not lawfull for any man to enter into possession or freehold of another without authority of the owner, or of the Law. The first Ground.

This Ground may be proved by many particular cases and authorities: for the Law of propertie would that every mans owne should bee private and peculiar unto himselfe; and therefore it is said, That

Nest loyal al un de enter en mon terre sauns mon licence. 12.H.8.2.b. Elliot.

Lou mes beasts sont damage fesant in auter terr, jeo ne puis enter pur eux enchaser hors ains convient a moy 21.Hen. 7. 27.b. Kingsmel. Reade.

moy primerment à tender amends.

If my beasts bee damage fesant in anothers ground, I may not enter and drive them out, but I ought first to tender an amends.

21.H.7.13. b. Rede. *Si home ad merisme gisant sur la terr d'un auter, il ne poit justifier le entry in le terr a veyer ceo si soit in bon plyte.*

If one have his timber lying on anothers ground, he cannot justifie his entry to see his timber in good case.

13.H.7.9.b. *Si maison soit lease a moy, & jeo mit mon biens en ceo; & puis mon lease expire les dits biens estant in le meason, nest loyal pur moy a ore pur enter en le dit meason de eux prender.*

If a house bee leased to mee wherein I put my goods, where they lye till the lease be expired, I cannot now enter into the house to take them.

14.H.8.1.b. Brudnel. *Si jeo mit mon chival in vostre stable & vous ne voiles ceo deliver a moy, & jeo enter & enfrend vostre stable, jeo sera puny pur l'entry, & le enfreinder del stable, mes nemy pur le prisel del chival.*

If I put my horse into your stable, and you will not deliver him unto me; if I enter and breake your stable, I shall bee punished for entring and breaking the stable, but not for taking my horse.

18.E.4.25.a *Si jeo command un a deliver a vous certaine beasts que sont en mon Park, nest loyal pur vous de enter en mon Park, & prender les dits beasts, ovesque cesti que jeo issent command per reason de cest commandement; car vous purra assets bien eux receiver coment que vous demurres hors del Park.*

If I command one to deliver you certaine cattell

tell out of my Park, it is not lawfull for you to enter into my Park with him whom I commanded to deliver them: for you may receive thē though you stay without the Park.

Si jeo baile biens al home, jeo ne puis justifier l'entry en son meason pur prender les biens, car ceo non fut per nul tort que ils viendra la mes per l'act de nous ambideux. 9.Ed.4.35.a 21.H.7.13.

If I deliver my goods unto a man, I cannot justifie the entring into his house to take them, &c.

Si le vicont ad fierifacias pur levier deniers recovers vers ascun, uncore si per force de ceo il ne voile enter et debruser le meason de cesti vers que le recovery fuit, il sera de ceo puny pur cest entry en trespas. 8. Ed.4.4.a.

If the Sherife hath a *fierifacias*, to levie money recovered, if by force thereof he enter, and break the house of the debtor, he is subject to an action of trespasse.

Si un Vicar ad offrings in un Chapel de quel Chapel le franktenement est in moy; il ne pur ceo justifiera l'entry et debruser de ma Chapel pur eux prender hors. 2.H.4.24.a.

If a Priest have offrings in a Chappell, the freehold of which is in me, hee cannot justifie the entry and breaking the Chappell to take out his offrings.

Si home esteant in sa Garren demesn springa un Feasant, et lessa sa falcon vola a ceo que vola in le Garren d'un auter home, & la prist le Feasant, nest loial pur le owner del falcon, pur enter in le auter Garren, & de la emporter. 38.E.3.10.b

If a man spring a Pheasant in his owne Warren, and let his falcon flye at her, and she flyes into anothers Warren, and there taketh the Pheasant, he that oweth the Hawke cannot enter into the others ground to take her.

Having proved the former ground with these sufficient former authorities, let us now descend unto the examination of such exceptions of the said proposition, as may exemplifie our former speeches: whereof some certaine being orderly delivered and confirmed with some authorities of booke cases, I hold it sufficient so to make manifest our meaning at this present; leaving a more exact consideration thereof to more fit place and opportunity.

We are therefore to conceive that there is an infallible rule of Law, That

Le Common wealth est destre prefer devan ascun private wealth.

The Common wealth is to be preferred before any private wealth.

By reason whereof lest contradiction betweene the said proposed rule and this now in hand should ensue upon some circumstance which may fall out; therefore the said last specified ground, concerning the benefit of the Common wealth, doth minister an exception for the better understanding of the aforesaid rule proposed, namely, That

The first Exception. *Home poit iustifie son entre en le franktenement ou sur le possession de un auter si soit pur le benefit del Common wealth.*

A

A man may justifie his entry into anothers freehold, if it be for the good and benefit of the Common wealth.

And therefore these cases following depending thereupon are produced to prove and manifest the same.

Si jeo vien in vostre terre, et occide un Fox, un Gray, ou un Otter, pur cest entry jeo ne sera my puny, pur ceo que sont beasts encounter le Common profit. 12.Hen. 8.

If I come into your ground to kill a Fox, Gray, 10.a.Brooke.
or Otter, for this entry I shall not bee punished; for they are beasts against the common profit.

Pur le Common wealth meason sera plucked down si 13.Hen.8.
le prochein meason soit ardent. 16.b.Shelley.

For the good of the Common-wealth an house shall be pulled downe if the next be fired.

Et Suburbes del Citie seront plucked downe in temps de Guerr, pur ceo q̃ ceo est pur le common wealth: Et 8.Ed.4.35.b
chose q̃ est pur le common wealth chascune poit faire Littleton.
sans aver action.

And the suburbs of a City shall be razed in the time of warre: And that which is for the good and profit of the Common wealth any man may doe without danger of anothers action.

Home justifiera son entry in auter terr in temps 21.H.7.b.
de Guerr pur faire Bulwarke in defence del Realme, Et Kingsmil.
ceux choses sont justifiable & loial pur maintenance del Common-wealth.

A man may justifie his going into another mans ground in time of warre to make a Bulwarke in defence of the Realme, &c.

Pur felony, ou pur suspicion de felony home poit de- 13.Ed.4.9.a

 bruser

bruser meason pur prender le felon, car il est pur le Common-wealth pur prender eux.

For felony or suspition thereof a man may breake a house to take the Felon; For it is the good of the Common-wealth, to have him taken. With such like.

Moreover because there is another Rule of Law, That

Nul prendra benefit de son torts demesne.

No man shall take benefit of his owne wrong.

And sometimes it falleth out that men, through malice to have others in danger, would not sticke to lay a traine to intrap them, to the intent, that they might, by some colour, for their further vexation, prosecute sute against them; To uphold the Conformity of Law upon those two grounds, that one of them doe not encounter the other, there is a second Exception to the former Rule namely, That

The second Exception. *Si home soit le Cause pur que un tortious Entry est fait sur son Possession, il navera de ceo Remedy: mes le party que ad issent enter, sur le matter disclose poit ayd luy mesme & justify tiel Entry.*

If a Man bee the cause that a wrongfull Act or Entry be made upon his possession, he shall have no remedy for it, but the party who hath entred may disclose the matter to justifie his entry.

9.Ed.4.35.a.b. *Home ad un Molyn, & l'eaw courge per le terr d'une auter al dit Molyn, le Tenant del terre mise stakes deins le dit eaw sur q̃s il edify un meason, per reason de quel l'eaw ne poit vener cy bien al dit Molin come devant: Le Tenant del Molyn enter en la dit terre, & enrasa les*

les stakes, per q́ la dit Meison eschew: Et in Trespas pur entry en la dit terr & enraser la meason; tout cest matter pur avoider le dit Nusance fuit plede per le defendant & tenus bon Iustification.

A Man hath a Mill, and the water running to it commeth through anothers ground, and hee fastneth stakes upon the ground in the water, and buildeth an house; by reason whereof the water commeth not to the Mill, as well as in time past, the Miller entreth unto the others ground and breaketh downe the stakes, and thereby the house falleth: If the other bring an Action of trespasse against him, for this, he may shew that hee did it, to avoyde wrong done to himselfe, and justifie the deed.

Home aver pris les beasts de I. S. & eux impound in sa terre, & vint un pur Replevy mesme les beasts, 20. Hen. 6.
Et pur ceo q́ cest q́ ad eux destreine ne voilet suffer les 28. a.
beasts deste Replevy, il ove arks & sagitts, sagitta al cesti q́ vint pur eux repleuy esteant in le port de mesme le close, lou ils fuere impound, pur q́ il pur doubt enfreint le close in auter lieu, & enchase hors les avers q́ fueront impound; Et per cest entry et infriender del Close, le Plaintife port trespas, Et sur tout cest matter disclose ceo, semble bone Iustification.

A man having taken *I. S.* his goods, and impounded them in his owne ground, a Replevin was brought for those Cattle, and hee that destrained them would not suffer any Replevin to be made, but standing in the gate of the Close where the Cattle were impounded, shot at him that came to make the Replevin, whereupon he

 broke

broke the Close in another place, and drew forth the said beasts: For which breaking the Plaintifes Close, he brought an Action of trespasse; but upon this matter disclosed, it was taken for a good justification.

21. Hen. 6. 39. b. *In travers, le defendant dit, q̃ pur ceo q̃ le Plaintife violet aver le defendant in son dainger, il commaund un son servant de chaser les beasts de defendant in les blees del plaintife mesme, & le defendant cy hastiment q̃ il avoit notice de ceo, il enter en le dit terre le Plaintife, et eux enchase hors: Et ceo fuit tenus bon*
9. Ed. 4. 35. a *Plea nient amountant al generall issue.*

Littleton. In an Action of trespasse, the Defendant said, that because the Plaintife would have the defendant within his danger, hee commanded one of his servants to drive the Defendants beasts into the Plaintifes Corne; And the Defendant assoone as he had notice thereof, entred into the Plaintifes Close, and drave them out; This was taken for a good Plea, and not amounting to the generall issue.

37. Hen. 6. 37. a. b. *In travers pur entry in le close, &c. Del Plaintife le defendant justifiera, pur ceo q̃ le Defendant fuit Chivanchant en le roial chimin q̃ gisoit pres le meason del Plaintife, quand il vint la encounter la dit mese, la vient le Plaintife ove Arke et sagitts et fist un assault sur le defendant, pur que il avoide son Chival, & fua in le dit mese, & ouster in le dit close; Et puis reveint in le dit chimin. Et ceo fuit tenus bon Iustification, si il voile adde a ceo q̃ le Chymin est in mesme le ville q̃ le meason est, ou in quel ville ceo est, & q̃ le huis del meale fut overt*

al temps: per q̃ le defendant issint dist accordant.

In an Action of Traverse for entering into the Plaintifes close, the Defendant justified, for that he ryding in the Kings high way, which lay neere to the Plaintifes house, the Plaintife set upon the Defendant, when hee came neere against the Plaintifes house, and assaulted him with bow and Arrowes; Whereupon he forsooke his horse and fled into the house, and so through it into his Close, and after returned into the high way; And this was taken for a good justification, if he had shewed further that the high way was in the same towne where the house was, and shewed in what towne the house was, and that the doore of the house was open, &c.

Moreover, where there is a ground or rule of Law, as hath beene often before remembred, That

Quando aliquis quid concedit, & id concedere videtur sine quo res concessa esse non potest.

Hereof ensueth a third Exception to be annexed unto the said former Ground: in this manner,

Si home ad interest ou authoritie derive de ascun person, owner, & possessor del soile: le quel cesty a q̃ le interest ou authority est done, ne poit accomply sans Entry in la terr ou measе de cesti q̃ issent done la interest ou authority, la son entry est imply in la dit interest ou authority: Et pur tlel cause son entry la sera justifiable. The third Exception.

Le Abbe de Hyde fait lease d'un ferm rendant Rent a son Monastery de Hyde, tandem le dit Monastery vient al mains le Roy, Hen. 8. per le statute de Dissolutions, *Com. Kidw. & Brand. 71.a.*

rions, q̃s puis ceo grant ouster al estranger : le lessee del dit ferme poit bien venir al dit Monastery la a tender la dit Rent, Et cesti q̃s ad le possession de ceo navera eint travers pur tiel entry.

Com. Kidw. & Brand. 71.b. Si A : soit tenus a B : in un obligation de 20. l. pur pair a luy 10.l. a tiel jour la intent q̃s nul lieu est expres pur le payment, A : est tenus a querer B. in quocumq̃s liew q̃s il soit : Et si B : est in son meason demesne, & vient a luy la, & tender le argent, il ne sera trespasser pur le vener la Mes s'il ust este in la meason de ascun auter home, la il seroit trespasser al dit home : Mes in l'auter cas intant q̃s il fut assentant q̃s il paiera a luy les dits deniers, & in ceo fut il containe q̃s il fut assentant que il vener a luy pur ceo purpose : il ensuitt ex consequenti que il ne puniera luy pur ceo chose a que luy mesme fut privy & agreement.

18.E.4.25.b Si jeo enfeoffe G. & face litre d'attorney a C. a deliver seisin a G : pur le veinder sur la terre, et pur l'entry fait per G. de prender la livery, G. ne sera punish in trespas; car il est impossibile que il receivera livery si non il entra in le terre, et il est imply in le fesance del feofment que il viendra sur la terr de prender Livery.

9.Ed.4.25.a. 13.H.8.15.b Englefield. Si home moy grant pur foder in son terre, & de faire un trenche de tiel font ou spring jusques a mon place, si puis le Pipe est estopp ou enfreint issint que l'eau issue hors, jeo ne poi foder in son terre pur mender le Pipe, car ceo ne fut grant, a moy, &c. Mes cest opinion fut deny per tout le Court, car fut dit, que il poit enter & foder pur ceo mender, pur ceo que est incident a tel grant a ceo discourer & d'amender.

9.Hen.6.29.b. In travers pur entry en un meason le defendant dit

dit que long temps devant le trespas que A. fut seisi del dit meason in fee, & q̃ ceo est in tiel ville & devisable per testament, per que le dit A devise le dit maison a un fem in taile, & que sil devy sans issue que son Executor ceo vendroit, & fait le defendant son Executor & devy, la fem entermary ove le Plaintife & puis devy sans issue, pur que le defendant enter sur le poss': le Plaintife a voir, si fut bien repaire al intent de scavoir a quel value le reversion fut a vender, & ceo fut tenus bone Iustification.

In Trespas pur Entry in meason & prisel del biens le defendant dit que le Baron del Plaintife fut possesses des dits biens & fuit seisy del dit meason in fee, et fait le defendant, & auter ses Executours, et devy possesses des dits biens, & le defendant vint al dit meason apres la mort le Testatour pur administer & trovant huys del dit meason overt il enter & prist les biens, et ceo fut tenus bon Plee per tout le Court. 2. Hen. 6. 15. b. 16. a.

By reason also that there is a Rule of Law, That

Le possession del terre de chescun home est subject al Iurisdiction del ley.

Thereof also this Exception following holdeth likewise place in restraint of the said former generall Rule or Ground, that is to say,

Lou le ley done al ascun authority de enter in auter ter ou sur le possession del auter, il justifiera son entry. The fourth Exception.

Si jeo suy seisi de terre in fee sur bon & indefesible title, et un estranger demand cest terre per precipe vers un auter estranger, & sur ceo le vicount per force del precipe vient sur la terre ove sommoners, & summon luy vers que le precipe est port, & puis le demandant Com. Manxel 13. a.

recover

recover vers luy per default ou per issue try sur certaine point, & perforce de Haberi facias seisinam le vic vient arere & mist cesty que ad recover in seisin; jeo ne puniera le vicont pur le primer vener, ne pur le second vener in le terre, pur ceo que le vicont ne fait riens mes execute le mandement le Roy come il ad in charge, & mon Possession est chargeable a cest Iurisdiction del Roy & ses ministers.

Littleton Villenage. Com. Manxel 13.a. *Si home fait lease pur vie, & un villeine purchase le reversion, semble a Litt. que le signior del villein poit maintenant vener al terre et claime mesme le reversion, et per tel clayme le reversion est maintenant in luy, et pur tel vener a le terr et act fait il nest trespassor.*

Com. Manxl 13. a. *Si villein purchase advowson plen d'incumbent, le signior del villein poit vener al dit Esglise, et claime le dit advowson, et pur ceo le Incumbent ne punishera luy per tiel vener al dit Esglise.*

11. H. 4. 75. b *In Trespas le defendant plede que il fut seisy del meason et terre et ceo lease al plaintife pur terme de ans, et que fut certifie que wast fut fait, et il enter in le close & meason pur viewer si wast fut fait, et le huis del maison fuit overt, & demand Iudgement, et ceo fut tenus bon barr; a que le Plaintife replica que il la demurr encounter le volunt le Plaintife un jour et un nuict, &c.*

Hitherunto have we expressed certaine exceptions of the fore-specified Grounds which are derived from the reason of some other grounds and Rules of the Law, and which reason would should be added, as restraints unto the said former Rule of Law first remembred for conformities sake,

and

and that the Law no way be impeached of contrarieties. Now resteth also that we deliver some few other exceptions unto the said generall Rule drawne likewise from the fountaine of equitie; which are such as doe ensue.

Sith it were voide of all reason and conscience that a man should punish a wrong done unto him, by the which he either sustaineth little or no detriment or damage, or at leastwise more benefit then he sustaines prejudice: Therefore this exception unto the said generall Rule, is among other likewise allowed for Law. That Exceptions ministred by equity.

Lou le party sur que possession home fait tortious entry, est plus benefit per tiel entry que prejudice, la home bien justifiera la dit tortious entry. The fift Exception.

Which the cases following do likewise at large sufficiently confirme.

Si jeo suy in peril deste murder in mon close, ou in mon meason, il est loial a chescun de enfrender mon meison ou close pur moy ayder, et pur ceo que est pur mon benefit. 12.H.8.2.b. Pollard.

Si jeo voy vostre beasts demesne in vostre corne, et jeo eux enchase hors, jeo ne sera my puny pur ceo que fut pur vostre advantage, et vous aves interest in les beasts. Mes si jeo chase les beasts d'un estranger hors de vostre corne, jeo serra puny pur ceo; car vous puisses aver remepy pur ceo; scil. per distresse. 13.H.8.15. b. Norwich.

Si jeo view le Chimney de mon voycin urant pur saver les choses que sont deins son meason, jeo justifiera l'entry in le meason, & deprender les biens que jeo trover dedans pur eux saver. 21.H.7.27. b. Palmes.

In trespas de Parco fracto, le defendant justifie le 20.H.6.37.

trespas pur ceo que fut controversie perenter luy, & le seigneur de Huntingdon Plaintife pur le overture d'un gorce, et pur ceo que le dit seigneur fut in le dit Park hunting, il enter pur les portes estēat overt a monstre a luy ses evidences concernant le dit gorce & ceo fut tenus per tout le Court bone Iustification.

Againe, the like equity doth minister one other exception of the like quality; for it were unconscionable and unreasonable that a man should be punished for a wrongfull entry, wheras he is compelled so to do, and cannot without his great prejudice eschew the same: And therefore it is holden for Law, That

The sixt Exception. *Si home enter sur le possession de un auter, lou il ne poit auterment faire sans son grand prejudice, ceo ne sera deeme tiel entry de que il sera puny.*

13.H. 8.16. b.Browne. *Si home ad Querck cressant in midds de trois maisons, et il decoupe ceo, et le Querck eschuet in terre d'un auter, si il justify in trespas il covient de alleager que il ne auterment puit faire.*

5.Ed. 4.7.b. *Home de coupa thornes que cresse in son terre & ils eschaont inter d'un auter, & il enter & eux prender hors, sil ne poit in auter maner faire, ceo luy excusera.*

Doctor and Student.ver. 10.Ed.4.7.b 22.Ed.4.8.b. 6.Ed. 4.7. b. *Si home chase avers per le chymin, et les beasts happont de escaper in les blees de son vicin, & cesty que eux enchase enter freshment in le terr de eux enchaser hors, pur ceo que ils ne ferront ascun damage, il justifiera ttel son entry in trespas.*

And thus much hath beene said touching the first Ground proposed in the said Dialogues of the said Doctor and Student, which hath beene proved

proved in particular with cases, and thereunto have beene annexed certaine exceptions which have likewise beene fortified with *Booke Cases*, and Authorities, whereby the former assertions have not onely beene exemplified, but also thereby it doth plainly appeare, That almost every disposition in the Lawes, *de qualitate*, or *de jure*, is in conference of Maximes, and resteth betweene the Rule and the Exception, which is either ministred by reason of equity, or upon some other Rule or Axiome. So that every difference shewed betweene Cases, is nothing else but the Rule and his exceptions; the effect whereof briefly is set forth by *Morgan*, who saith: That

Maximes ne doient este impugne, mes touts temps admit; mes les maximes per reason poient este confer & compare l'un ove l'auter, coment que ils ne varient: Ou per reason poit este discusse quel chose est plus prochein al Maxime ou meane perenter les Maximes & quel nemy: mes le Maximes ne unque poient este impeach ne impugne, mes touts dits doient este observe & tenus come firme Principles de eux mesmes. *Com. Colth. 27. a*

For the better understanding whereof, we may note that all matters of debate which may be referred to the controversies or questions *de qualitate* or *de jure*, as hath been said, have either commonly a Maxime of the one part, & a Maxime of the other; or severall reasons of each part derived from sundry Maximes; or else that there is a Maxime of the one part, and there is equity and reason which doth minister an exception to that Maxime or generall Rule: So that all disceptation

tion herein is, as hath beene ſaid, in conference or comparing of Maximes and Principles together, diſcourſing which thing is directly under the reaſon of the ſaid Maxime; and what matter or circumſtance may make a difference, and will be by exception exempted from the ſame; as more at large hereafter in the declaration of the uſe of theſe Maximes may be made manifeſt and apparent.

Now reſteth moreover to proſecute the ſecond Axiome or Principle propoſed in the ſayd Dialogues, namely, that which followeth there in the ſevententh chapter of his firſt booke, that is to ſay:

The ſecond Ground.

It is not lawſull for any man to enter upon a deſcent.

Which ground being expounded by *Littleton* in his chapter of deſcents to extend onely to deſcents of an eſtate of Inheritance and freehold, and not of a reverſion or remainder, all which follow after in the ſayd Chapter, are nothing but Caſes of Exceptions unto the ſaid Grounds, as it is evident unto every one that conſidereth the ſame, and therefore ſhall it here bee needleſſe long to inſiſt thereupon. Neverthele ſſe it ſhall be expedient to ſhew ſome exceptions therunto, eſpecially ſome certaine, of ſuch of them as being exceptions unto the ſaid Rule, are againe reſtrained with other exceptions. Becauſe there is a Rule of Law, That

Firſt exception Littleton Garranty 279.

Laches ou folly ne ſera impute a un enfant de luy prejudice.

There-

Therefore lest contrarietie might happen in consequence of reason betweene the sayd Rule of descents, and this Rule last remembred: there is ministred by the meanes of this latter Rule, an exception unto the said former ground, namely, That

If an infant have right of entry, hee may enter upon a descent. *Littleton descents cas. 402* *20. H. 6. 28. b*

This exception, although it doth import great probability of truth, yet is the same like unto the Ground in this respect, namely, that it is also subject to bee restrayned with another exception, *viz.*

If an infant, or such priviledged or excepted person have a right of entry, and a descent of those lands is had to one that hath a more ancient right; the party having such ancient right shall be remitted: and both the right and entry of the infant taken away.

And this exception ensueth of another general Rule of Law, which is, That

An ancient right shall alwaies be preferred before another meane right or title.

The said exception upon exception, grounded upon the last remembred Rule, may bee plainly proved by this case.

If Tenant in Taile do discontinue and after do disseize his discontinuee, and during this disseisin the discontinuee dyeth, his heire within age; and after the Tenant in Tayle doth dye seised; and this land descendeth unto the issue in tayle, the heire of the discontinuee being still within age; *11. E. 4. 1. b.*

This

This is a remitter, and the entry of the heire of the discontinuee is tolled, notwithstanding that the Ground and Principle is, that the laches of the infant shall not prejudice the infant. And the cause is the ancient right the issue had.

The second exception.

Moreover the former Generall Rule touching descents that toll entries, hath among other, also this exception.

Litt. fol. 59. case 403. 9. H. 7. 24. a. 2. Ed. 4. 24 a 7. Ed 4. 7. b. 20. H. 6 28. b

A descent had during the Coverture, shall not toll the entry of the woman or her heires after the Coverture dissolved.

But because there is a Generall Rule of Law, That,

None shall be favored in any Act wherein folly may be imputed to him.

From whence is derived also this more speciall Rule or Ground.

Com. Zouch. 366. a. 42. E. 3. 12. b 9. H. 7. 24. a.

Coverture shall not ayde a woman where the taking of a Husband which respecteth not her benefit may be imputed to her folly.

Hereof ensueth this exception upon exception to the said former remembred Rule, That

42. E. 3. 12. b 9. H. 7. 24. a. Litt. fol. 95. cas. 404. 3. 4. Ph. Ma. 144. n. 57.

Where folly may be imputed to the woman for taking of such a Husband as will be heedless of her benefit, there a descent, during the coverture shall bind the woman and her heires.

Much more might bee said of like effect, but this for example sake shall suffice.

Com. 72. b. Com. 268. a. Com. 294. a.

Now resteth briefly to say something touching the first proposed Latine Rules: Of which the former was this,

Sublata causa tollitur effectus.

This

This Rule is not absolutely true; for the Philosophers from whence it is borrowed, doe understand it, *De causis internis, non de externis.*

The Civill Lawyers do restraine it in this manner, *Hæc autem Gnosis sine Regula, de causa finali, non de causa impulsiva intelligitur.* *Prateus.*

The common Law of the Realme, thus;

Sublatâ unâ causâ, si alia remanet, non tollitur effectus.

The second Rule; which was this, *Qui tacet, consentire videtur,* is verified with this exception.

Si ad ejus commodum & utilitatem spectat, præsens & tacens pro consentiente habetur. *Prateus l. 7. c. 3. fol. 911.*

The third Rule was this,

Quod initio non valet, id tractu temporis non convalescit.

Which Ground may be confirmed with many cases, yet is the same Ground restrained with this exception, because That

Habet locum in his tantum quæ statim debent valere, & nullam suspensionem habent. *Decius.*

If a man make a lease for life of land unto *I. S.* and after doth make a lease for yeares unto *I. N.* of the same land to beginne presently, This lease being made by word is voyd; for the freehold in the first lease is more worthy, and by law intended to be of longer continuance then the terme in the second lease: yet if the first leasee die, or surrender afore the second be expired, the residue of the terme is good. *37. Hen. 8. Brooke. Leases 48. Com. Smith & Stapleton 433. a. Com. Griesbrooke. 422. a.*

If the father devise his land unto his daughter

5.Ed.4.6. Per Billing quod fuit concessum & Abridge per Fitzh.tit. Assi. 27.

and Heire apparant, and after leaving his Wife *encinct*, or with child with a son, upon the death of the father this devise unto the daughter is void for that she is his heire; but after, when the sonne is borne it is good.

The fourth Rule of the said Latine rules before set downe, was this,

Quando duo jura in uno concurrunt, aequum est acsi esset in duobus.

This Rule hath exception grounded upon another Rule, that is, That

Com. 375.b. *Vigilantibus & non dormientibus jura subveniunt.*

Or to the same effect;

Unicuique sua mora nocet.

And therefore

Com. Stowell. 372.b. *In causes de negligence ou laches divers droits concurrant in un person ne seront deeme si come ils fustent in divers persons.*

Where, if *Tenant pur auter vie* be, the remainder for life over to another, the remainder in fee to the right heires of the *Tenant pur auter vie*, If the said *Tenant pur auter vie* be disseised, and the disseisor levie a fine with proclamations, and the five yeares doe passe, and after *Cesti que vie* dyeth; and after also dyeth he in remainder for life; he which was *Tenant pur auter vie*, shall not have other five yeares after the death of the *Tenant* for life in remainder to pursue his right for the feesimple.

Upon like reason, if a Bishop bee seised of an Advowson in the right of his Bishopricke, and the

the Church become voyd, and sixe moneths doe passe; the Bishop shall not have other six moneths as Ordinary, the same Church being in his Diocesse, as he should have if the same Church were of the patronage of another person, although he be in one respect Patron, and in another Ordinary.

Hitherto wee have entertained discourse as touching the verity of Axiomes, Rules, and Grounds; which, as hath beene shewed, is either necessary or contingent.

Contingent verity was divided into two branches; the one resting upon the entendment of Law; the other being derived from the disposition and nature of humane things, by debate and discourse of reason.

Of the first sort there are two kinds; for some propositions there are, although of themselves but only probable, yet neverthelesse are supposed of such certainty, that no averment shall be received to encounter the same. Othersome, although they be by the Law intended true, *Prima facie*, yet neverthelesse the same Law alloweth an averment, and admitteth proofe to impeach the same.

Those moreover which rest upon discourse, of reason, are subiect to divers exceptions, the materiall cause whereof is, the infinite variety of circumstances that in all humane actions doe happen.

The forme and nature of the exception is perceived and knowne by this effect following; in that it restraineth the ground unto which it is connexed.

The efficient causes are two, *viz.* Equity or some other Ground of the Law importing contrariety. And the end thereof is conformitie and coherency of Law agreeable unto Iustice, whose minister the Law is.

Moreover as occasion hath beene offered in the declaration of the causes from whom Exceptions of Rules doe spring, there hath beene shewed the use of equitie in the common Law, Statute Law, and Chancery, by the two effects thereof, application and restraint; the one enlarging, and the other abridging.

Wherefore now resteth to speake of the second principal part, concerning the forme of Aixomes, namely, generality: The consideration whereof, bringeth to memory, that GOD in his most excellent worke of the frame of transitorie things, though hee hath furnished the world with unspeakeable variety, thereby making manifest unto all humane creatures, to their great astonishment, his incomprehensible wisedome, his omnipotent power, and his unsearchable providence, yet being the God of order, not of confusion, hath admitted no infinitenesse in nature (howsoever otherwise it seeme to our weak capacities) but hath continued the innumerable variety of particular things under certaine specialls; those specialls under generalls; and those generals

a-againe under causes more generall, linking and conjoyning one thing to another, as by a chaine, even untill wee ascend unto himselfe, the first, chiefe and principall cause of all good things. And this is that which *Plato* out of *Homer*, was wont to call *Iupiters golden chaine*.

The eye whereby we doe see and view, and the inward hand whereby wee doe reach and apprehend these things, is mans understanding, which is wholly imployed about universality as about his proper object, by meanes wherof, in all things rationall, being discovered by the use of reason, mans understanding for the attaining of knowledge proceedeth from the effect to the cause, and againe from the cause to the effect; that is, from the particular to the speciall, and from the special to the generall; and so to the more generall, even to a principall and primary position or notion, which needeth no further proofe, but is of it selfe knowne and apparant. And so againe from such chiefe & primary Principles and propositions to more speciall and peculiar Assertions, descending even to every particular matter.

But that, of this which hath beene said, some example might be shewed, especially in this matter, which we now have in hand, namely, concerning the Grounds & rules of the Law of *England*; let one of the proposed grounds first before mentioned stand here for an example, *viz*.

Nihil est magis rationi consentaneum, quam eodem modo quodque dissolvere quo conflatum est.

 This

This principle being a Rule of Reaſon contayning great probability, and being of the number of thoſe that before we ſaid to have beene derived from the obſervation of the nature of things, which though it bee ſubiect to manifold exceptions, yet neverthеleſſe as a generall Rule, the ſame is verified in many ſpeciall Axiomes; and they againe diverſly ſubdivided into many more peculiar propoſitions; as the example of theſe following may make manifeſt.

1 *Ceſty que eſt charge per Record doit luy diſcharger per Record.*

2 *Ceſty que eſt charge per fait doit luy meſme diſcharge per fait, ou per auter matter cy haut.*

3 *Ceſty q̃ eſt charge forſq̃ per parol, poet eſte diſcharge per parol.*

Of which generall Propoſitions there can bee made no better reaſon then by the commemoration of the ſaid firſt aforeſhewed generall Rule.

Moreover, the firſt of the laſt above remembred comprehendeth under the generality thereof certaine other more ſpeciall Rules:

As

In det ſur arrerages de accompt que eſt matter de Record, le party doit diſcharger luy per matter cy haut, & nemy per ſpecialty, ou fait ou auter matter que neſt cy haut. 6.*Hen*.4.6.*a*. 3.*Hen*.4.5.*a*.11.*Hen*.4.79.*b*. 13.*Hen*.4.1.*a*. 8.*Hen*.5.3.*b*.3.*Hen*.6.55.*a*. 4.*Hen*.6.17.*b*.20.*Hen*.6.55.*b*.

In det ſur recovery, home ne ſera diſcharge mes per matter cy haut: ou a tiel effect, 6, *Hen*.4.6.*a*.

Vnder

Vnder the second Rule or Ground before proposed touching a discharge where the party is charged by matter of specialty; those speciall Rules following are likewise comprehended.

In nul case home ne poit avoide single obligation, sans auter specialty de auxy haut nature, 1.*Hen*.7.14.*b*.5.*Hen*.7.33.*b*. 11.*Hen*.7.4.*b*.

Home que ad enfreint covenant ne pledera matter in discharge de ceo sans fait, 3.*Hen*.4.1.*b*. 1.*H*.7.14.*b*. 21.*Hen*.6.31.*a*.

Home ne discharger a luy mesme dun annuity que charge son person sans specialty, 5.*Hen*.7.33.*b*. 35.*H*.8.51.*a*. *Dyer*.

The first rule of these last remembred Grounds, namely, touching obligations, is againe divided into divers particulars; as for example.

Arbitrement ne dischargera home de un duty due per un obligation, 8.*H*.7.3.*b*. 6.*H*.4.6.*a*.

Si le obligee deliver l'obligation al obliger come acquittance, & puis ceo prist de luy, & commence sute sur ceo, cest delivery ne sera discharge del obligation, 1 *Hen*. 7.17.*a*. 33.*Hen*.8.51.*a*. *Dyer*.22.*H*.652.*b*.

The other following concerning indentures of Covenants, may likewise be divided into other more particular assertions: but to avoyde tediousnesse, these already shewed abundantly manifest our meaning, and therefore may suffice.

The use of this kind of observation of the generality of Rules and Propositions is manifold.

The use of generall Rules, and the observations of their specialls.

First, things proposed in the generality are best knowne and most familiar to our conceipt, sith

ſith they be the proper object of our underſtanding,as before is declared.

Secondly,they doe better adhere and ſticke in memory,ſith Intellective memory is (as the underſtanding is) imployed about univerſall and generall things.

Thirdly, univerſall Propoſitions are the precepts of Art, and therefore they are called perpetuall and eternall : for no Art, Science, Method, or certaine knowledge can or may conſiſt of particularities : for the orderly proceeding of every Art, Methodically handled, is from the due regard had of the generall,to deſcend unto the ſpecialls contained underneath the ſame : wherefore it enſueth hereof, that generall Propoſitions are the moſt ſpeedy inſtruments of knowledge : for experience, which wholly is gotten by the obſervation of particular things (being deprived of ſpeculation) is ſlow, blinde, doubtfull, and deceiveable, and truly called the miſtreſſe of fooles.

IF perchance upon occaſion of ſome former ſpeeches here publiſhed touching the univerſality of Grounds, there bee demanded this queſtion.

Queſtion. Why the Lawes of *England* at the firſt and from time to time, had not beene publiſhed after this Method of generall and ſpeciall Rules with their exceptions.

I anſwer

I anſwer thereunto, that many ancient writers attempted that kinde of writing, and accompliſhed the ſame according to their ſeverall and ſundry gifts more or leſſe perfect each than other: as by the treatiſes of *Glanvile, Bracton, Britton*, and others appeareth. Anſwer 1.

2 Secondly, I ſay that foraſmuch as dayly new queſtions came in debate whereof before had bin no reſolution, and wherein many times the leaſt variety of circumſtances doth alter the Law; therefore our Anceſtors thought it more convenient, to be rather governed by an unwritten law, not left in any other monument, than in the mind of man; and thence to be deduced by deceptation and diſcourſe of reaſon: and that when occaſion ſhould be offered, and not before.

3 Thirdly, it is more convenient and profitable to the ſtate of the common wealth to frame Law upon deliberation and debate of reaſon, by men skilfull and learned in that faculty, when preſent occaſion is offered to uſe the ſame, by a caſe then falling out and requiring Iudiciall determination: for then is it likely, with much more care, induſtry and diligence to bee looked unto; and much more time of deliberation is there taken for the mature deciſion thereof, then otherwiſe upon the eſtabliſhing of any poſitive Law, might bee imparted concerning the ſame.

4 Laſt of all, ſith all good Lawes require perſpicuity and plainneſſe; and that in generality, for the moſt part, lurketh *obſcurity*; therefore there is nothing of more force and effect touching the

making and framing of a good Law, then the present occasion offered, sith thereby is brought to light, that which otherwise would not as much (many times) as be thought upon, and giveth occasion to dispute that which none would have thought ever should have come in question. And therefore not without due consideration among the Romanes, *Disputationes fori*, and with us *Demurrers* have ever beene allowed as originals of Law.

As touching the manifestation of Rules, all are affirmative or negative: wherein though the affirmative be, for many causes, the more worthy; yet such negation as implyeth affirmation (and therefore called pregnant) is not without some use in the setting downe and delivering of exceptions and generall Rules. And thus much touching the forme of Rules, Grounds, and Axiomes.

The efficient cause of Rules, Grounds, and Axiomes is the light of naturall reason tryed and sifted upon disputation and argument. And hence is it, that the Law (as hath bin before declared) is called reason; not for that every man can comprehend the same; but it is artificiall reason; the reason of such, as by their wisedome, learning, and long experience are skilfull in the affaires of men, and know what is fit and convenient to bee held and observed for the appeasing of controversies and debates among men, still having an eye and due regard of justice, and a consideration of the common wealth wherein they live; for well saith *Aristotle, Hoc quidem perspicuum est, leges pro ratione*

Reipub.

Reipub. esse scribendas. And of this reason that we speake of, *Tully* hath a notable saying. *Ratio est societatis humanæ vinculum, ut oratio, quæ dicendo, communicando, disceptando, judicando, conciliat, inter se homines conjungit, & retinet naturali societate.* Wherefore sith the Grounds of Law are the foundation of Law, or at leastwise the Law it selfe delivered in manner of compendious and short sentences & propositions; that which is the efficient cause of Law, must likewise be the efficient cause of those Rules and Axiomes. Cic. 1. Offic.

Inasmuch then as *Primaria efficiens causa juris, est natura & ratio civilis, ex quibus potissimum leges emanant, & veluti scaturiunt.* The same nature and reason are likewise the principall and originall efficient cause of the Rules, Axiomes, Grounds, and Propositions of the Law; I meane *Civilis ratio*, that is, reason respecting justice and the Common wealth. *Iohannes Corasius de arte juris lib. 1. cap. 20.*

This reason hath in the written workes of the Lawes of this Land, either been plainly published and expressed in the bookes of Law, upon deceptation of cases in debate, and left unto posterity, as the Lights, Rules, and Directions, whereby the said cases so called into question, were at the last decided and determined.

Or else it is not at all expresly published in words, but left neverthelesse implyed and included in the cases so decided, and therein doth as it were lye hidden; and yet neverthelesse to bee easily, with industry collected and inferred upon those Cases decided, and doth necessarilie follow upon the resolution of the same, and being thence drawne, may aboundantly serve to infinite uses, in the determinating of other doubts, which daily doe and may come in debate. Wherefore sith in the Law (as in other sciences) all arguments and disputation doe either consist of expresse proofe and allegation of Authority (which are called *Inartificiall Arguments*) or else of application and inference; as well the Rules to bee collected upon inference and application of other Cases, are to be regarded and to bee produced, as those which are direct authorities. And forasmuch as in very few cases of doubt newly rising in debate, and called into question and controversie, expresse proof and pregnant authority can be found; the Lawyer is most beholding to Inference and Application, wherewith he is instructed and taught, that Cases different in circumstance, may be neverthelesse compared each to other in equality of Reason; so that of like Reason, like Law might be framed. And by how much Application and Inference doth more depend upon wit and Art, than the producing of expresse Authoritie, by so much the more it excelleth the same, sith the Allegation of expresse Authority, resteth wholy upon Industry and Memory in publishing and noting that which he findeth already framed to his hand.

Expresse Rules, Axiomes, Grounds and Positions of the former sort are published in the bookes of Law, either in the Latine tongue, as are the former generall rules first mentioned, and also so infinite other of that kinde; or else in the French; in which tongue the Reports of forepassed Cases are published unto the use of posterity, and wherewith the said booke of yeares and tearmes (almost in every case therein found) are fully furnished. So that all, though it shall bee needlesse to make manifest that by Example, which of it selfe is evident; yet still to pursue the former Method and order hitherunto observed, we shall easily perceive the same in this short case hereafter expressed.

Vn home avoit a luy & ses heires le nomination del Clerke d'un Esglise a un Abbe, & le Abbe doit presenter ouster le Clerke nominate al ordinary, oré le Roy ayant les possessions del Abbey ad present son Clerke al dit Esglise estant voide sans ascun nomination. Et le opinion del Court fut, que le party que averoit le nomination, avera Quare impedit vers le Incumbent tantum, sans ascun deste nosme Patron: Car le Roy ne poit este sue come disturber: Tamen fut dit q̃ le Roy ne poit este Instrument al ascun home. Et Shelley dit que il est Instrument a chacun home: Car per luy chacun Subject ad Iustice a luy minister.

The Principles, Maximes, Rules, or Grounds expressed in plaine words in this case, and which are indeede the very reason of the Resolution therein taken are these.

1 *Le Roy ne poit este sue Come disturber.*

2 *Lou le Roy present per tort, Quare Impedit sera port vers L'incumbent sole sans ascun deste nosme Patrone.*

3 *Le Roy ne poit este instrument al ascun home, si come son servant.*

4 *Per le Roy chescun subject ad Iustice a luy minister.*

5 *Le Roy est instrument a chacun home pur minister a luy Iustice.*

So that the Reasons of every Resolution in any booke-Case being reduced into short Sentences, Propositions or Summarie Conclusions are the Grounds, Rules, and Principles that we do meane and speake of in this place.

Such Summarie Conclusions, Corolaries, Reasons, Grounds, or Propositions therefore as afore declared, are delivered in the bookes of Reports in two manners.

Sometimes without any note or marke that they are Grounds or Rules, but onely as laid downe and dispersed in the Arguments and Resolutions as short Reasons of the opinion or determination there expressed; as in the last example appeareth.

Sometimes with a note or marke that they are Grounds, or Rules and Maximes, and are expresly invested with such names, as in the entrance of this treatise hath appeared. And thus much of the Grounds or Propositions expressed in the bookes.

Now as touching the second sort, which are to be collected, and inferred out of the Cases left reported, we plainly may perceive the notable use of such collection, in reading advisedly the Commentaries of M^r^. *Plowden*, or other the best bookes

bookes of Reports; or diligently obſerving any notable Argument made at this day in any the Kings Courts in matter of *Demurrer*, where we may not thinke that every caſe cited or allead-ged out of the bookes for proofe of the Contro-verſie, is therefore alleadged becauſe it hath ex-preſſe matter therein publiſhed in plaine words, and tending to the reſolution of the point in que-ſtion: but at ſometimes, and that moſt common-ly, ſuch proofe is produced upon inference, and yet neverthelesſ, ſufficiently pregnant to approve the matter whereunto it is rightly applyed: which inference and application proceedeth wholly up-on collected Rules and Axiomes included in the reſolution of thoſe Caſes produced, although the ſame be not expreſly ſpoken or publiſhed therein.

Wherefore notwithſtanding the beſt meanes of the collection of the ſaid Rules, depending on-ly upon Meditation, and reſting wholly upon the ſagacity, wit, induſtry, and judgement of the Stu-dent, (becauſe every mans ſeverall conceit is in it ſelfe ſundry) may beſt be referred unto the ſtudent himſelfe: yet neverthelesse, ſhall it not be amiſſe here to manifeſt ſuch direction therein as may be obſerved with ſome fruit.

1 Firſt, after the caſe read, let us conſider with our ſelves, & meditate in our minds, to what ſeve-rall purpoſes the ſame caſe may bee applyed, and what matter, or ſeverall matters the reſolution of the ſaid Caſe can confirme. Which when wee have conſidered of, it ſhall be good for our me-morie to commit them to writing, in manner, and

33.H.8.48. b.n.1.Dyer. and according to this example following;

Fut move si Tenant in tayle d'un Manour, a que vilains sons regardant, en feoft un des vilains d'un acre per cel del Manor, et devy, coment que le Manor discend al issue in tayle, uncore il ne poit seiser son vilain tanque le acre soit recover.

Vpon meditation had of this case, what it will prove, these Propositions or Rules following may easily be collected.

1 *Lou home ad forsque un action al principal chose la il naver benefit del accessary, tanque il ad per recovery continue le principal.*

And because here the whole principall is not discontinued, but onely one Acre, thereof may be collected,

That

2 *Regardancy ou Apendancy nest solement al tout le Manor, mes chachun acre del demeanes.*

Moreover, because the principall in this Case, *viz.* the acre discontinued, cannot be recontinued without suit to be attempted against the Villein, it followeth in Reason, that he shall not be infranchised thereby: Whence also this Axiome is to be confirmed or proved, That

3 *Necessary suite ew vers un villein per le signier ne enfranchise le villein.*

Hereof hath appeared that although none of these Propositions be expressed in the resolution of the said Case, in the booke wherein the same is left reported; yet neverthelesse are they necessarily implyed in the resolution of the said Case, as before hath beene declared.

But

But if the Caſe ſo read doth conſiſt of many points or ſeverall queſtions ſunderly debated, every of them may likewiſe bee ſunderly and apart conſidered of, according to the manner before ſhewed.

A ſecond meanes, by Inference to collect ſuch Rules and propoſitions as are before declared, is 2
by way of Argument by Syllogiſme: For ſuppoſing the ſaid Caſe to be denyed to be Law which we have read; let us endeavour to draw the immediate reaſons thereof into a Syllogiſme for confirmation of the ſame. So that thereby, foraſmuch as all Rules out of the Law are of two ſorts, that is, either being the Reaſons of the Caſe, or the Caſe contracted ſhortly it ſelfe, by ſuch manner of Argument, the Major, and firſt Propoſition of the ſaid ſyllogiſticall Argument, will bee the generall reaſon of the ſaid Caſe: The Minor or ſecond Propoſition, will be the particular reaſon: and the Concluſion will be the contracted caſe it ſelfe: Which alſo will ſerve as a ſecondarie Rule to determine other Caſes of equall Reaſon called into controverſie. For example herein, wee will take the opinion of *Hulls* in *9. Hen. 4.8. a.* in the end of a Caſe there argued, where hee holdeth for cleere Law,

That

Si un home fait fine pur un treſpas dont il fut endite ſon boache ſera eſtopp a dire que il neſt my culpable, ſil ſoit eint implead apres. *9.H.4.8.a.*

But becauſe the ſame is denyed in *Hen. 6.* wee endeavouring to prove the ſame by Syllogiſme, ſhall not onely confirme it, but alſo exemplifie our former ſpeeches.

Major] Nul ſera permit a denyer ceſt injury pur que il ad fait ſatisfaction, ou ad ſuffer puniſhment.

Minor] Mes ceſty que ad fait fine pur un offence ad fait aſcun ſatisfaction & in ceo ad eſte puny.

Concluſio] Il q. ad fait un fine pur une treſpas ou auter offence ſera eſtopp a ceo denier apres.

Every of theſe propoſitions be eſt-ſoones confirmed not onely with the Caſe before ſpoken (for as they doe prove the Caſe, being the immediate Reaſons thereof; ſo are they to be proved againe by the Caſe as by their effect) but alſo with ſundry other Authorites found in the bookes of like effect.

3 A third obſervation of Propoſitions and Axiomes may bee drawne from the conſideration of the Titleing words, or words which doe yeeld matter of effect; whereof in the caſe laſt remembred are ſuch as doe follow; namely;

Fyne, Eſtoppel, Enditement, Non culpable, Party, &c.

And herein is to be meditated and conſidered what Rules may be derived and collected out of the ſaid caſe, and be referred to every of the ſayd Titles; as namely,

Vnder Fines.

1 *Fine fait pur un offence prove, ceſty q. fait le fine voluntarunt, deſte culpable del dit offence.*

2 *Fine fait per un offence cauſera ceſty q. fait le offence q. il ne ceo deniera apres.*

Vnder

Vnder Enditement, these.

SI home soit convince, d'un offence sur un Enditement, q̃ est al sute le Roy, il ne deniera le dit offence, s'il soit apres de ceo implede al sute del Party.

Vnder Estoppel, these.

HOme sera estopp per matter de Implication q̃ imply le contrary de son disant de Record.

Vnder Non Culpable, these.

NOn Culpable ne sera plede per ascun lou per implication il ad confess le cause del action.

Vnder Party, these.

SI offence soit commit cy bien al Roy que come al Party condemnation al sute d'un d'eux, aydera l'auter in son sute.

A fourth manner of observation is to referre unto every Ground or Rule so collected, a Rule, more generall, so proceeding from the speciall Rule unto the generall Reason, and from that generall Reason unto a more generall: As out of the sayd first Case may bee drawne this generall Rule. 4

Home ne sera permit a denier ceo que devant il ad confess per implication de Record. 9. H. 4. 8. a.

Vnder which Ground not onely the first proposed Case of *9.Hen.*4. 8.*a*.may bee comprehended;and divers others of like effect and purpose, and which doe concurre under the said Generall Rule; As for example.

*Stamf.*155.*a* *cap.* 62. *Stamf.* 98.*b.* 22.*E.*4.39.*b* He which is arraigned, after he hath pleaded either in Barre or in Abatement of the Appeale wheron he was arraigned,may plead over *not guilty* to the felony: Except the Bar or Plea do comprehend such matter as doth acknowledge the felony; as a Release or pardon. But if he doe plead any such Plea or Barre,*viz*. Release,or Pardon in in any Appeale or Enditement, he cannot plead over *Not guilty* to the Felony, because thereby he confesseth the Felony by implication.

11.*H.*4.69.*a* *Culpepper.* If in a Præcipe,the Tenant say that he is Leassee for life,and pray in ayde, the demandant saith he hath fee, which the Tenant denyeth not, and therefore he is owted of the ayde: If after he will say he is Tenant for tearme of life, and vouch, hee shall not be thereunto received.

These Cases with many other may bee comprehended under the generality of the last specified Rule, and are one in Reason, not under one immediate Reason, but under this Reason, *viz. Home ne serra admitt a contradize ceo q̃ il ad confess de Record.*

Moreover there is another Case, one in effect of Reason with the former proposed Case, which because it is neverthelesse in circumstance more generall, therefore it cannot bee comprehended under the last specified Rule,as namely.

If

If a man bee indicted of Travers, and thereupon be found guilty by verdict at the suite of the King; If after, the party against whom the Travers was committed, bring an action for the same Travers; the other shall not pleade *Not guiltie* thereunto. 7.H.4.35.b.

In the former Grounds, and Cases thereupon, the partie was concluded by an implyed confession; but in this last Case, he is convinced by an open tryall or verdict. And whosoever will comprehend both this and the former Cases under one Ground or Rule, must make the same more generall then the former, in this manner.

Home ne serra permit a denier tiel offence de que il poit este convince per matter de Record.

And forasmuch as a man may be convinced of an offence as well by confession, as by verdict; and that as well by implicature confession, as by expresse confession: Therefore every of the said former Cases may bee concluded and comprehended under the amplenesse of this last remembred Ground.

A speciall Ground may be reduced unto a rule or Proposition generall, by seeking the Genus or generall Notion of every Titeling word found in the said speciall Ground, As for example, the said Proposition before remembred, and which hath beene exemplified with Cases, was this.

Home ne serra permit a denier ceo q̃ devant il ad Confess per implication de Record.

Vpon the word (*denier*) it may be drawne more generall, thus;

Home ne sera permit de contrary son act demesne que devant il ad conuz.

A more generall Reason whereof may againe be yeelded, thus.

Seroit inconvenient que le ley alloweroit a dize, & a dedize une mesme chose de Record.

Vpon the word (*Confession*) these Reasons also may bee assigned more generall than that first ground.

Confession de un est le plus pregnant proofe que poit este encounter luy.

A reason hereof: For, *Le Confession de chacun que concerne luy mesme sera intend vray.* For,

Nul convoit le offence melious que cesty que ad ceo commit & perpetrat.

Vpon the word (*Implication*) these generall Rules may be proposed.

Confession per Implication est cy fort encounter le Party come Confession express. For

Pregnant Implication est equivalent al matter express.

Vpon the word (*Record*) somewhat likewise may be said of like effect; *viz.* thus;

Matter de Record que est grounded sur le act del Party mesme luy issint liera que il ne contra dira ceo apres. For,

Le credit d'un Iudicial act ne sera impeach per ascun que est privy a ceo, For,

Matter de Record est plus hault testimony in ley.

Vnder

Vnder the word *(Fine)* there was mentioned this Ground or Rule.

Fine que est fait pur un offence prove home culpable del offence.

Here hence these Propositions being more generall, may be derived.

Nul per Common presumption voit faire voluntary fine pur le offence de quel il nest culpable.

A reason whereof may be thus.

Pœna culpam implicat. And *Le Consequent importa son Principal.*

Hereof you see what abundance of Rules and Propositions one Case containeth; and that we may descend from the particular case, to the speciall Reason, from that to a more generall, untill we finde out the very primarie ground of naturall reason, from whence all the other are derived.

Herein this Caution is to bee considered and had in minde, that in collection of Grounds and Principles out of any proposed Case, the same may be native, & alwaies appliable & reduceable to the immediate Reason of the said Case, so that in any occasion of Argument, the same Case may be a pregnant and efficient proofe thereunto.

Furthermore collection of Propositions may bee drawne and reduced from all the principall places of Logicall invention.

1 As from the Causes unto the Effect.

2 And contrariwise from the Effects unto their Causes.

3 So likewise from the Consequent unto the Antecedent.

4 And

4 And from the Antecedent to the Consequent.

5 Moreover *a Pari*,as from the Equall or like.

6 *A majori* from the more likely unto that which is lesse probable.

7 And againe,from that which is lesse Likely or Probable to that which is more Probable.

8 Finally,from the Contrary to his Contrary; sith that *Eadem est ratio & proportio Contrariorum*.

THe reasons and causes wherefore these Propositions,Rules,and Axioms (as hath been declared first in manner as aforesaid) are not onely to be considered,observed and collected, but alway to be had,and carefully to bee kept in memorie; and the *end* and *scope* whereto they serve and tend, will manifestly appeare, as well by the observation of the right use of them,and the manifold utilitie and great helpe, which riseth by the daily meditation therein, as likewise by the consideration and amendment of some inconsiderate abuses which have crept into the daily handling of them, both in judiciall places abroad, and in private exercises at home.

The necessary use of them therefore consisteth in two parts.

1 The one serving to the obtaining of the knowledge of the Law.

2 The other in use and practice of the Law learned by these Propositions and Rules,reducing them, as occasion serveth,to publike and private behoofe.

The

The first is Speculative.

This last Practique.

As touching the first, the profit hence springing may soone be seene and discovered, if we call to our memory, that no manner facultie whatsoever to be learned by the light of Reason, can consist or be comprehended by the capacity of mans understanding, except (as before also in part hath appeared) it be furnished with certaine Assertions, Precepts, Rules, and Propositions, and the same adorned with these two qualities, *Universalitie* and *Veritie*. And as none may worthily take upon him the name of a Divine, which is ignorant of the Principles of his Science; nor any man may well arrogate the title or name of a Philosopher or Physitian, who knoweth not the severall Rules, whereupon, as upon sundry foundations, the said severall faculties are built and erected; so none may be deemed a Lawyer, or admitted, or can give good advise therein, which knoweth not the Precepts whereon his Art dependeth; or hath not read the determination of former doubts left reported in bookes, being the greatest part of the written Law in this Land; And thence, not collected Conclusions for the decisions of present and future controversies.

Moreover seeing the Law of this Land is wholly Rationall (as hath been said) wherein, as in all other Sciences, the minde of man holdeth and keepeth the former published proceeding, by apprehension and discourse, collecting Primary and Secondary Conclusions and Grounds, it cannot

 be

be otherwise, but that the observation of these Primarie and Secondarie Conclusions, must needs be the best, most approved, profitable and speedie meane, for the attaining of the right, sound, and infallible knowledge of the said Lawes.

And if there be any way extant, or to be found by mans wisedome, to purge the English Lawes, from the great Confusions, tedious and superfluous iterations, with the which the Reports are infested; or quit it of these manifold contrarieties, wherewith it is so greatly overcharged, so that the Coherencie, constancie, and conformitie thereof, is almost utterly lost, and not without some blemish and reproach of our Nation and Common-wealth, in manner cleane abolished; Surely, as to me seemeth, there is likelihood by that way and meanes to bring the same to passe, or by none. For, by Rules and Exceptions, all Sciences are and have beene published, put down and delivered: out of Rules and Exceptions, a method is framed, by which meanes men may view a perfect plot of the coherence of things: Even as in a large spred tree, from the lowest root to the highest branch; from the most ample and highest Generall, by many degrees of descent, as in a Pedigree or Genealogie, to the lowest speciall and particular; which are combined together as it were in a consanguinity of blood and concordancie of nature.

And yet therewithall perusing the particular differences and degrees of distinction betweene

them,

them, in all the course of humane studies, there is none that doth more commend unto your cogitations the wonderfull force of mans wisedome, then doth this discourse, which treateth of the Principles, Grounds, Rules and Originals of Law and Iustice, being the chaine of humane society, without the which it cannot consist; and which, besides the exceeding pleasure that the consideration therof breedeth in the well-affected mind, is able to bring us speedily to ripenesse and maturitie in that profession. For,

Principium est dimidium totius, saith *Aristotle.*

Short refined Reasons of long perplexed cases, doe, through their soundnesse, satisfie our judgements, through their brevity and shortnesse, wonderfully delight the minde, through their pithinesse, they may bee deemed incomparable treasures, yeelding a great shew of wit, and wonderfully sharpning our understanding, of infinite use, in all humane affaires, containing much worth in few words, no burthen to memory, but once obtained, are ever retained.

Sith all Sciences do tend to Verity (as hath bin before often affirmed), which is the object of the intellectuall part of our minde; And sith Veritie and Truth cannot be obtained or found without due knowledge of the causes; *Tunc enim* (as saith the Philosopher) *unumquodque scire arbitramur, cum ejus causas & Principia cognoscimus*. And not unfitly said the Poet,

Fœlix qui potuit rerum cognoscere causas.

Then must the right and due observatiõ of these

and ſuch like principles containing the Cauſes of things, be a direction to conduct and lead us to the knowledge of that faculty and ſcience, whereof they are Principles. For from hence all artificiall Demonſtrations are, and have beene drawne and deduced.

To adhere therfore and wholly to reſpect particular caſes, without any obſervation of the generall Rules and Reaſons, and to charge the memory with infinite ſingularities, is utterly to confound the ſame; a labour of unſpeakable toyle, & wherin we ſhall never free us from confuſion; but engender in our ſelves, that wrong opinion which many have (amiſſe) entertained, that there is nothing certaine in our Lawes.

Finally, if the Law be every mans inheritance borne under the ſame, as notably (beſides our owne Lawes) ſaith the Prince of Oratours, *Tully*, *Major hæreditas venit unicuique noſtrum à jure & legibus, quàm ab iis à quibus illa bona relicta ſunt. Nam ut perveniat ad nos fundus, teſtamento alicujus fieri poteſt: ut retineamus quod noſtrum factum eſt, ſine jure civili fieri non poteſt.* And all mens inheritance ſhall be certaine both for the private repoſe of the people, and publike good and quiet of the Common wealth. We muſt needes thinke the Law of this Land full of defect, except we thinke and deeme it to be (as indeed it is) certaine.

M.T. Cicero pro Cecinna.

Who then can, without the conſideration of theſe univerſall Maximes, Propoſitions, Rules, and Principles, wherein certaintie is alone contained, attaine unto the certaine knowledge thereof?

thereof? for as it hath beene truly published; *Principiorum est unumquodque sibi ipsi fides*; Insomuch that *cum negantibus ea, non est disputandum*, 10.*Eliz*.271.*a*. *Dyer*, 26.

Hitherto hath beene spoken what profit the carefull consideration and observation of Principles, Rules, and Maximes of the Law of this Realme doth give us, and what assistance we may finde therein toward the study and speculation of the same. It resteth therefore now, that somewhat be said of the commodity which may come to him, that shall mannage and practise the same Lawes, and to what use this observation therein likewise serveth.

Two kindes of Arguments are noted by *Morgan*.

Il y sont deux principall choses sur que Arguments poient estre fait, s. nostre Maximes, & reason, le Mere de touts Leyes, &c. *Com. Colthurst.* I thinke by the latter of these, the use of Argumentation upon reasons drawne from the logicall place of invention, are to be understood; as namely, to argue and reason in cases of debate, from the causes, effects, parts, consequents, mischiefes, and inconveniences, and such like; which aptly may bee called naturall reason, because all Art therein observed, is but the imitation of nature: which kind or course of Argument is much used in ancient bookes, when as there were fewest bookes of reports extant.

But by the former of these two specified kindes of Arguments, is meant as manifestly appeareth, the helpe that Grounds and Maximes do yeeld in that kinde. For the underſtanding therefore of the right uſe thereof, it behooveth to conſider, that the ſame wholly doth conſiſt in the apt and convenient application of the ſaid Rules, unto ſuch particular caſes daily falling in debate, as may bee comprehended under the generality of the ſame Rules, and may in every reſpect be rightly reduced therunto; ſo that the Rule might ſerve as a well-grounded reaſon of the matter called in queſtion.

To this effect the Author of the Dialogues betweene the Doctor and Student, after he had at large ſpoken of the credit and ſuppoſed certainty of a Principle or Maxime of the Lawes of this Land, addeth further that ſuch Maximes bee not onely holden for Law, but alſo other caſes like unto them, and all things, that neceſſarily follow upon the ſame, are to be reduced to the like Law.

2 A ſecond uſe of the obſervation of principles in Argumentation may be this.

We are taught (as ſaith *Ariſtotle*) and as likewiſe hath afore beene remembred, by the electiõ of principles to abound in matter fit for Argumentation. Our propoſitions may bee framed as parts of Syllogiſmes, or as antecedent propoſitions of Enthymemes, by which forme of Arguments, this profit and commodity is reaped, that he which rightly uſeth the ſame, in proofe or diſproofe of any propoſed matter ſhall not need to fall into any unneceſſay and extravagant matter, or digreſſe from the point that hee hath in hand. For if the parts of our argument ſo to bee concluded,

ded,doe consist of Propositions which are Principles in Law, and be in due and expedient manner framed and combined together, the Conclusion,which is the point in question, will follow, either necessarily or probably, according to the truth of the said propositions, for as we have before shewed, that by reducing a Case to a Syllogisme, we might finde some of the principall reasons and propositions, whereupon the verity of the said case,being the conclusion, dependeth; as trying out the cause by the effect: So of the contrary part, to frame the effect by the cause; the same propositions will,as they confirme one case, so likewise establish all other speciall cases,which shall happen to concurre in equall and like reason, or be reducible to, or under, the generalitie of the said proposition.

And although the Lawyer be not tyed to this short course of Argument current in schooles,yet in whatsoever large discourse of Argument, if this forme be respected, though amplified and enlarged with Prosyllogismes, after the manner of Rhetoritians or Orators, it will yeeld the fruit afore remembred. There are in our bookes extant of both,as namely, by *Conisby*, to prove that a man might grant his Lease for yeares without Deed,useth this plaine and expresse Syllogisme; whereof every proposition being a Ground and Principle in the Law, the Conclusion necessarily doth follow. *14.H.7.3.b.*

1 *Major*] *Chose que jeo poy prender in lease sans fait poiet passer hors de moy sans fait.*

2 *Minor*]

2 *Minor*] *Et un lease de terre pur terme d'anus est bon sans fait.*

3 *Conclusio*] *Ergo per mesme le reason il poit passer hors del Lessee, & ceo sans fait.*

10·H.7.13 b Likewise a question grew whether the heire or executor were to have a furnace fixed unto the soile, or such chattels as were annexed to the freehold after the death of the Testator, or no; where the Reporter putteth downe the opinion of *Reede* chiefe Iustice, *Fisher* and *Kingsmill*, that the executors should not have the same under the frame of this forme of Syllogisme; whereof every proposition is a Rule of Law.

1 *Major*] *Ceux choses que ne poient este forfeit per utlary in personall action, ne este attache in Assise ne distraine per le signior pur Rent, tiels choses executours naveront.*

2 *Minor*] *Mes un furnace ou table fix sur la terre, ou posses, ou un pale, ou un covering de un lict merisme, ou bord annex al franktenant, ou house & fenesters, & auters tiels semblables queux sont annex al franktenement, & sont fait, pur un profit del inheritance, ne poient este forfeit per utlary, ne attach, ne distraine.*

3 *Conclusio*] *Ex consequenti sequitur que executours naveront tiels choses.*

As touching the second sort of Argument by Syllogisme, in the Commentaries of *Plowden* the same is very frequent and usuall. And herein to take example out of the first case, because it first commeth to memory; All the said Argument of *Griffith* in the case of *Fogossa*, may be reduced into this Syllogisme set forth in the entrance thereof.

Major]

Major] Chascun agreement covient este perfect, plein & compleite.

Minor] Et le evidence icy ne prove le agreement deste perfect, ne plain, ne compleit, mes plus tost un communication ou parlance que un agreement.

The conclusion is suppressed, for that it apparently followeth of the premises, untill the end of the argument; where at last it is expressed in this manner.

Conclusio] Et issint le agreement est imperfect a doner action pur le subsedy per que le agreement intend per le statute nest accomply.

The Major Proposition is amplified with this Prosyllogisme.

Car agreement concernant personall choses, est un mutuall assent des parties, & doit este execute ove un recompence, ou auterment doit este cy certaine & sufficient que doit doner actio, ou auter remedy pur recompence, & sil issent nest, donque ne sera dit agreement mes plus tost un nude communication.

And this proposition he prooveth by the cases thereafter by him alleadged.

The Minor proposition of the first Syllogisme is there enlarged, where he further addeth.

Et issint in nostre case entant que estatute de Ann. 1. *Regis nunc, cap.* 3. *&c.* untill the end of the case.

The like may bee observed in every good and effectuall argument; but wee stand not upon example.

A third profit may be considered herein : for many times it falleth out, that we perceive a coherence and likenesse betweene divers and sun- 3 dry cases, which therefore we know are applyable to our purpose; and yet neverthelesse, except we draw the unity of reason so found and considered in the said cases, unto a short Sentence, Ground, Rule or proposition, wherein they may concurre, and doe agree; we shall bee driven with long circumlocution and many words, to make manifest our meaning in the allegation of the same, especially if the cases doe not concurre and agree in one mediate reason or likenesse, but are upon some conformity further off, to be resembled each to other. As for example.

1 Hen.7.4.b. *Le Roy ne poit arrest un home de suspition de treason ou felony, luy mesme, come un subject poit faire, pur ceo que si il fait tort in ceo feasant, le party issint injury ne poit aver action envers luy.*

49.Ed.3.5.a 50.Assis.p.1. 9.Eliz. 262. *Si home soit indebt a un sur contract sans specialty; si apres cesty a que le det est due soit utlage in action personall, le Roy naver cest dett pur l'utlary a luy forfeit, pur ceo que donq; le defendant perderoit le benefit del ley gager que il puis aver in sute de ceo commence vers luy per le Creditour.*

25.Ed.3.48. a.b. Com.Walsingh. *Coment que lestatute de W.2.cap.3. done resceit a cesty in le reversion generalment uncore si le tenant pur vie soit lou le Roy ad le reversion; & il estant implede fait default apres default, le Roy ne sera receive come common person seroit. Car, sur le resceit, le demandant doit counter vers cesty que est receive, Mes issent ne poit ascun counter vers le Roy, ne luy suer, mes per petition; Et pur ceo, si le Roy seroit resceive le breve, le demandāt abateroit maintenant, & pur cest mischiefe, al demandant le Roy ne sera resceive: mes son droit sera save per auter meane.*

These

These three cases greatly do differ both in the circumstance of matter, and in the immediate reasons, and yet neverthelesse have some resemblāce, and a kinde of conformity and likenesse, between them each to other.

1 First they all concerne the King.

2 Secondly the King in every of them is restrained from that power or benefit that his subject hath. For

1 In the first, he cannot arrest one as his subject may.

2 In the second hee shall lose that debt which his subject, in whose right he claimeth it, should recover.

3 In the third he shall not bee received where the subject might.

And lastly, in every of these cases, if the King should bee admitted to doe as a common person might, the subject in suit with him should sustaine great prejudice. For

1 In the first hee should not bee permitted to punish the injury done to his person.

2 In the second hee should lose the benefit of waging his Law. And

3 In the third and last have his action debated without his default.

The likenesse of which cases cannot so well be conceived without many words, except wee reduce unto some generall Axiome the unity and resemblance of reason found in them. And therefore this proposition without more might have sufficed for all.

Where the ſubject by reaſon of ſome Prerogative, that is in the King, ſhould otherwiſe be put to a prejudice; there the King ſhall not be allowed that benefit which every of his ſubjects by Law enjoyeth.

In which generall Axiome or Rule, a generall reaſon of all the ſaid ſeverall Caſes doth equally concurre.

4 By this obſervation wee may reape likewiſe a fourth commodity, after this manner. All the Reports do conſiſt of particular Caſes. Every particular Caſe hath his ſeverall Circumſtance. Circumſtances are ſingular, and hardly retained in memorie. For, true is that ſentence, which *Bracton* hath borrowed out of the Civill Law, *Omnia habere in memoria, & in nullo errare, divinum eſt potius quam humanum.* Wherefore when the Caſe is out of memory, and the circumſtances thereof quite forgot, the Reaſon yet remaineth, and is had in memory. For, *Memoria intellectiva eſt univerſalium, ut eſt ipſemet intellectus.*

Bracton li. 1. cap. 1. §. 3.

It is not the Caſe ruled this way, nor that way, but the reaſon which maketh Law; For, *Non quid ſit intelligere ſufficiat, ſed cur ſit diligentius inquiratur.* So that hee which by obſervation of theſe Grounds & principles, remẽbreth but the reaſon (as he eaſily may) ſhall ſo ſufficiently reſolve all doubts of like degree, as if he had remembred the expreſſe Caſes from which the ſame reaſon is deduced. Although in argument, I confeſſe, not only the generall reaſons, but likewiſe the ſpeciall Caſes are as proofes produced and alleadged.

Math. Gribaldus de ratione ſtudij juris lib. 1. cap. 4.

Laſtly,

Laſtly, ſith the choſen and collected Propoſitions and principles in manner as aforeſaid, for our better uſe behooveth to be cōmitted to writing; we may eaſily without great trouble, by diſpoſing of them orderly, frame a Directory, in manner either of a methodicall Treatiſe, or of an Alphabeticall Table, fit and convenient both for the ſpeedy finding of that we would ſeeke, and the ready having of that we can wiſh for, ſurpaſſing the benefit of any Abridgement heretofore extant. 5

And thus much touching the commodities growing by the conſideration and collection of Principles, Rules, Axiomes, Grounds & Maximes: and of the ſcope and end whereunto they tend in managing of our Lawes, as well for the behoofe of the Student, as for the uſe of the Practiſer. And now remaineth that a few words bee ſayd to forewarne both, of certaine abuſes ordinarily bred herein.

1 The firſt Abuſe is, that neither the Ground often-times produced doth come neere the Reaſon of the Caſe, in queſtion; nor the Caſes alleadged to prove and fortifie that Ground, do directly confirme the ſame. A fault very uſuall in publike exerciſes; and may be redreſſed, if we do call to minde that any caſe alleadged ought not to be wreſted to prove the Rule or Ground alleadged; but the Rule, Ground or Principle ought to be the very immediate or ſecondary reaſon of the Caſes whence it is drawne, and which caſes are brought to confirme the ſame, in ſuch ſort, that all the

Cafes alleadged doe concurre in equality of reafon,likeneffe, and proportion; and in full proofe of the Principle fo produced. And that the groũd or principle bee a reafon of the queftion in variance, to fubvert or confirme the fame. Wherein alfo let this be weighed,that a few principles cannot fufficiently ferve to fupply al occafions in that behalfe, but the fame muft be drawne and deduced of all Caufes, Titles, and matters in the Law fit for argument and ufe.

2 A fecond principall overfight is this. Many to prove their opinion in the controverfie propofed, frame their reafon rightly from fome notable Ground, and knowne principle or Rule, which though it be well applyed, yet not regarding the manifold Exceptions whereunto the fame Principle is fubject,they doe fet it forth fo generall,that it giveth their adverfary fome caufe of challenge and cavill thereunto, by objecting fome inftance or cafes upon exception of the faid Rule: and thereby doth not only feem to enfeeble the fame, in fhewing the fallacies thereof; but fometime in fhew, weakeneth the whofe reafon and argument grounded thereupon.

3 The third abufe of thefe Principles or Propofitions,is, in the too much frequenting and often needleffe ufe of them. For fometimes the obfcurity of the caufe, may require fome other manner of argument,drawn from places of invention, which may content and fatisfie the minde of the hearers much better. And fometimes the clearneffe of the matter it felfe, needeth not fuch preparation

paration of proofe and confirmation of thofe principles and rules. For then is the moft and beft of them, when that both propofitions and Cafes to confirme the fame, have great coherence with the queftion; when both the circumftance of the Cafe in queftion,and the caufe of doubt,doe give occafion to ufe them;fo that which thereby is affirmed,may rightly be reducible to the purpofe.

4 Finally,it fometimes falleth out to be a fault overmuch to abound in well doing.*Omne nimium vertitur in vitium*, faith the Proverbe; for fundry times it happeneth, that it is very convenient and direct to the matter to make argument upon a well applyed Principle , Rule or Ground, which by men of great learning and reading is fometimes fo fufficiētly handled,with fuch abundance and ample furniture of notable and direct Cafes, that their endeavour herein deferveth high commendations: yet more convenient were it, that their paines were leffe. For to what purpofe behooveth it, to heape Cafe upon Cafe, as it were one on the neck of another,*Pelion* upon *Offa*? whereas many probable reafons, though confirmed with few good Cafes, breed greater contentation to the hearer,by reafon of the feverall proofe made thereby then many Cafes.

FINIS.

www.ingramcontent.com/pod-product-compliance
Lightning Source LLC
LaVergne TN
LVHW091527200926
848483LV00002B/323